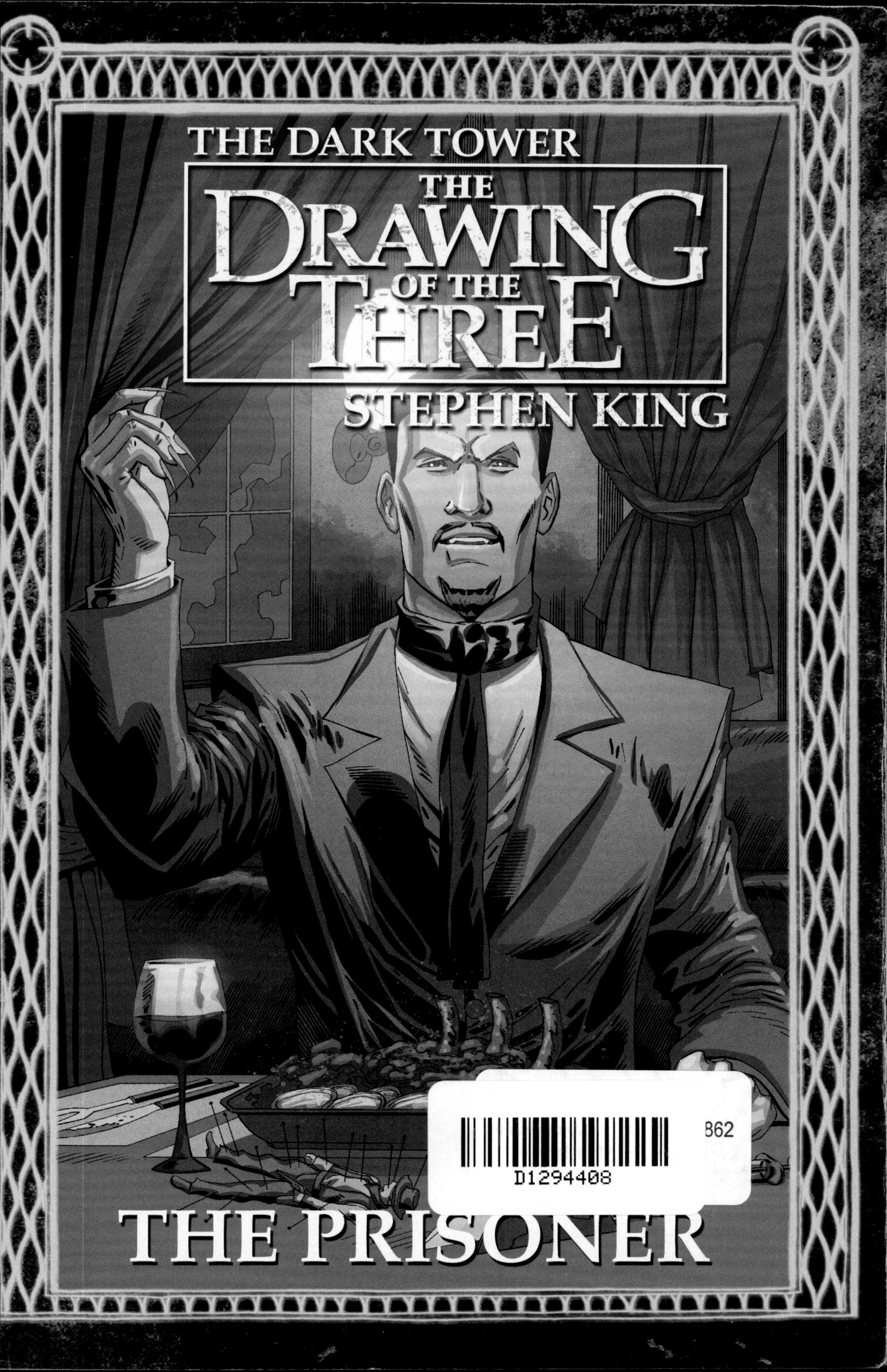
THE DARK TOWER
THE DRAWING OF THE THREE
STEPHEN KING
THE PRISONER

THE DARK TOWER

THE DRAWING OF THE THREE

STEPHEN KING

CREATIVE DIRECTOR AND EXECUTIVE DIRECTOR
STEPHEN KING

PLOTTING AND CONSULTATION
ROBIN FURTH

SCRIPT
PETER DAVID

ARTIST
PIOTR KOWALSKI

COLOR ART
NICK FILARDI

LETTERING
VC'S JOE SABINO

COVER ARTIST
JULIAN TOTINO TEDESCO

ASSISTANT EDITOR
MARK BASSO

CONSULTING EDITOR
RALPH MACCHIO

EDITOR
BILL ROSEMANN

THE PRISONER

COLLECTION EDITOR
MARK D. BEAZLEY

ASSISTANT EDITOR
SARAH BRUNSTAD

ASSOCIATE MANAGING EDITOR
ALEX STARBUCK

EDITOR, SPECIAL PROJECTS
JENNIFER GRÜNWALD

SENIOR EDITOR, SPECIAL PROJECTS
JEFF YOUNGQUIST

SVP PRINT, SALES & MARKETING
DAVID GABRIEL

EDITOR IN CHIEF
AXEL ALONSO

CHIEF CREATIVE OFFICER
JOE QUESADA

PUBLISHER
DAN BUCKLEY

ARK TOWER: THE DRAWING OF THE THREE — THE PRISONER. Contains material originally published in magazine form as DARK TOWER: THE DRAWING OF THE THREE — THE PRISONER #1-5. irst printing 2015. ISBN# 978-0-7851-9157-5. Published by MARVEL WORLDWIDE, INC., a subsidiary of MARVEL ENTERTAINMENT, LLC. OFFICE OF PUBLICATION: 135 West 50th Street, New ork, NY 10020. Copyright © 2014 and 2015 Stephen King. All rights reserved. All characters featured in this issue and the distinctive names and likenesses thereof, and all related indicia are ademarks of Stephen King. No similarity between any of the names, characters, persons, and/or institutions in this magazine with those of any living or dead person or institution is intended, and ny such similarity which may exist is purely coincidental. Marvel and its logos are TM & © Marvel Characters, Inc. **Printed in Canada.** ALAN FINE, EVP - Office of the President, Marvel Worldwide, ic. and EVP & CMO Marvel Characters B.V.; DAN BUCKLEY, Publisher & President - Print, Animation & Digital Divisions; JOE QUESADA, Chief Creative Officer; TOM BREVOORT, SVP of Publishing; AVID BOGART, SVP of Operations & Procurement, Publishing; C.B. CEBULSKI, SVP of Creator & Content Development; DAVID GABRIEL, SVP Print, Sales & Marketing; JIM O'KEEFE, VP of Operations Logistics; DAN CARR, Executive Director of Publishing Technology; SUSAN CRESPI, Editorial Operations Manager; ALEX MORALES, Publishing Operations Manager; STAN LEE, Chairman Emeritus. or information regarding advertising in Marvel Comics or on Marvel.com, please contact Niza Disla, Director of Marvel Partnerships, at ndisla@marvel.com. For Marvel subscription inquiries, lease call 800-217-9158. **Manufactured between 1/2/2015 and 2/9/2015 by SOLISCO PRINTERS, SCOTT, QC, CANADA.**

0 9 8 7 6 5 4 3 2 1

THE DARK TOWER
THE DRAWING OF THE THREE
STEPHEN KING

THE PRISONER
CHAPTER ONE

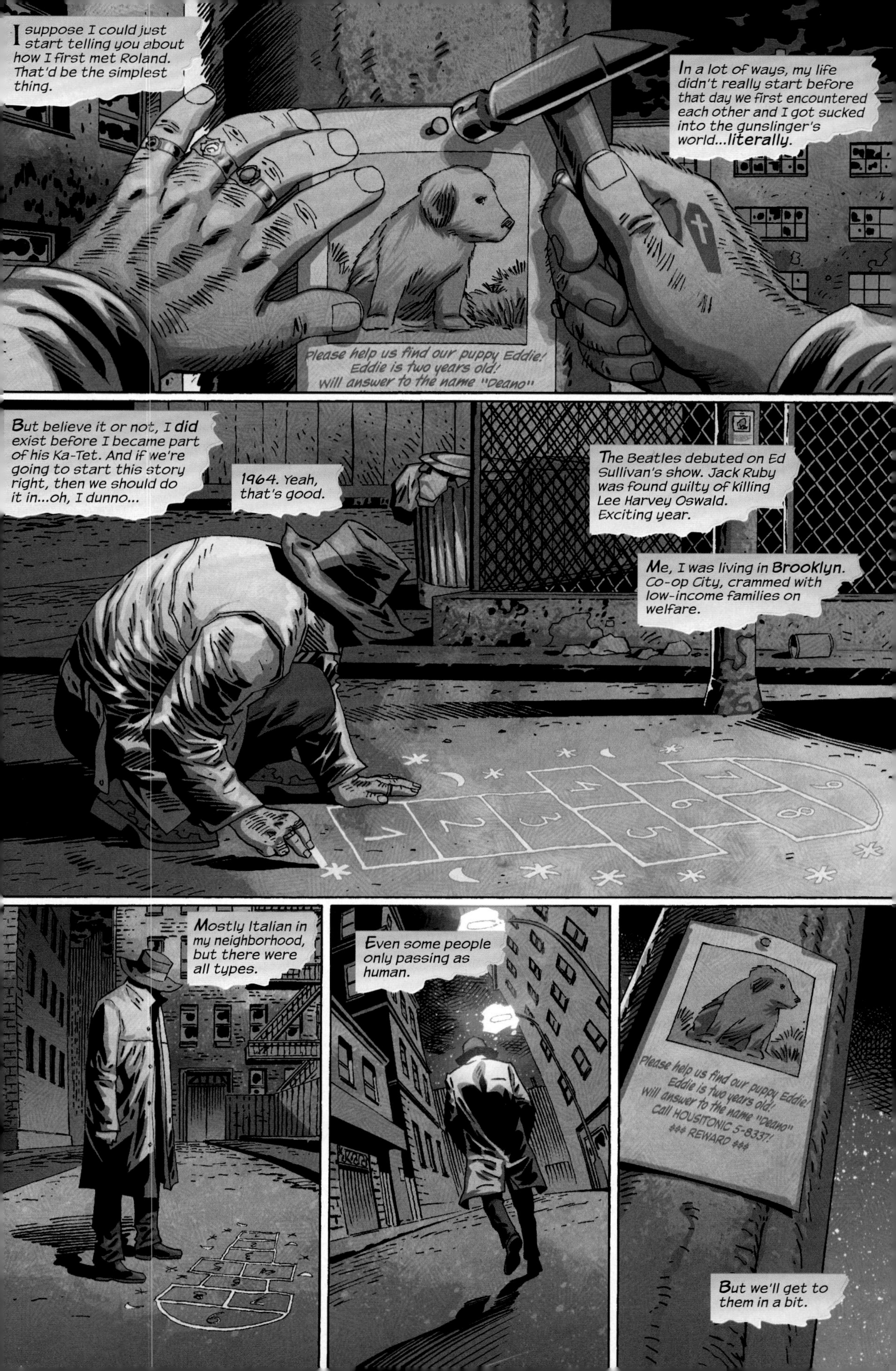
I suppose I could just start telling you about how I first met Roland. That'd be the simplest thing.
In a lot of ways, my life didn't really start before that day we first encountered each other and I got sucked into the gunslinger's world...literally.
Please help us find our puppy Eddie! Eddie is two years old! Will answer to the name "Deano"
But believe it or not, I did exist before I became part of his Ka-Tet. And if we're going to start this story right, then we should do it in...oh, I dunno...
1964. Yeah, that's good.
The Beatles debuted on Ed Sullivan's show. Jack Ruby was found guilty of killing Lee Harvey Oswald. Exciting year.
Me, I was living in Brooklyn. Co-op City, crammed with low-income families on welfare.
Mostly Italian in my neighborhood, but there were all types.
Even some people only passing as human.
Please help us find our puppy Eddie! Eddie is two years old! Will answer to the name "Deano" Call HOUSITONIC 5-8337! $$$ REWARD $$$
But we'll get to them in a bit.

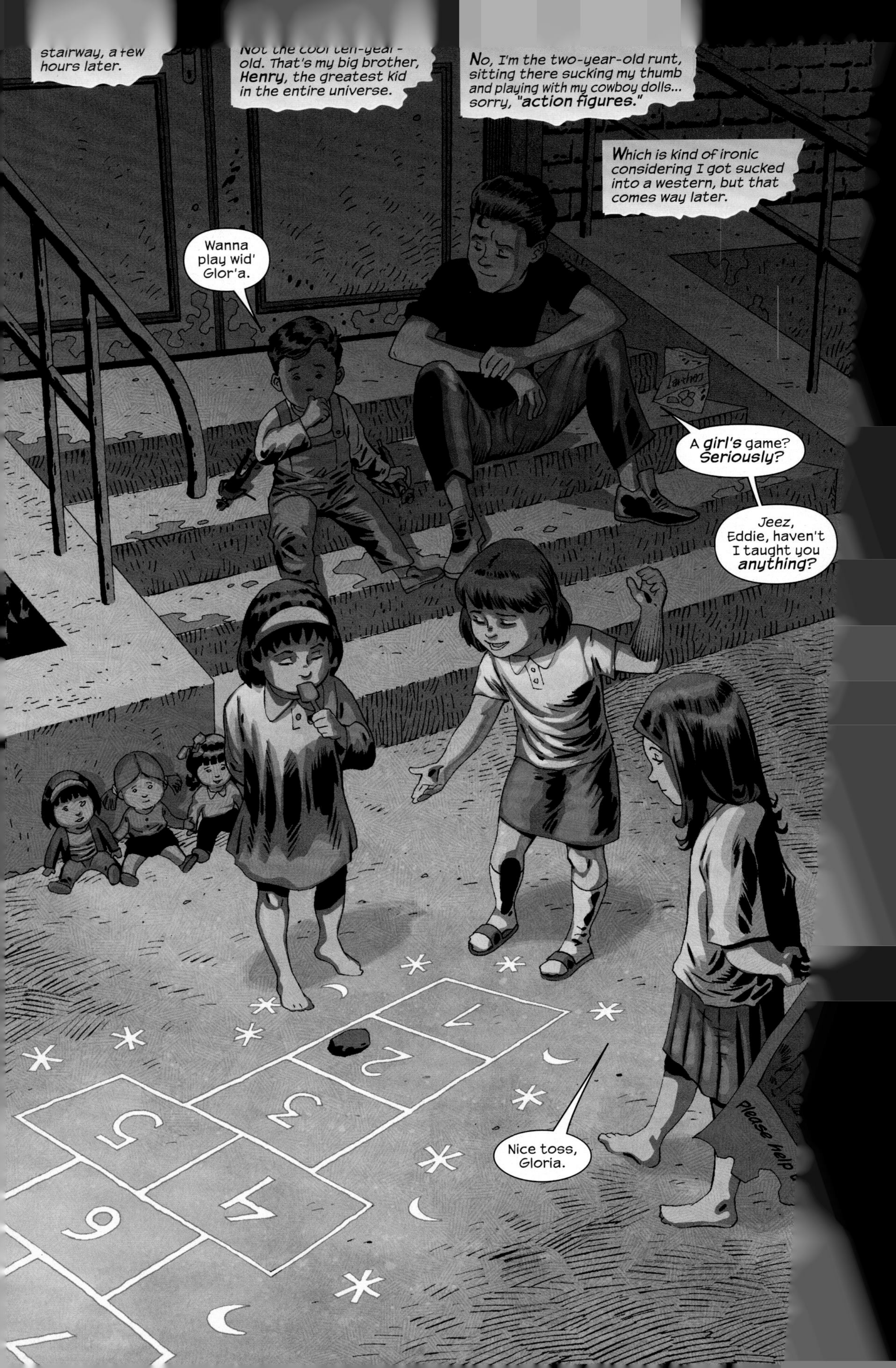
stairway, a few hours later.
Not the cool ten-year-old. That's my big brother, **Henry**, the greatest kid in the entire universe.
No, I'm the two-year-old runt, sitting there sucking my thumb and playing with my cowboy dolls... sorry, **"action figures."**
Which is kind of ironic considering I got sucked into a western, but that comes way later.
Wanna play wid' Glor'a.
A ***girl's*** game? ***Seriously?***
Jeez, Eddie, haven't I taught you ***anything?***
Nice toss, Gloria.
Please help

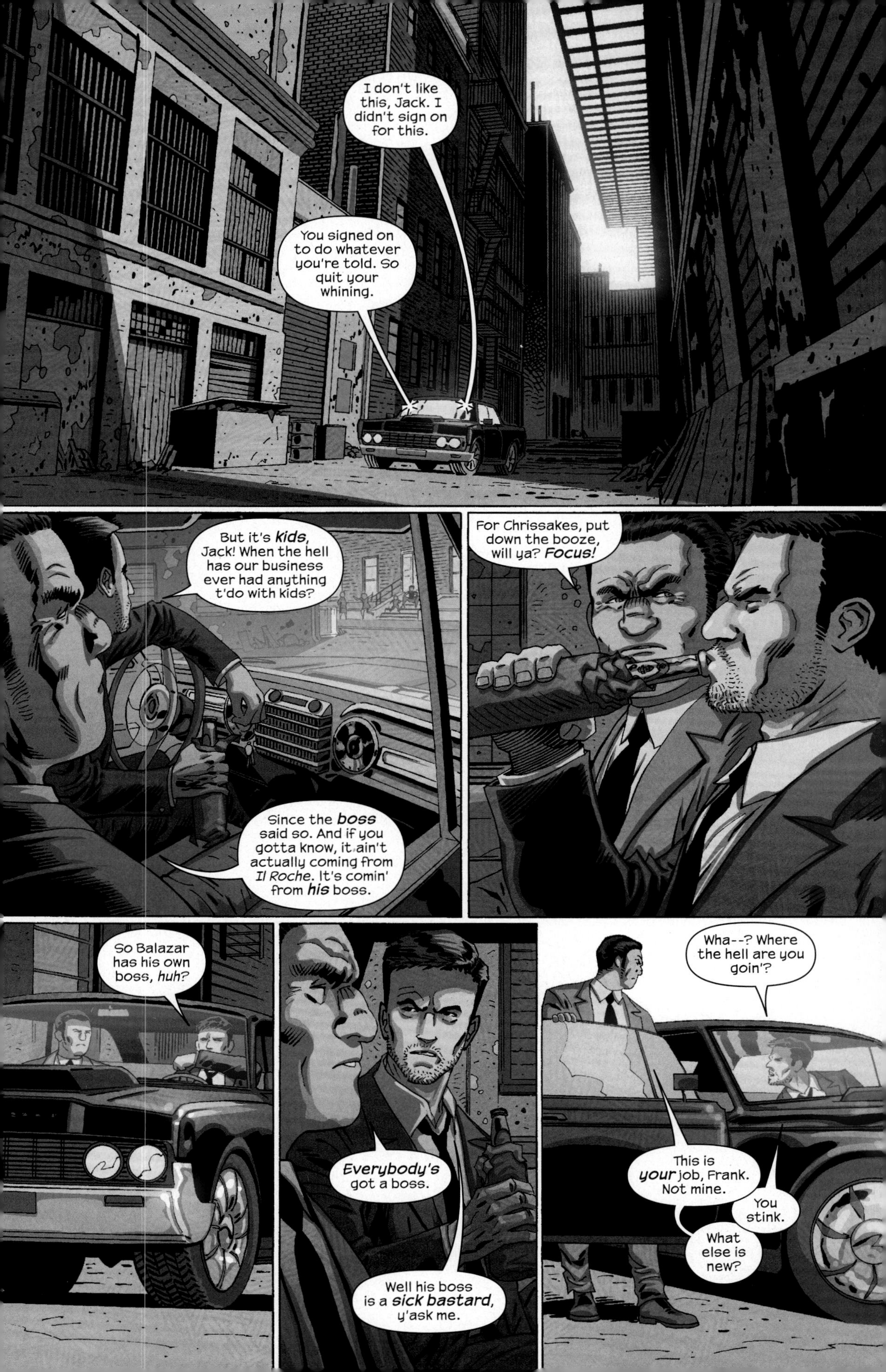
I don't like this, Jack. I didn't sign on for this.
You signed on to do whatever you're told. So quit your whining.
But it's *kids*, Jack! When the hell has our business ever had anything t'do with kids?
Since the *boss* said so. And if you gotta know, it ain't actually coming from *Il Roche*. It's comin' from *his* boss.
For Chrissakes, put down the booze, will ya? *Focus!*
So Balazar has his own boss, *huh?*
Everybody's got a boss.
Well his boss is a *sick bastard*, y'ask me.
Wha--? Where the hell are you goin'?
This is *your* job, Frank. Not mine.
You stink.
What else is new?

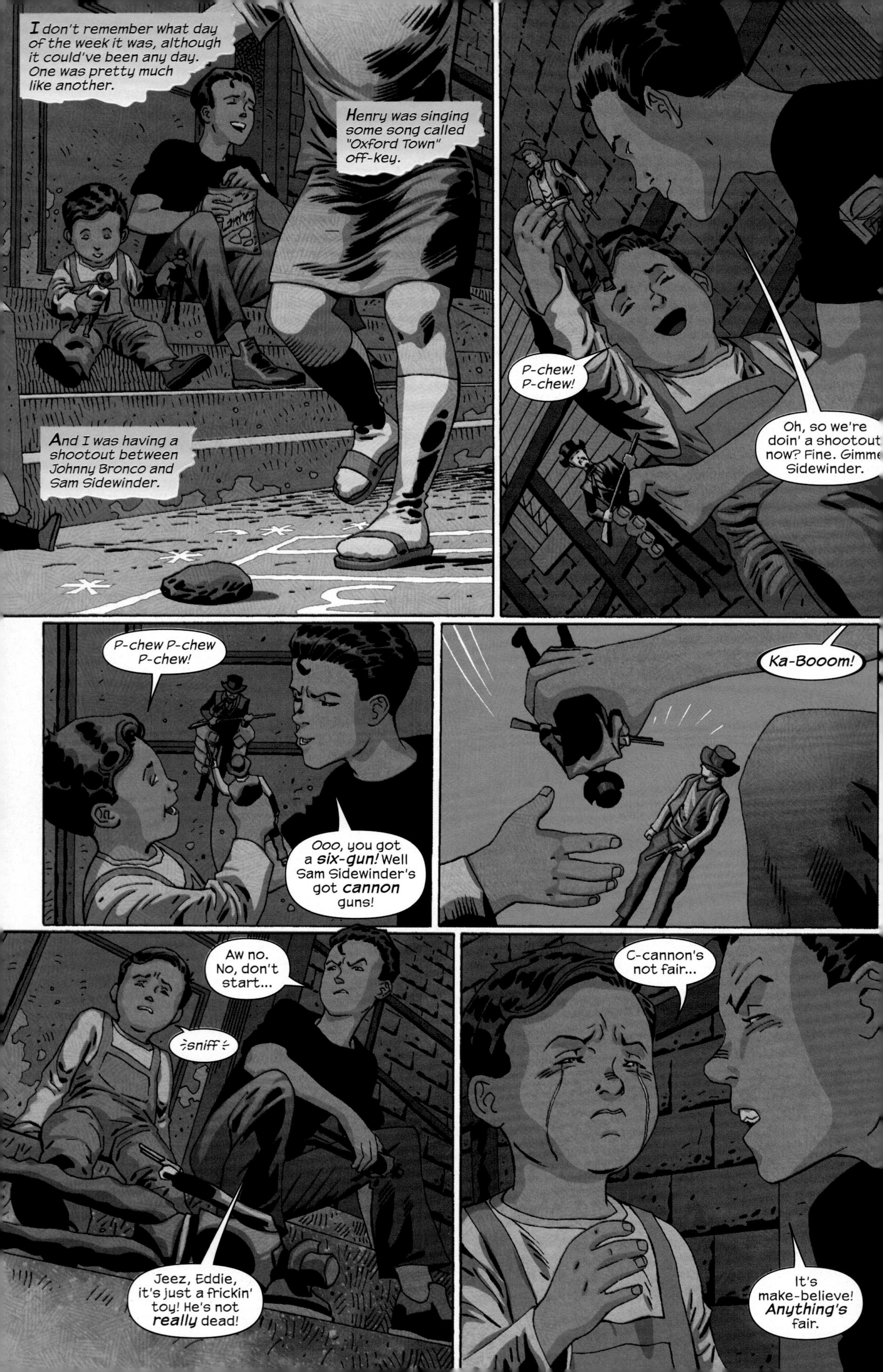
I don't remember what day of the week it was, although it could've been any day. One was pretty much like another.
Henry was singing some song called "Oxford Town" off-key.
And I was having a shootout between Johnny Bronco and Sam Sidewinder.
P-chew! P-chew!
Oh, so we're doin' a shootout now? Fine. Gimme Sidewinder.
P-chew P-chew P-chew!
Ooo, you got a six-gun! Well Sam Sidewinder's got cannon guns!
Ka-Booom!
Aw no. No, don't start...
sniff
Jeez, Eddie, it's just a frickin' toy! He's not really dead!
C-cannon's not fair...
It's make-believe! Anything's fair.

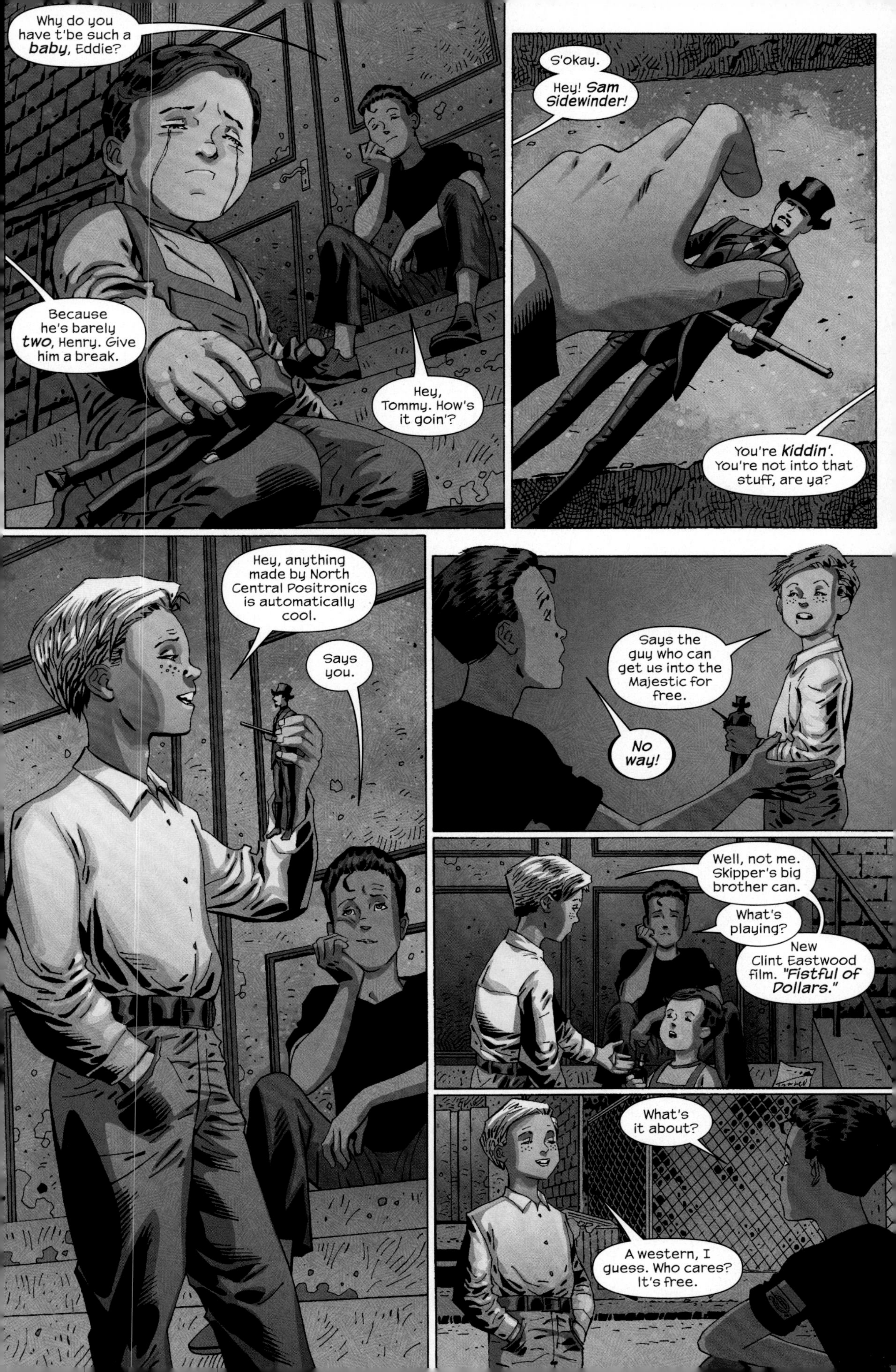
Why do you have t'be such a *baby*, Eddie?
Because he's barely *two*, Henry. Give him a break.
Hey, Tommy. How's it goin'?
S'okay.
Hey! *Sam Sidewinder!*
You're *kiddin'*. You're not into that stuff, are ya?
Hey, anything made by North Central Positronics is automatically cool.
Says you.
Says the guy who can get us into the Majestic for free.
No way!
Well, not me. Skipper's big brother can.
What's playing?
New Clint Eastwood film. *"Fistful of Dollars."*
What's it about?
A western, I guess. Who cares? It's free.

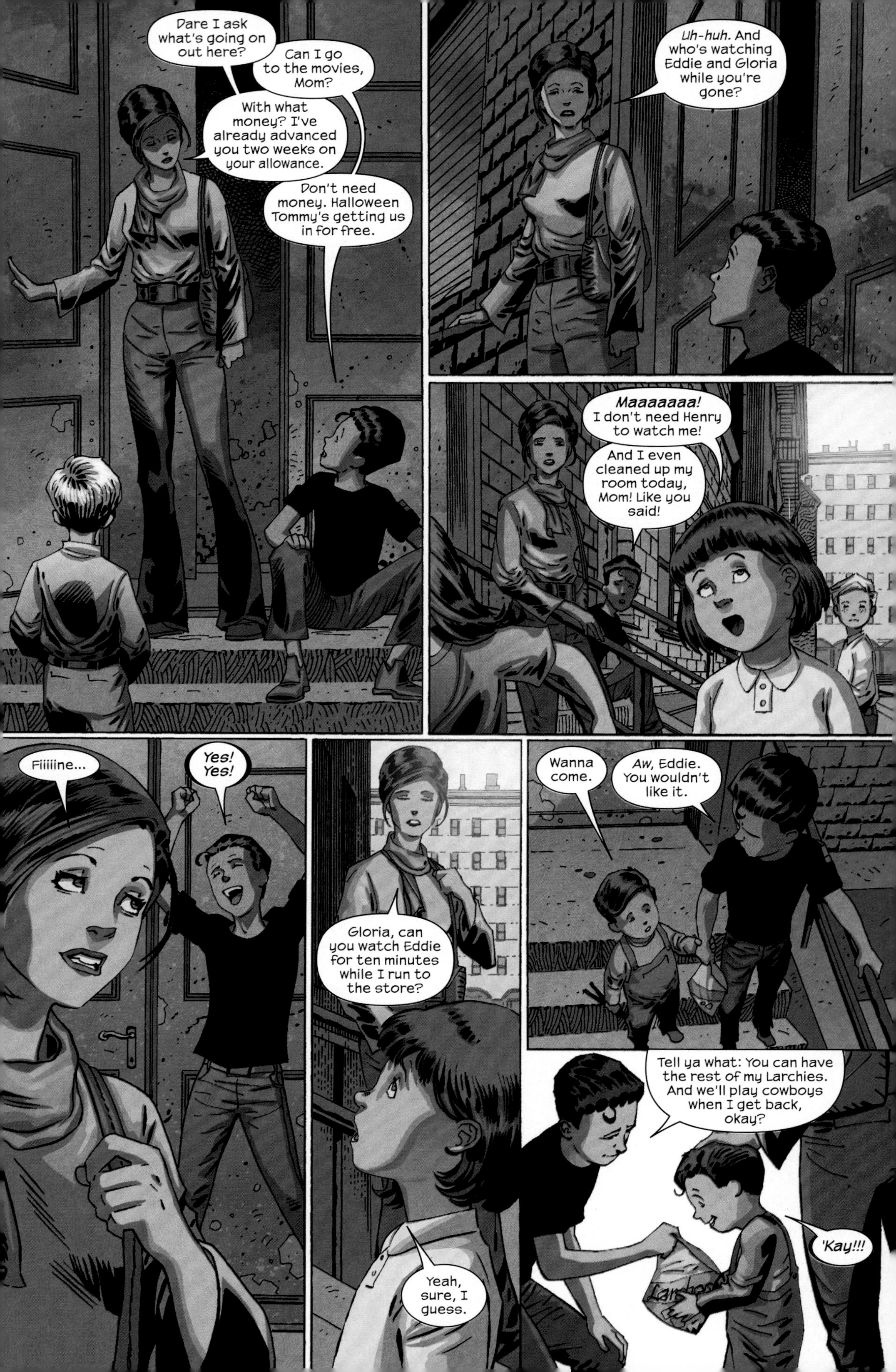
Dare I ask what's going on out here?
Can I go to the movies, Mom?
With what money? I've already advanced you two weeks on your allowance.
Don't need money. Halloween Tommy's getting us in for free.
Uh-huh. And who's watching Eddie and Gloria while you're gone?
Maaaaaaa! I don't need Henry to watch me!
And I even cleaned up my room today, Mom! Like you said!
Fiiiiine...
Yes! Yes!
Gloria, can you watch Eddie for ten minutes while I run to the store?
Yeah, sure, I guess.
Wanna come.
Aw, Eddie. You wouldn't like it.
Tell ya what: You can have the rest of my Larchies. And we'll play cowboys when I get back, okay?
'Kay!!!

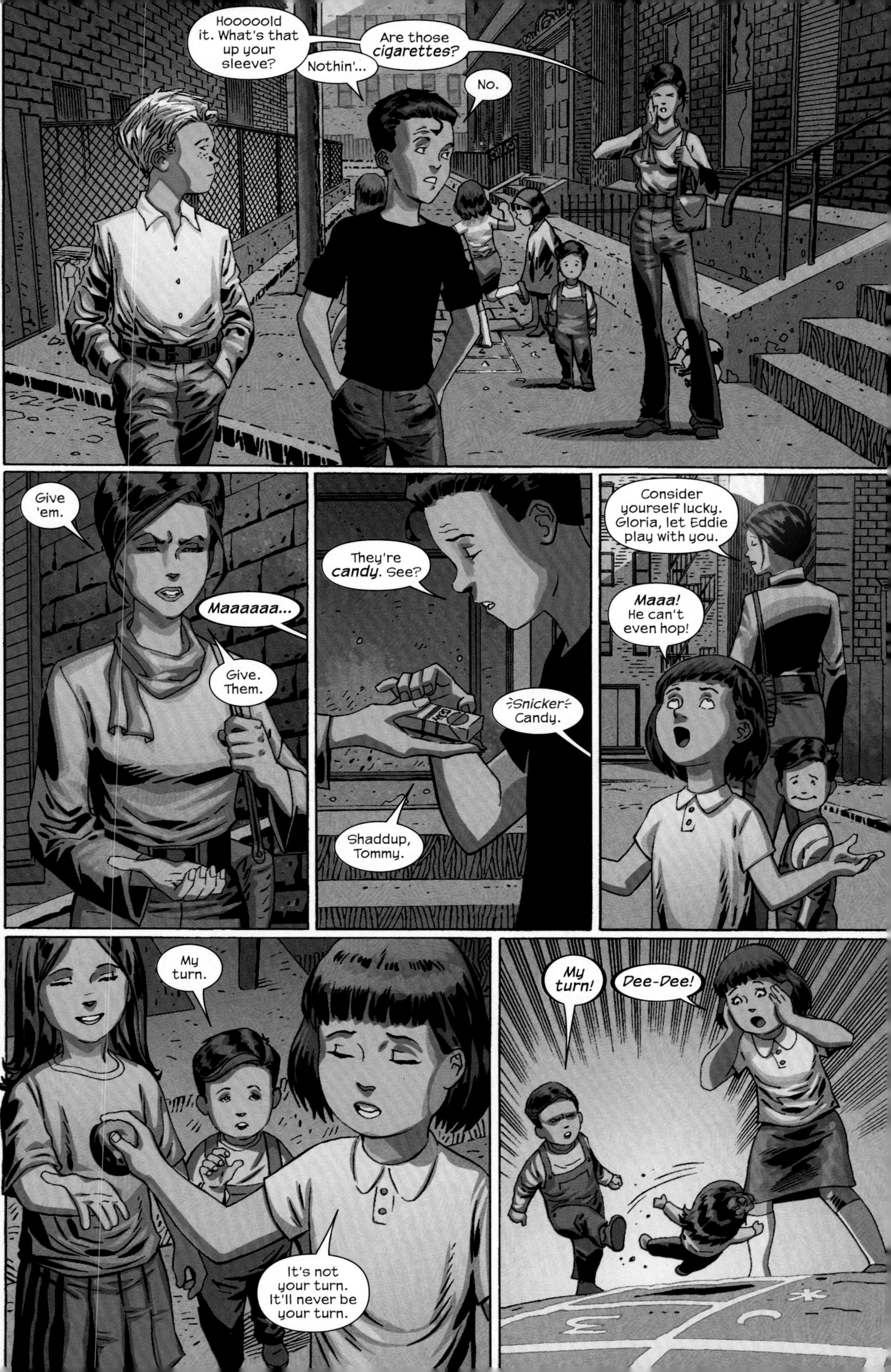
Hoooold it. What's that up your sleeve?
Nothin'...
Are those *cigarettes?*
No.
Give 'em.
Maaaaaa...
Give. Them.
They're *candy*. See?
Snicker
Candy.
Shaddup, Tommy.
Consider yourself lucky. Gloria, let Eddie play with you.
Maaa! He can't even hop!
My turn.
It's not your turn. It'll never be your turn.
My turn!
Dee-Dee!

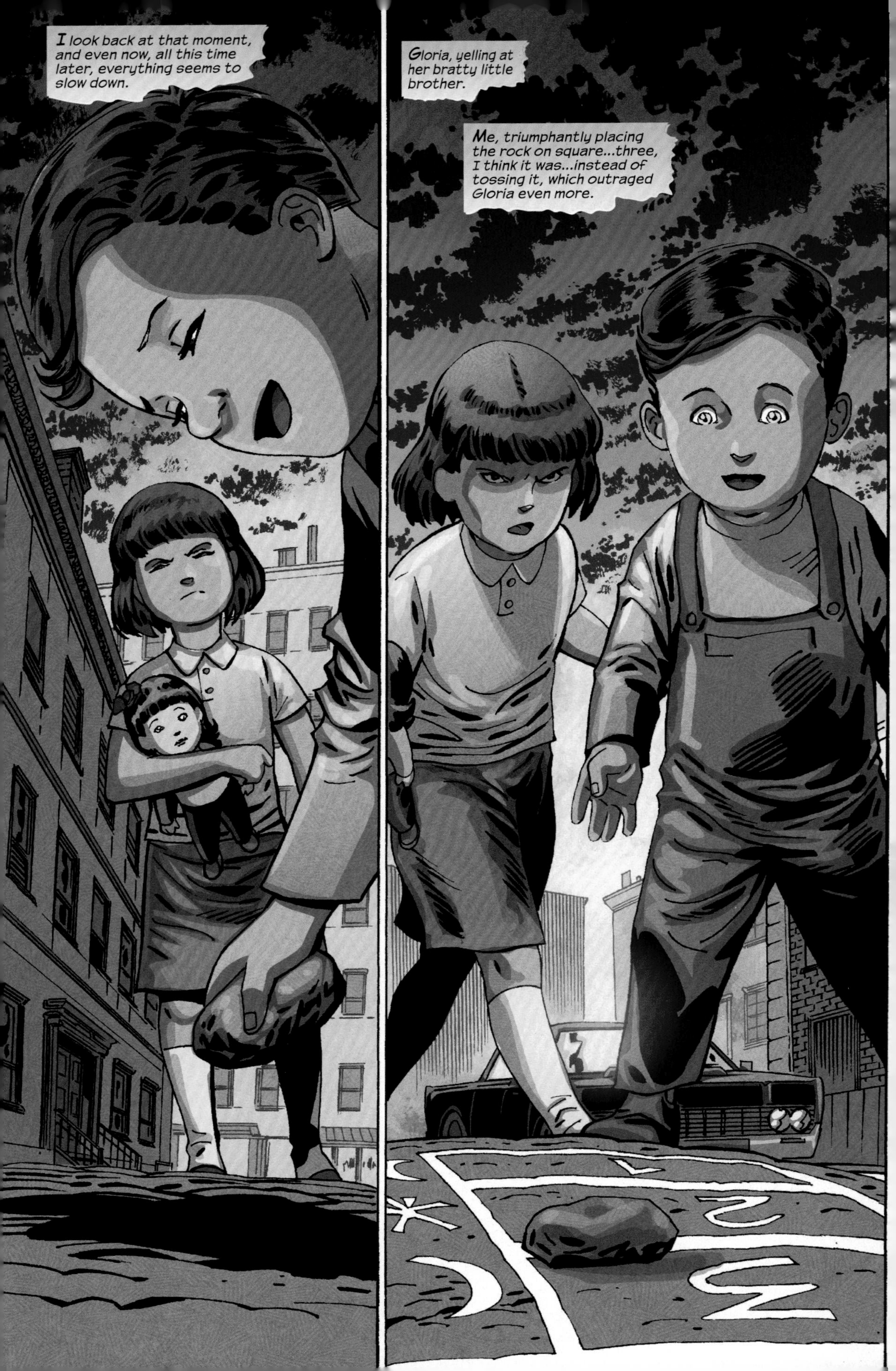
I look back at that moment, and even now, all this time later, everything seems to slow down.
Gloria, yelling at her bratty little brother.
Me, triumphantly placing the rock on square...three, I think it was...instead of tossing it, which outraged Gloria even more.

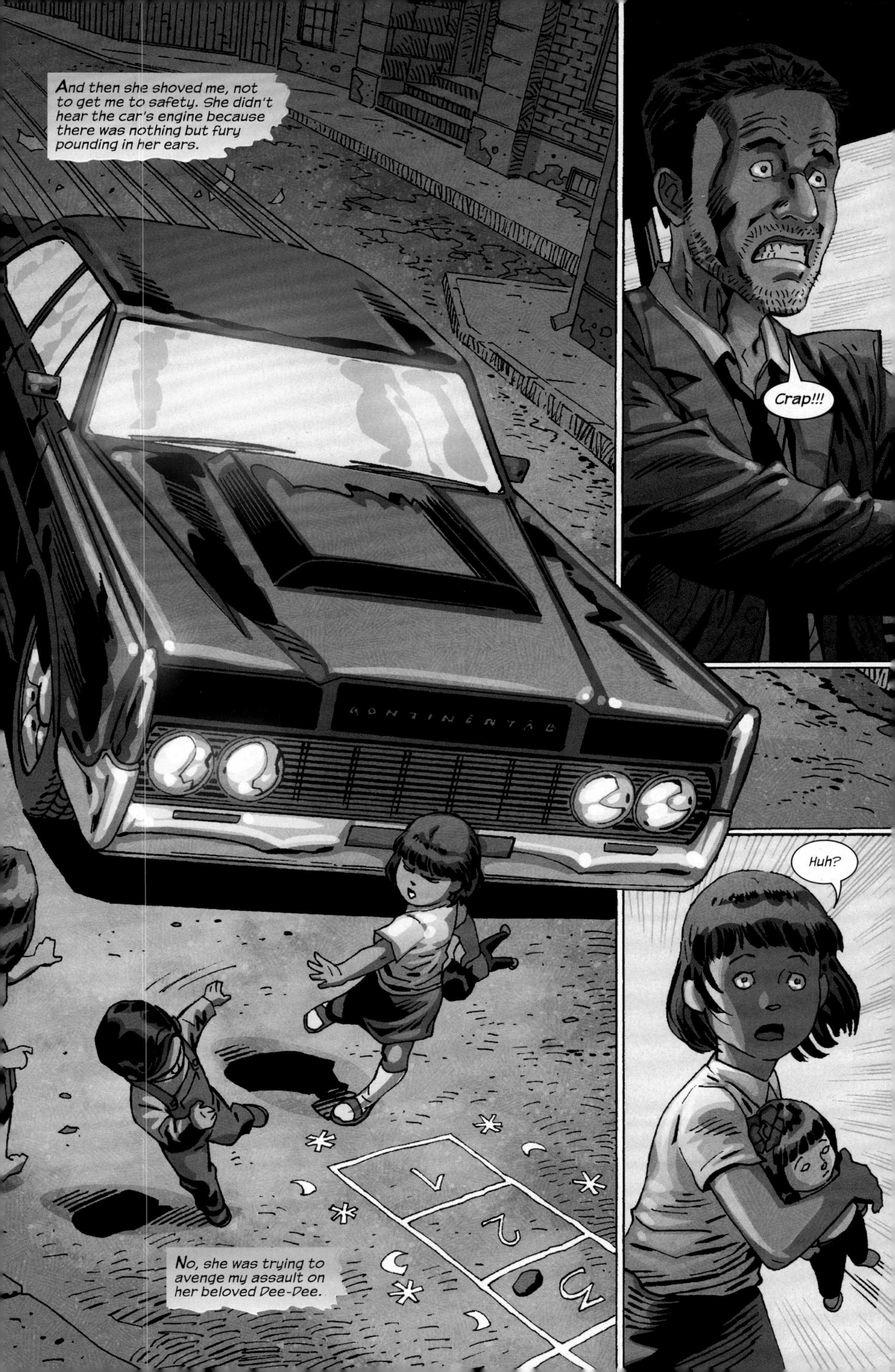

And then she shoved me, not to get me to safety. She didn't hear the car's engine because there was nothing but fury pounding in her ears.
CONTINENTAL
1
2
3
No, she was trying to avenge my assault on her beloved Dee-Dee.
Crap!!!
Huh?

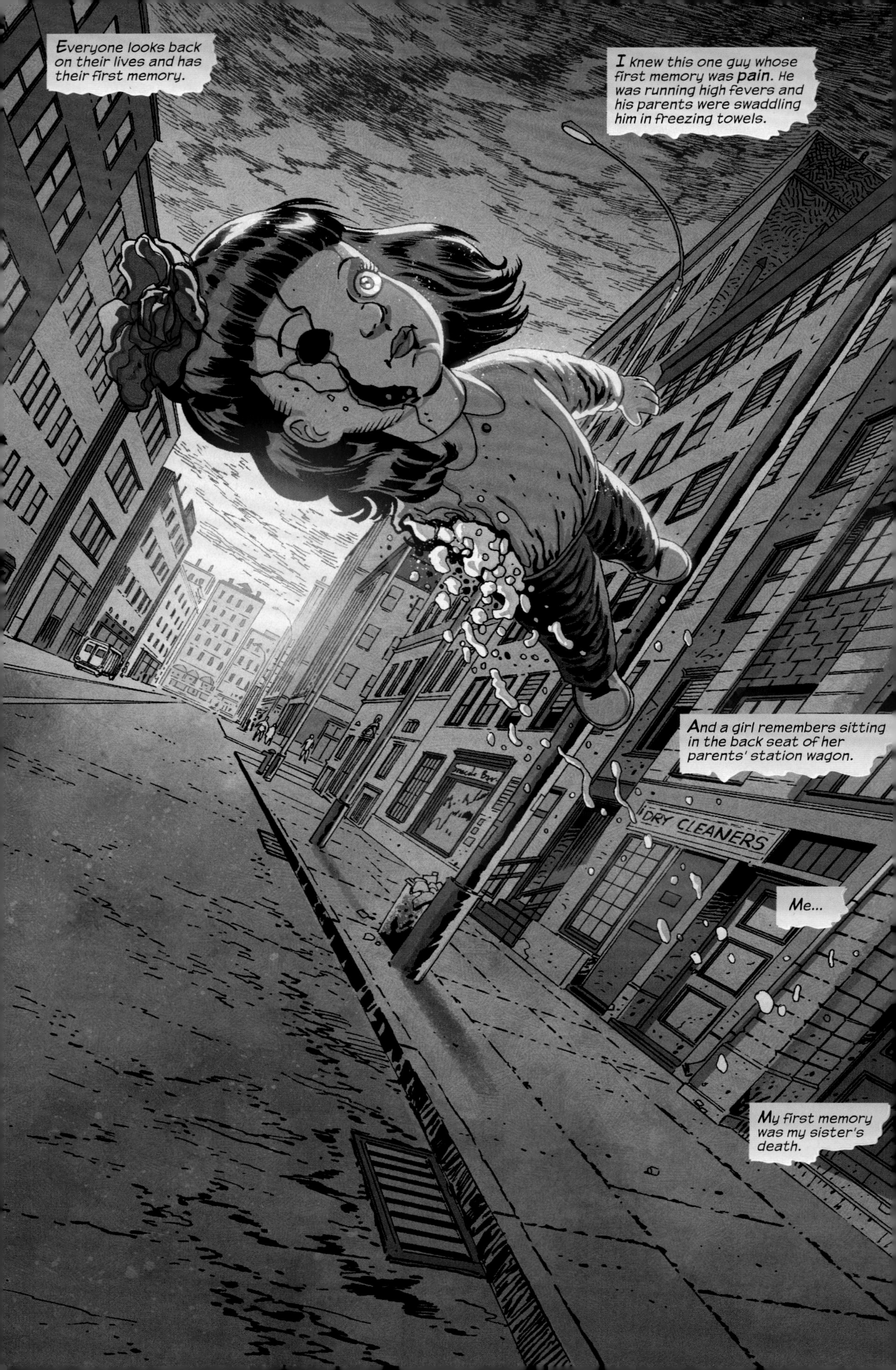
Everyone looks back on their lives and has their first memory.
I knew this one guy whose first memory was pain. He was running high fevers and his parents were swaddling him in freezing towels.
And a girl remembers sitting in the back seat of her parents' station wagon.
DRY CLEANERS
Me...
My first memory was my sister's death.

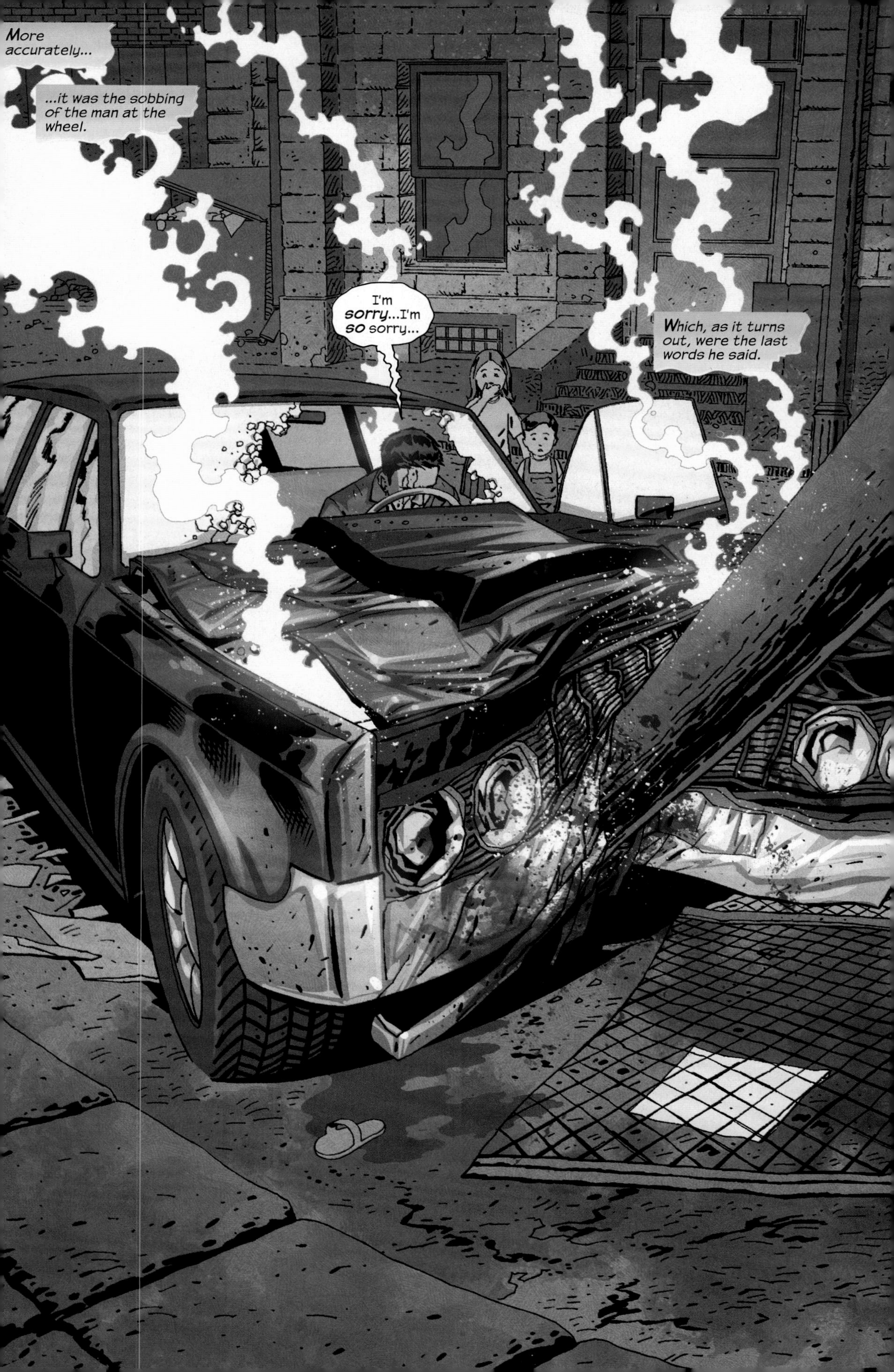
More accurately...
...it was the sobbing of the man at the wheel.
I'm sorry...I'm so sorry...
Which, as it turns out, were the last words he said.

Neighbors came running, screaming from every direction.

Me, I had no idea what had happened. I was only two. I didn't have any grasp of death.

I mean, I understood it enough, in that I knew my cowboy could die in a shootout. But I had no grasp of its **permanence**.

I kept waiting for Gloria to stand up. Brush herself off.

I didn't know that the rattle I'd heard from the driver's throat was the last noise he was going to make.

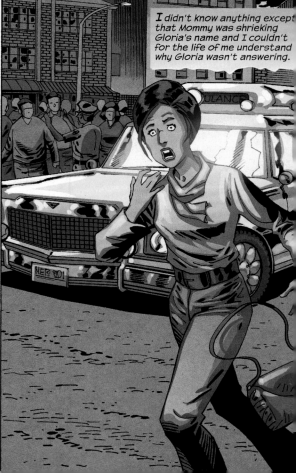

I didn't know anything except that Mommy was shrieking Gloria's name and I couldn't for the life of me understand why Gloria wasn't answering.

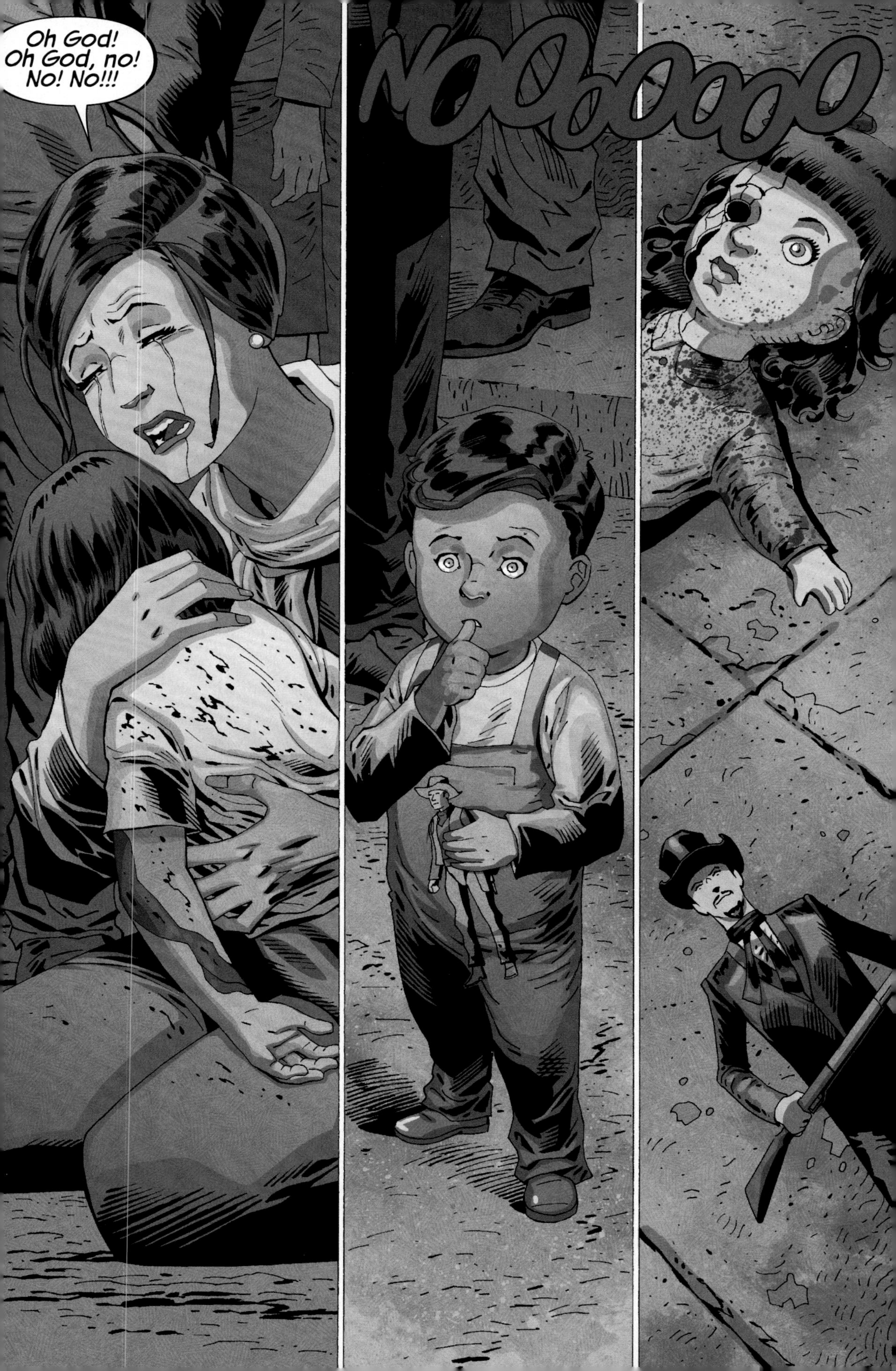
Oh God!
Oh God, no!
No! No!!!
NOOoOOOOO

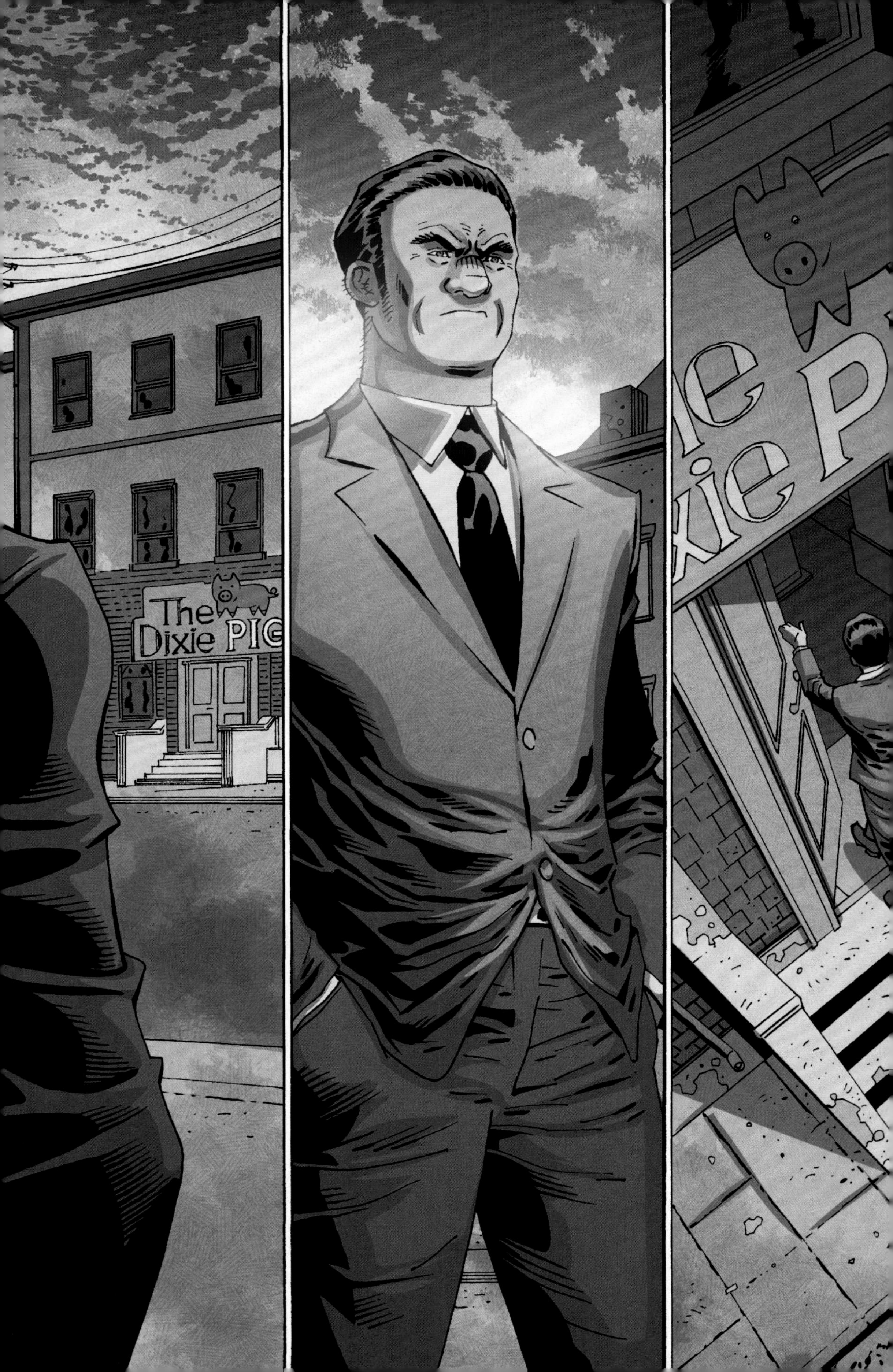
The Dixie PIG

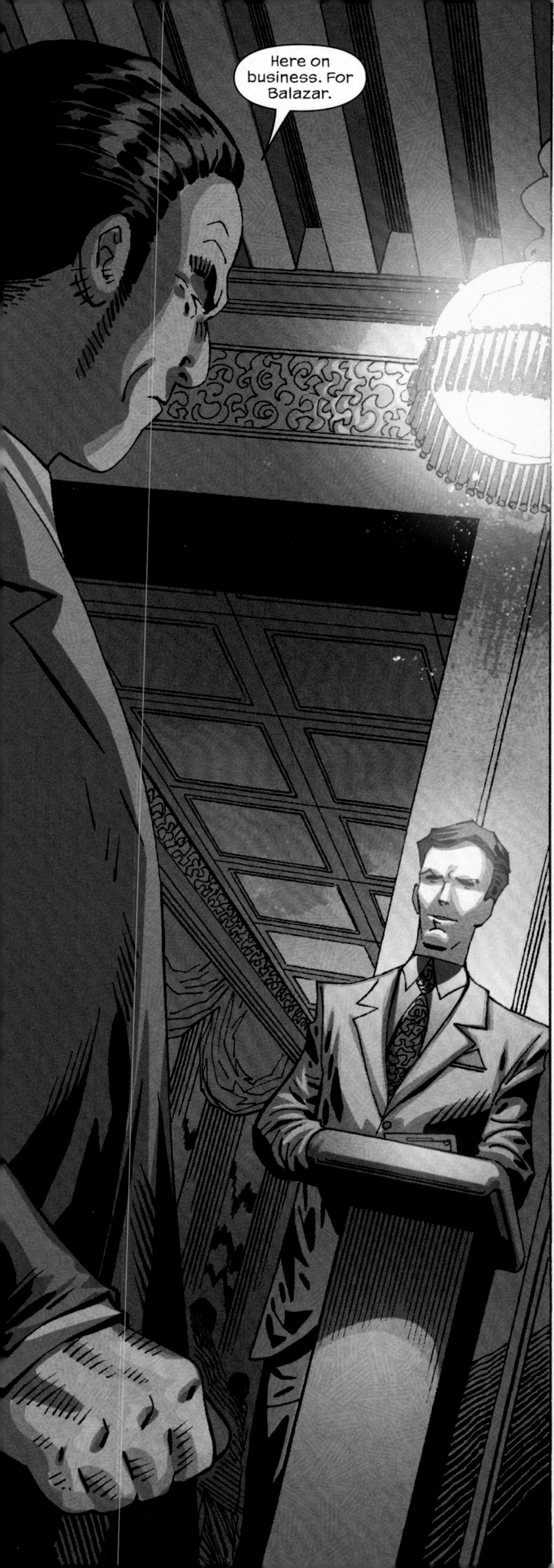
Here on business. For Balazar.

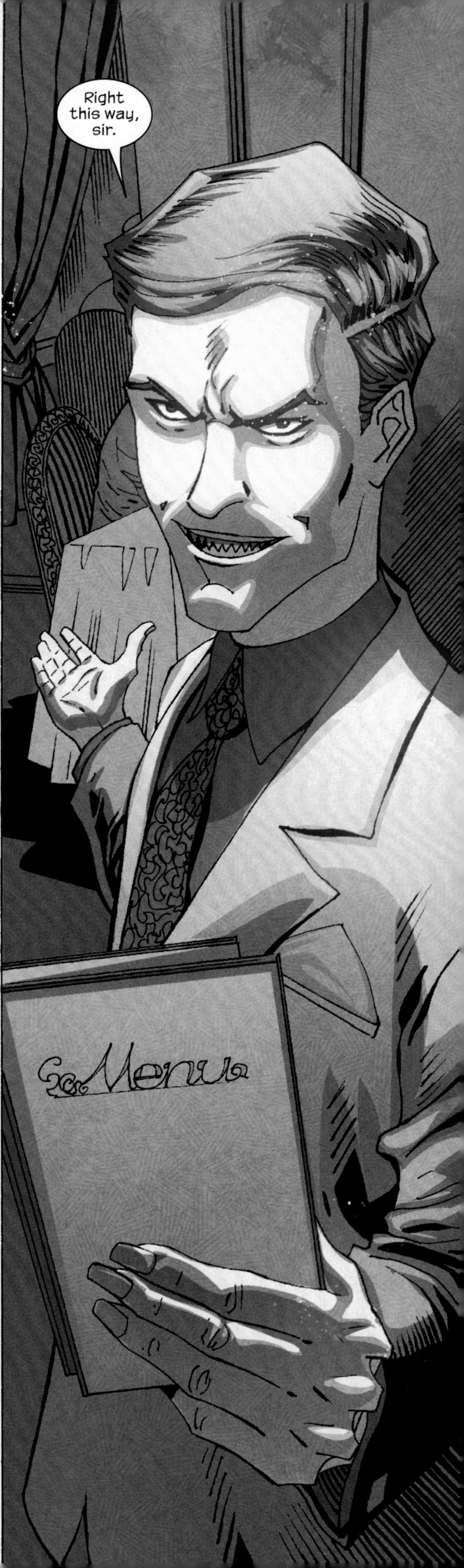
Right this way, sir.
Menu

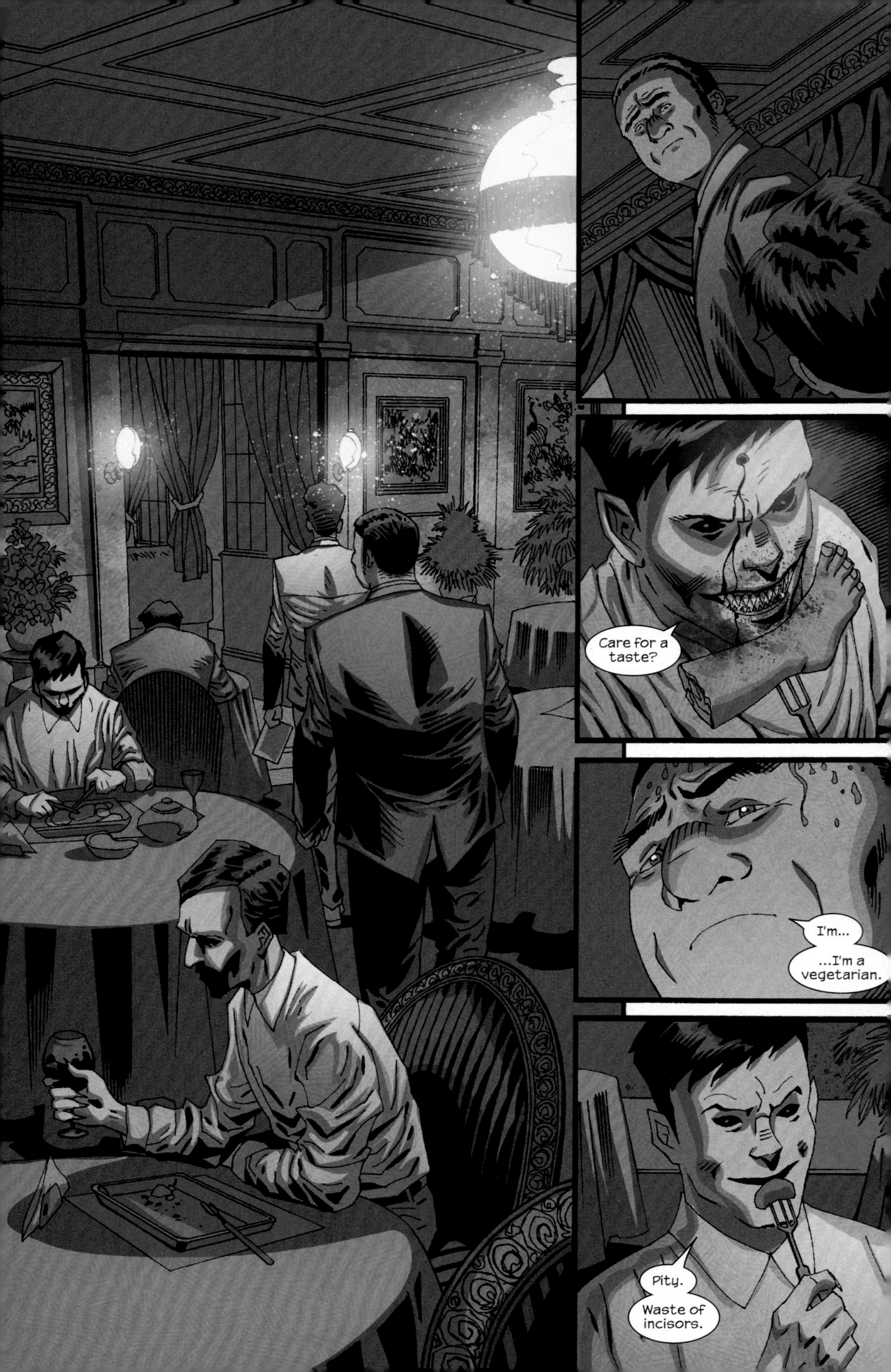
Care for a taste?
I'm...
...I'm a vegetarian.
Pity.
Waste of incisors.

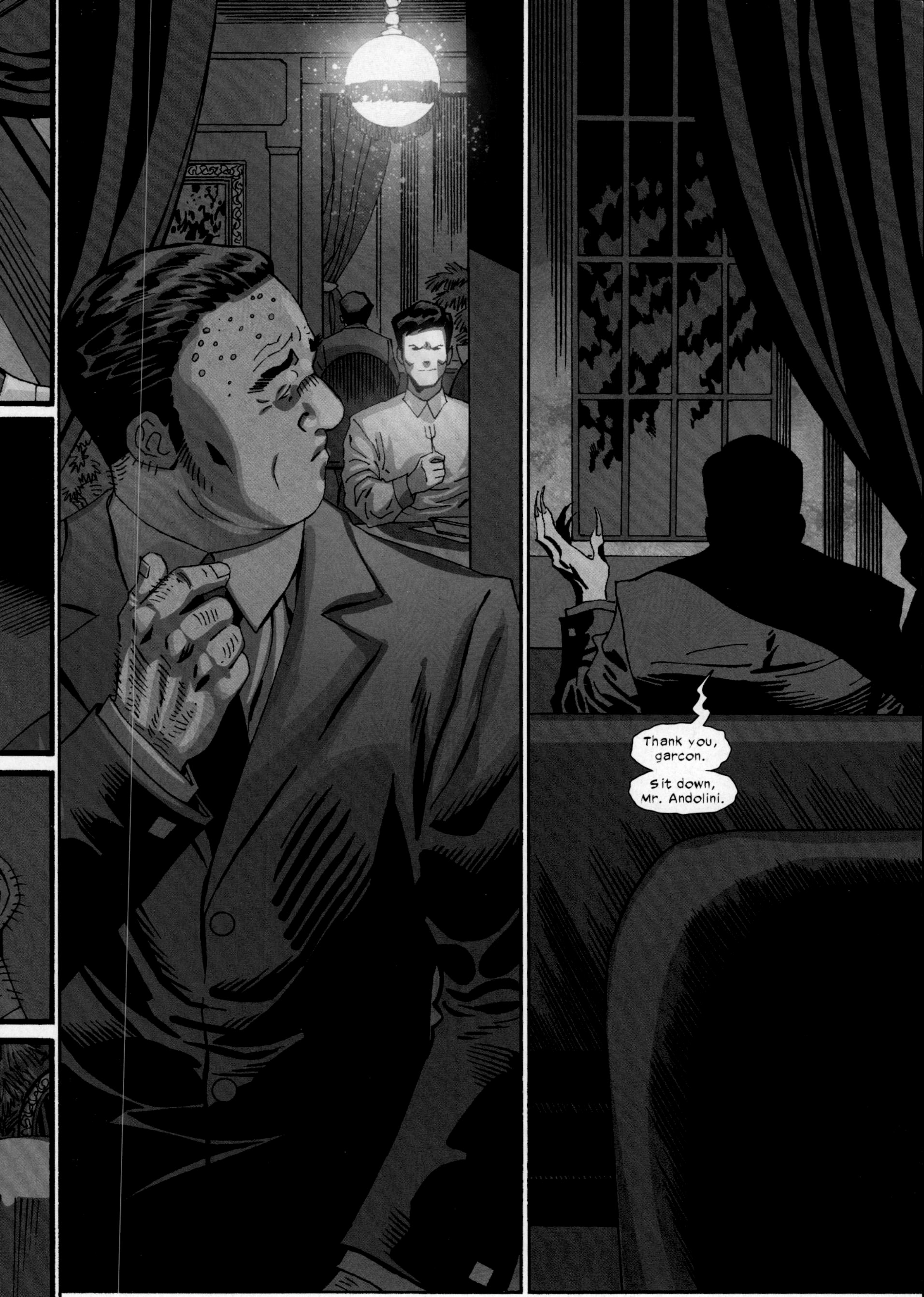
Thank you, garcon.
Sit down, Mr. Andolini.

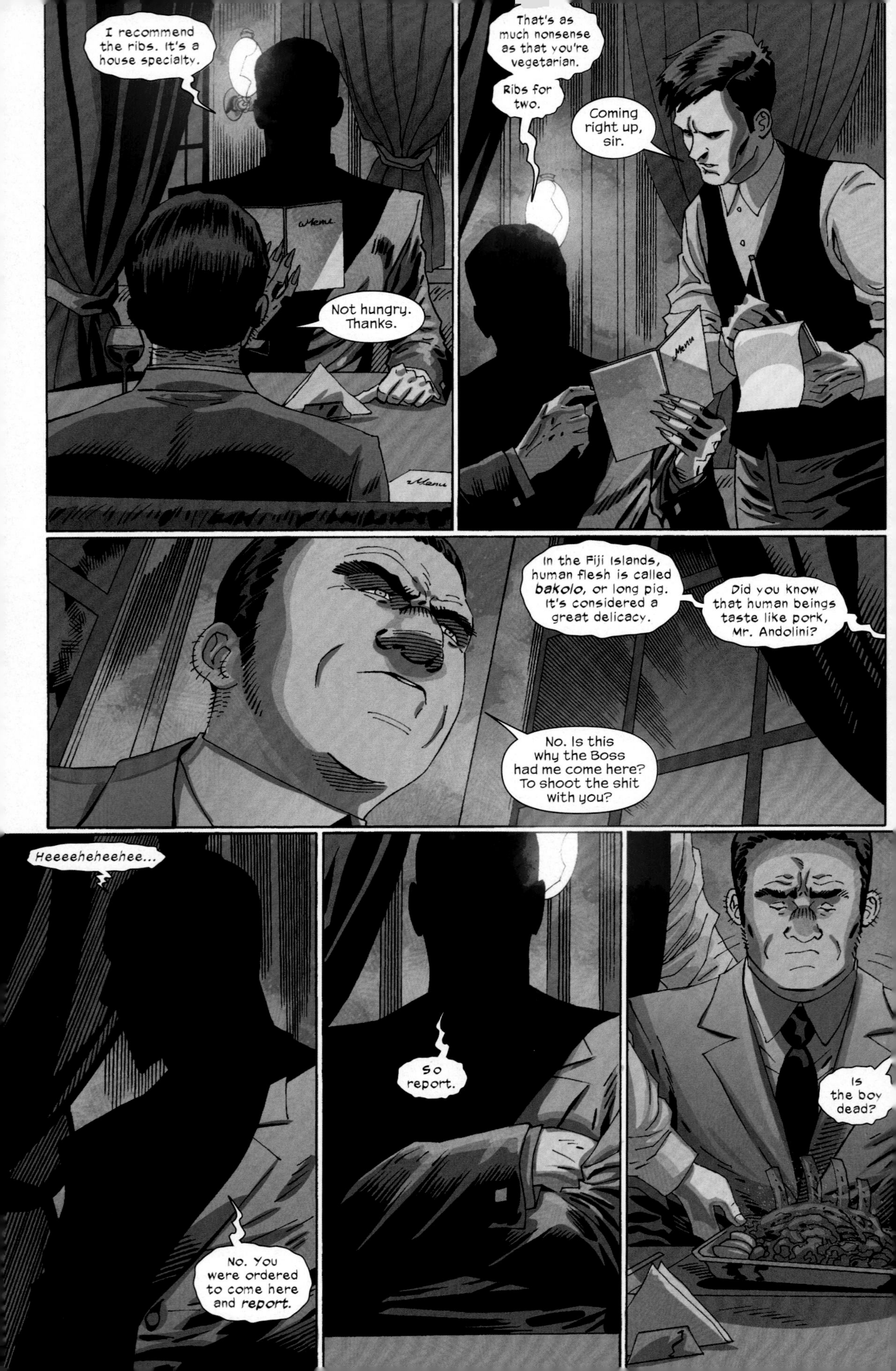
I recommend the ribs. It's a house specialty.
Not hungry. Thanks.
That's as much nonsense as that you're vegetarian.
Ribs for two.
Coming right up, sir.
No. Is this why the Boss had me come here? To shoot the shit with you?
Did you know that human beings taste like pork, Mr. Andolini?
In the Fiji Islands, human flesh is called *bakolo*, or long pig. It's considered a great delicacy.
Heeeeheheeehee...
No. You were ordered to come here and *report*.
So report.
Is the boy dead?

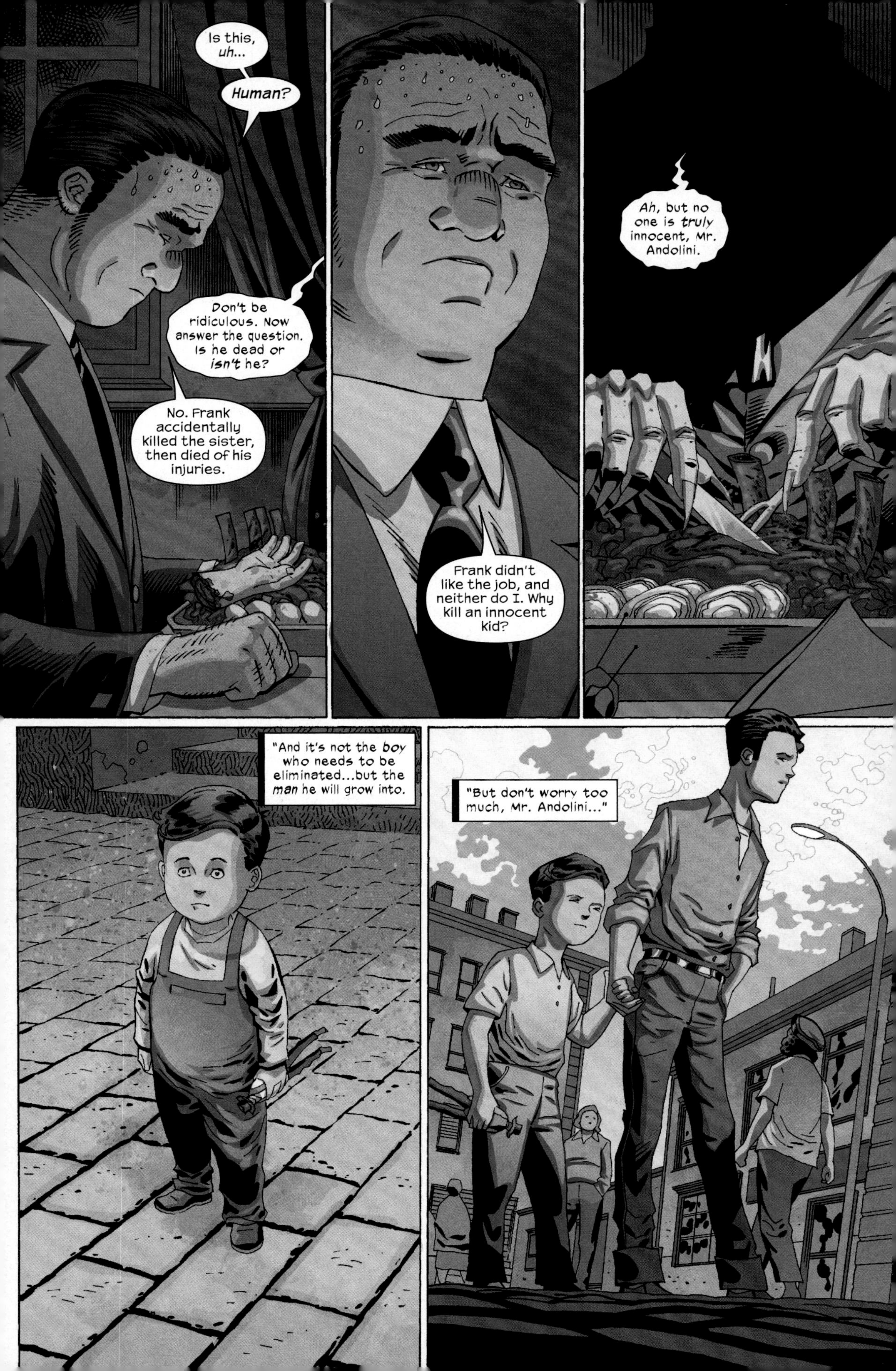
Is this, uh...
Human?
Don't be ridiculous. Now answer the question. Is he dead or isn't he?
No. Frank accidentally killed the sister, then died of his injuries.
Frank didn't like the job, and neither do I. Why kill an innocent kid?
Ah, but no one is truly innocent, Mr. Andolini.
"And it's not the boy who needs to be eliminated...but the man he will grow into.
"But don't worry too much, Mr. Andolini..."

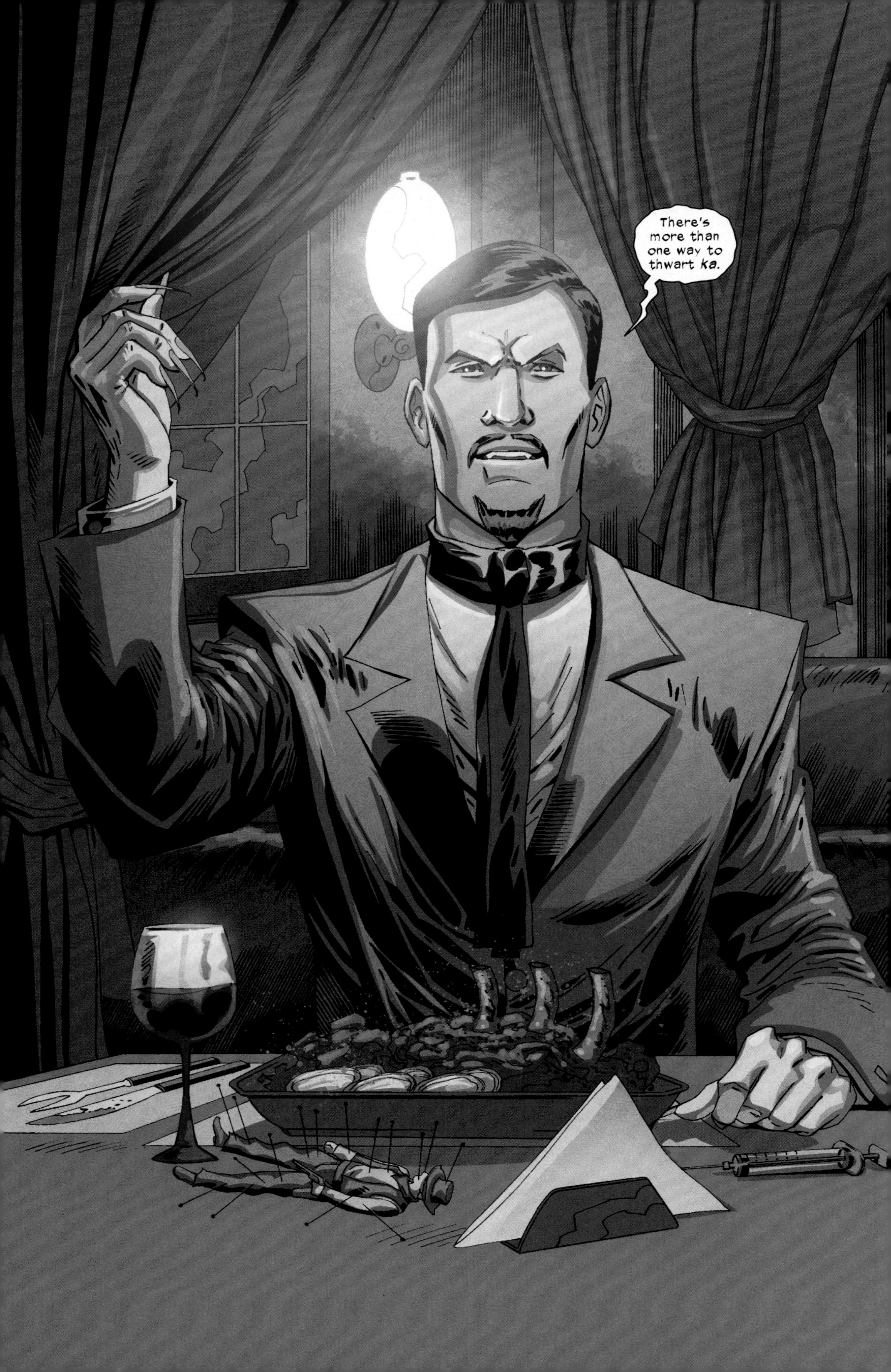
There's more than one way to thwart ka.

THE DARK TOWER
THE DRAWING OF THE THREE
STEPHEN KING

THE PRISONER
CHAPTER TWO

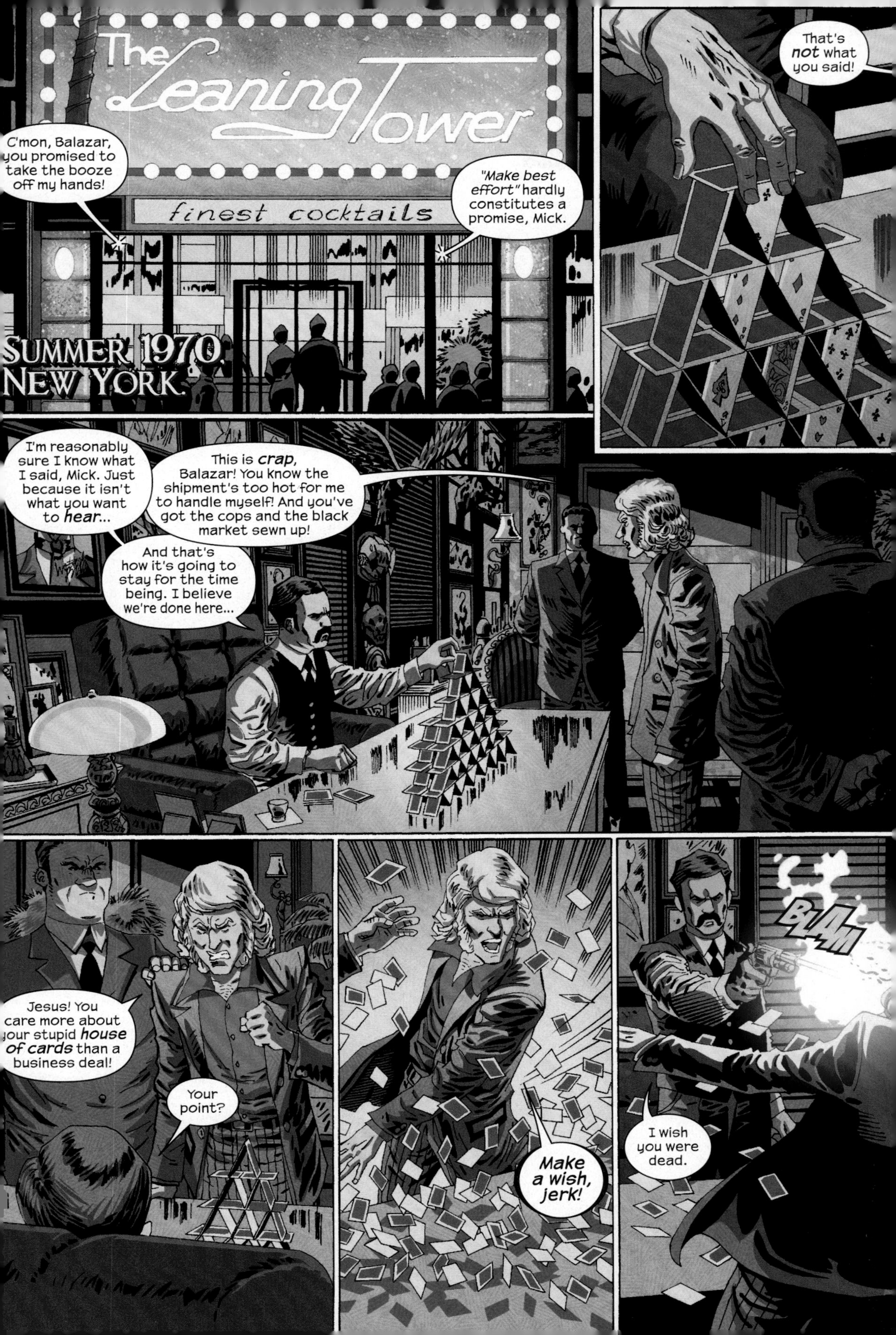
The Leaning Tower
finest cocktails
SUMMER 1970. NEW YORK.
C'mon, Balazar, you promised to take the booze off my hands!
"Make best effort" hardly constitutes a promise, Mick.
That's not what you said!
I'm reasonably sure I know what I said, Mick. Just because it isn't what you want to hear...
This is crap, Balazar! You know the shipment's too hot for me to handle myself! And you've got the cops and the black market sewn up!
And that's how it's going to stay for the time being. I believe we're done here...
Jesus! You care more about your stupid house of cards than a business deal!
Your point?
Make a wish, jerk!
BLAM
I wish you were dead.

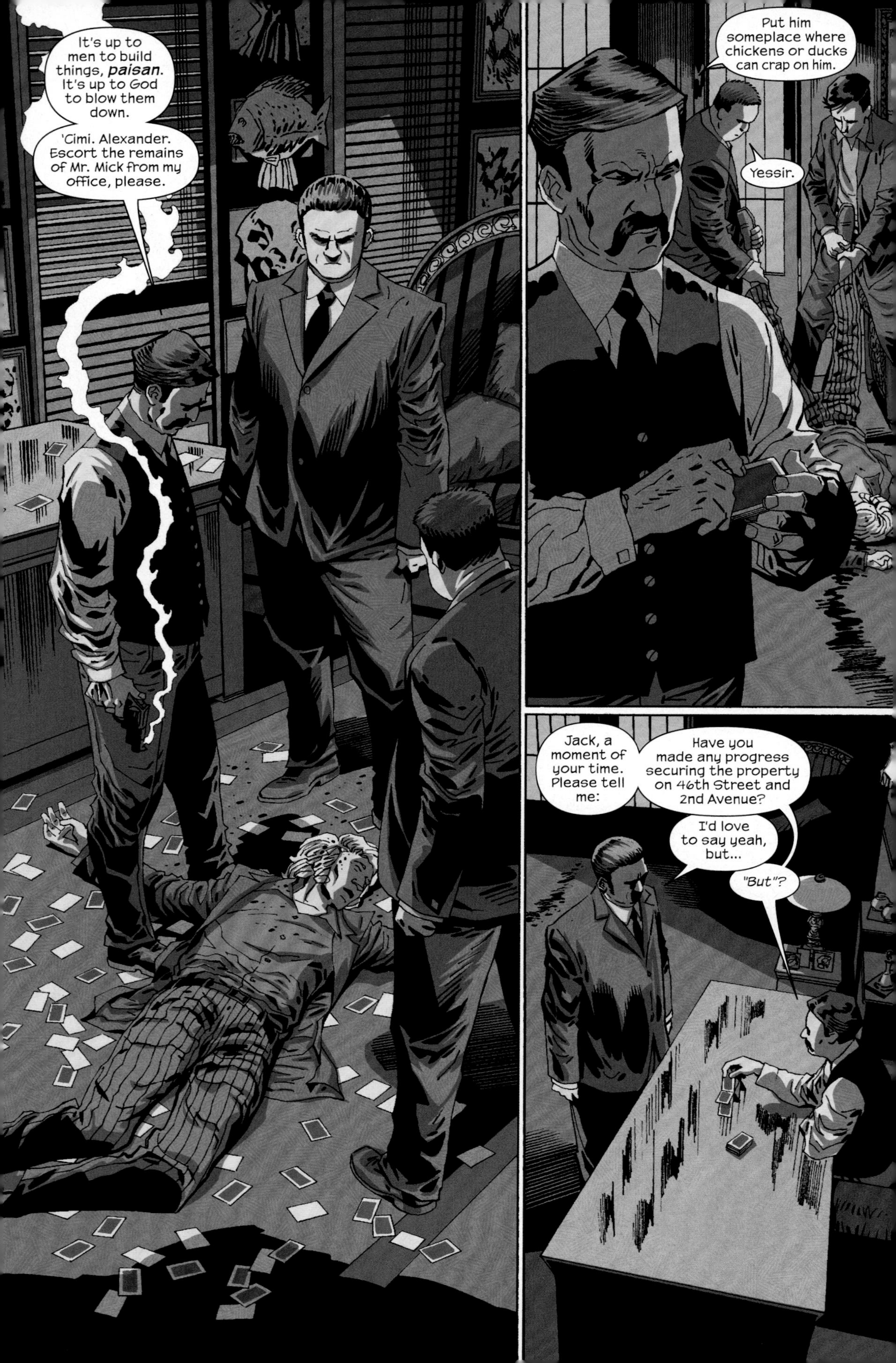
It's up to men to build things, *paisan*. It's up to God to blow them down.
'Cimi. Alexander. Escort the remains of Mr. Mick from my office, please.
Put him someplace where chickens or ducks can crap on him.
Yessir.
Jack, a moment of your time. Please tell me:
Have you made any progress securing the property on 46th Street and 2nd Avenue?
I'd love to say yeah, but...
"But"?

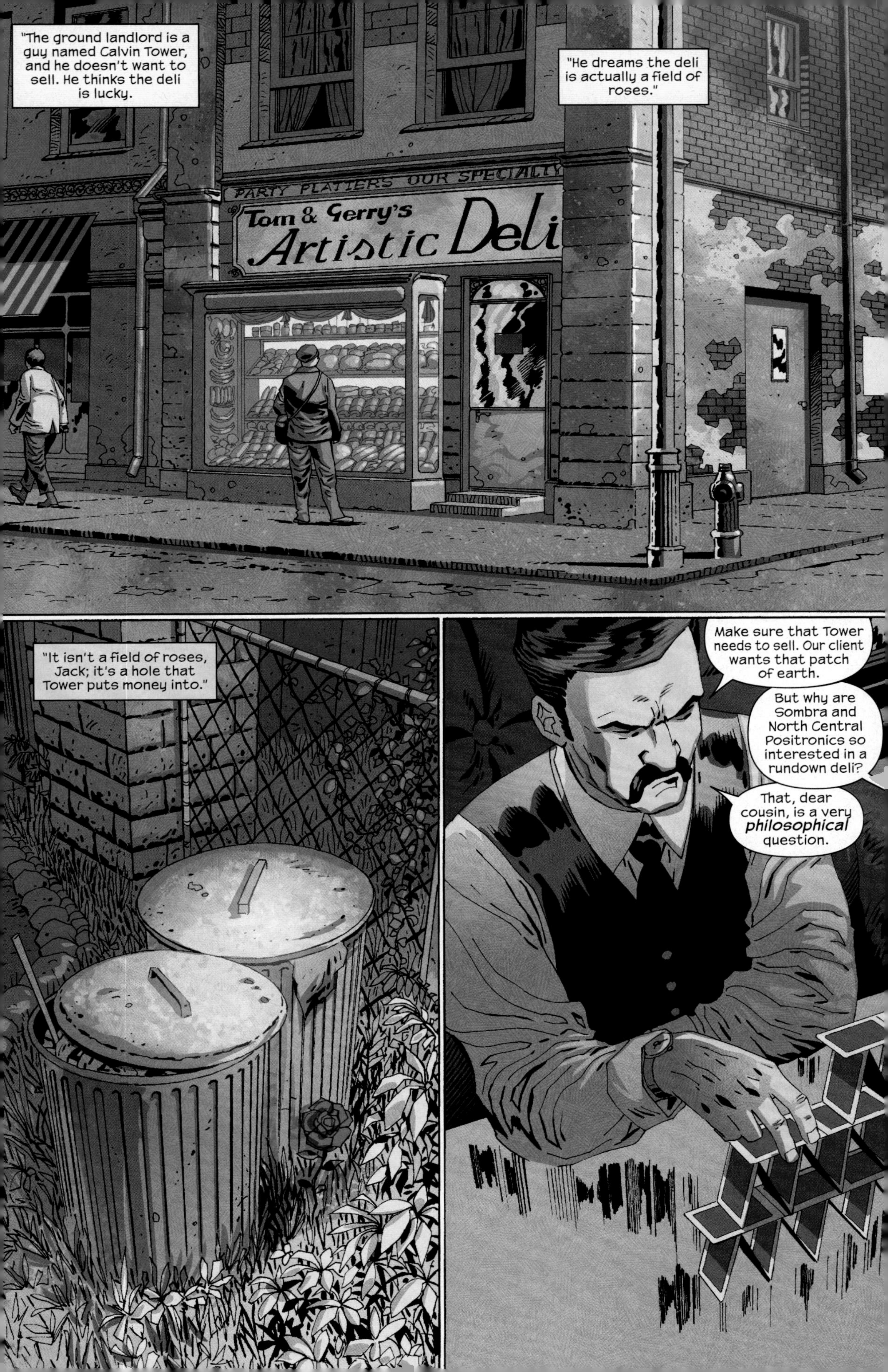
"The ground landlord is a guy named Calvin Tower, and he doesn't want to sell. He thinks the deli is lucky.
"He dreams the deli is actually a field of roses."
PARTY PLATTERS OUR SPECIALTY
Tom & Gerry's Artistic Deli
"It isn't a field of roses, Jack; it's a hole that Tower puts money into."
Make sure that Tower needs to sell. Our client wants that patch of earth.
But why are Sombra and North Central Positronics so interested in a rundown deli?
That, dear cousin, is a very *philosophical* question.

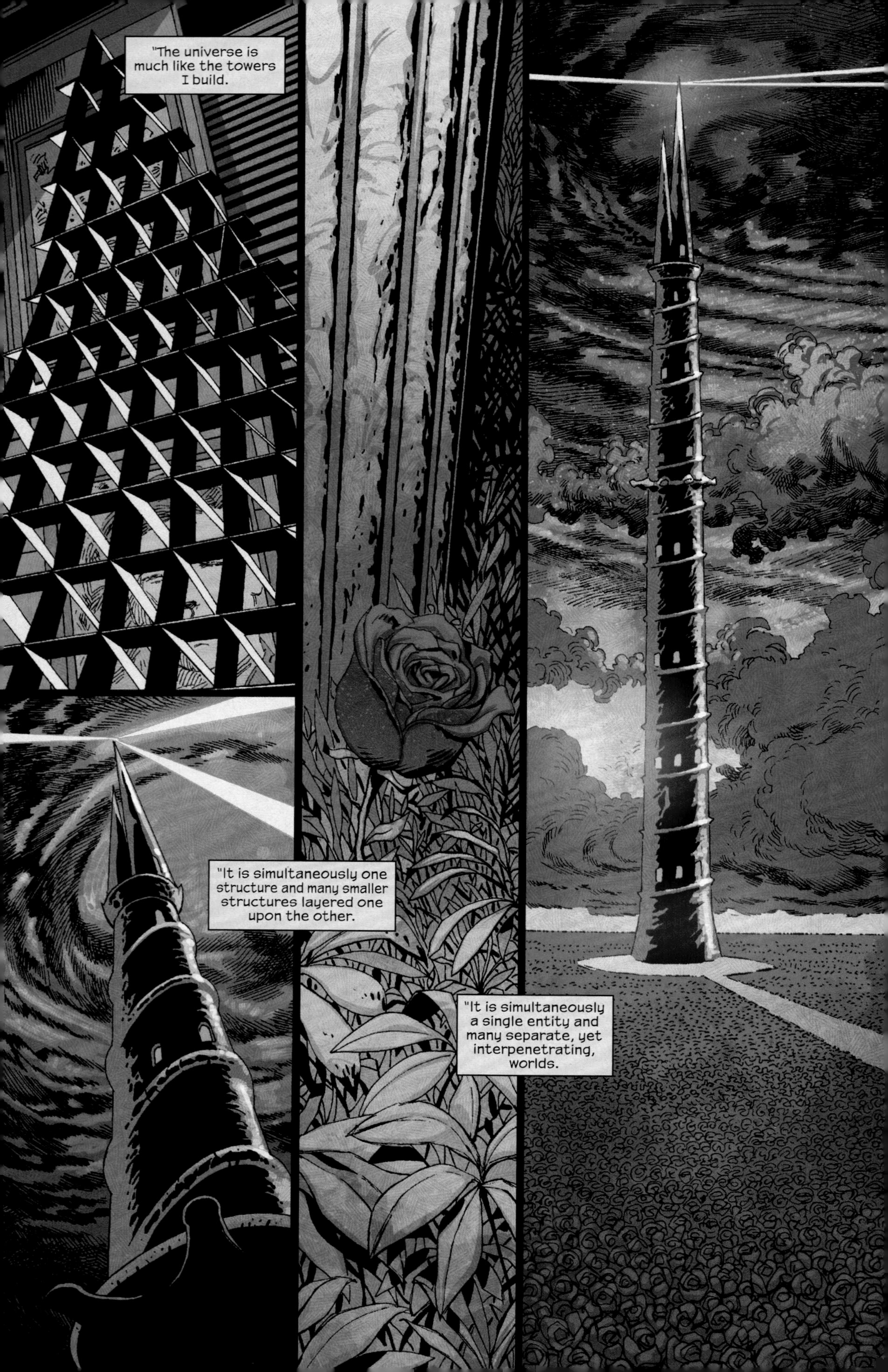
"The universe is much like the towers I build.
"It is simultaneously one structure and many smaller structures layered one upon the other.
"It is simultaneously a single entity and many separate, yet interpenetrating, worlds.

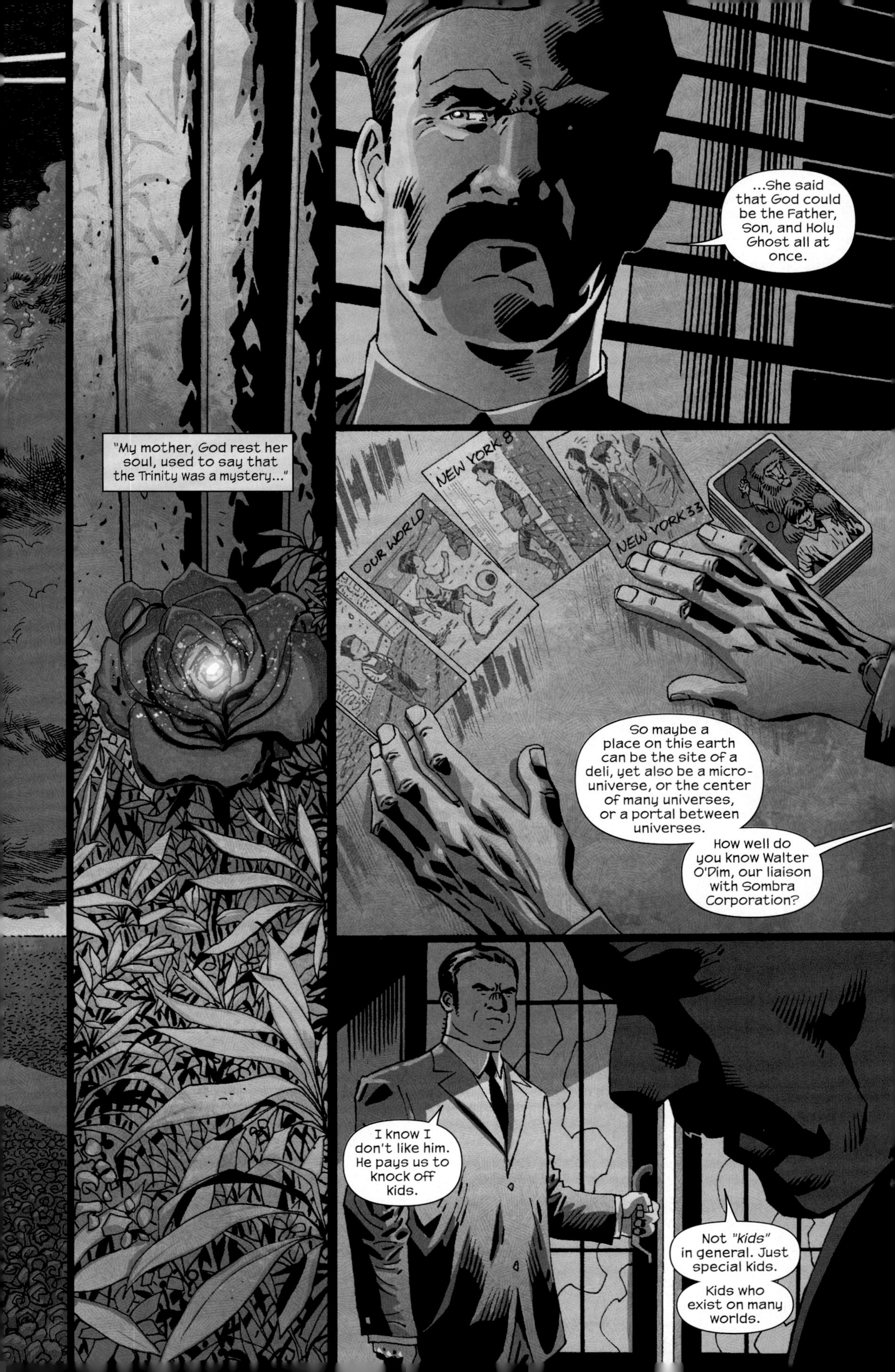

...She said that God could be the Father, Son, and Holy Ghost all at once.
"My mother, God rest her soul, used to say that the Trinity was a mystery..."
NEW YORK 8
OUR WORLD
NEW YORK 33
So maybe a place on this earth can be the site of a deli, yet also be a micro-universe, or the center of many universes, or a portal between universes.
How well do you know Walter O'Dim, our liaison with Sombra Corporation?
I know I don't like him. He pays us to knock off kids.
Not *"kids"* in general. Just special kids.
Kids who exist on many worlds.

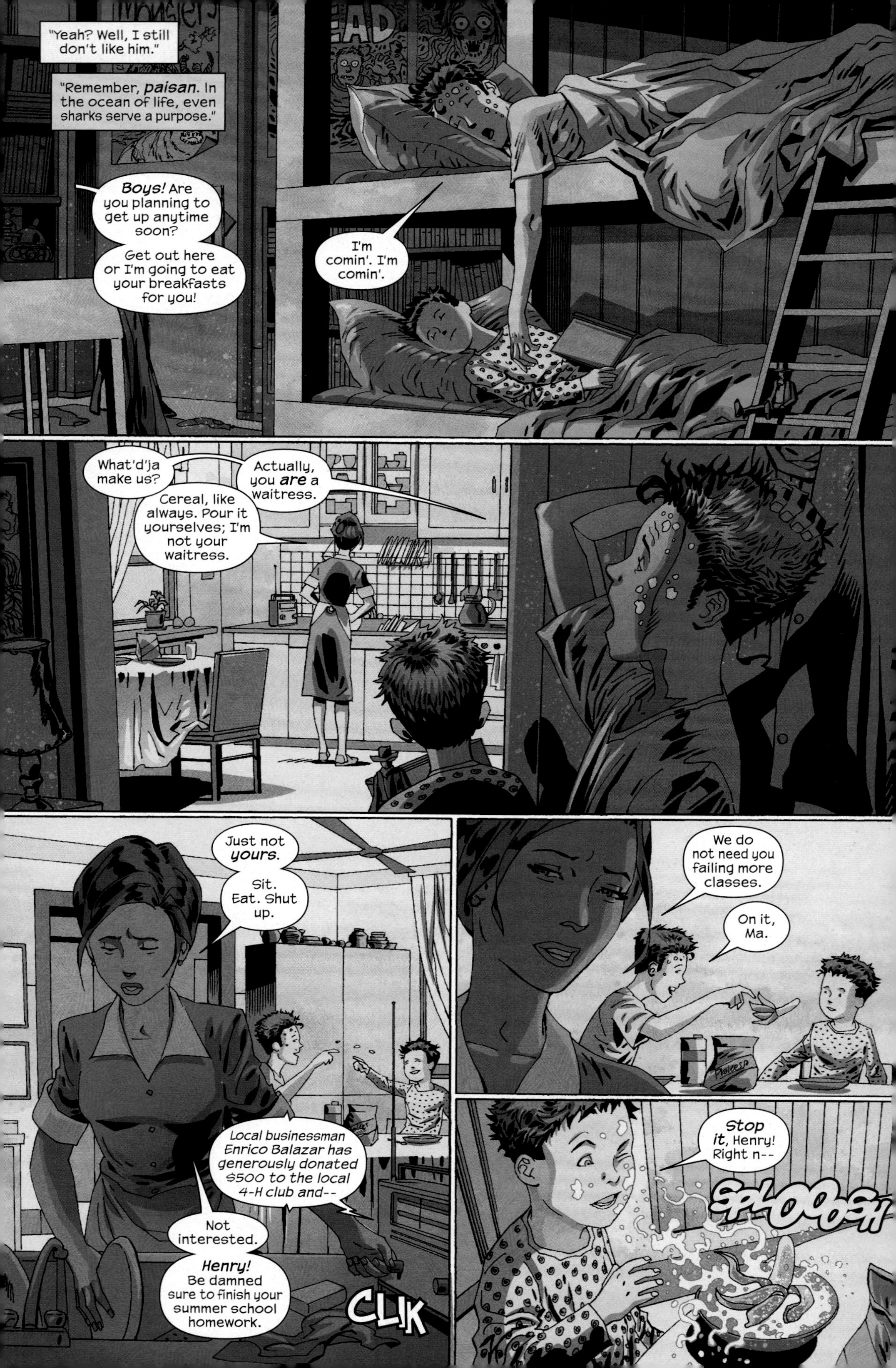
"Yeah? Well, I still don't like him."
"Remember, paisan. In the ocean of life, even sharks serve a purpose."
Boys! Are you planning to get up anytime soon?
Get out here or I'm going to eat your breakfasts for you!
I'm comin'. I'm comin'.
What'd'ja make us?
Cereal, like always. Pour it yourselves; I'm not your waitress.
Actually, you are a waitress.
Just not yours.
Sit. Eat. Shut up.
Local businessman Enrico Balazar has generously donated $500 to the local 4-H club and--
Not interested.
Henry! Be damned sure to finish your summer school homework.
CLIK
We do not need you failing more classes.
On it, Ma.
Stop it, Henry! Right n--
SPLOOOSH

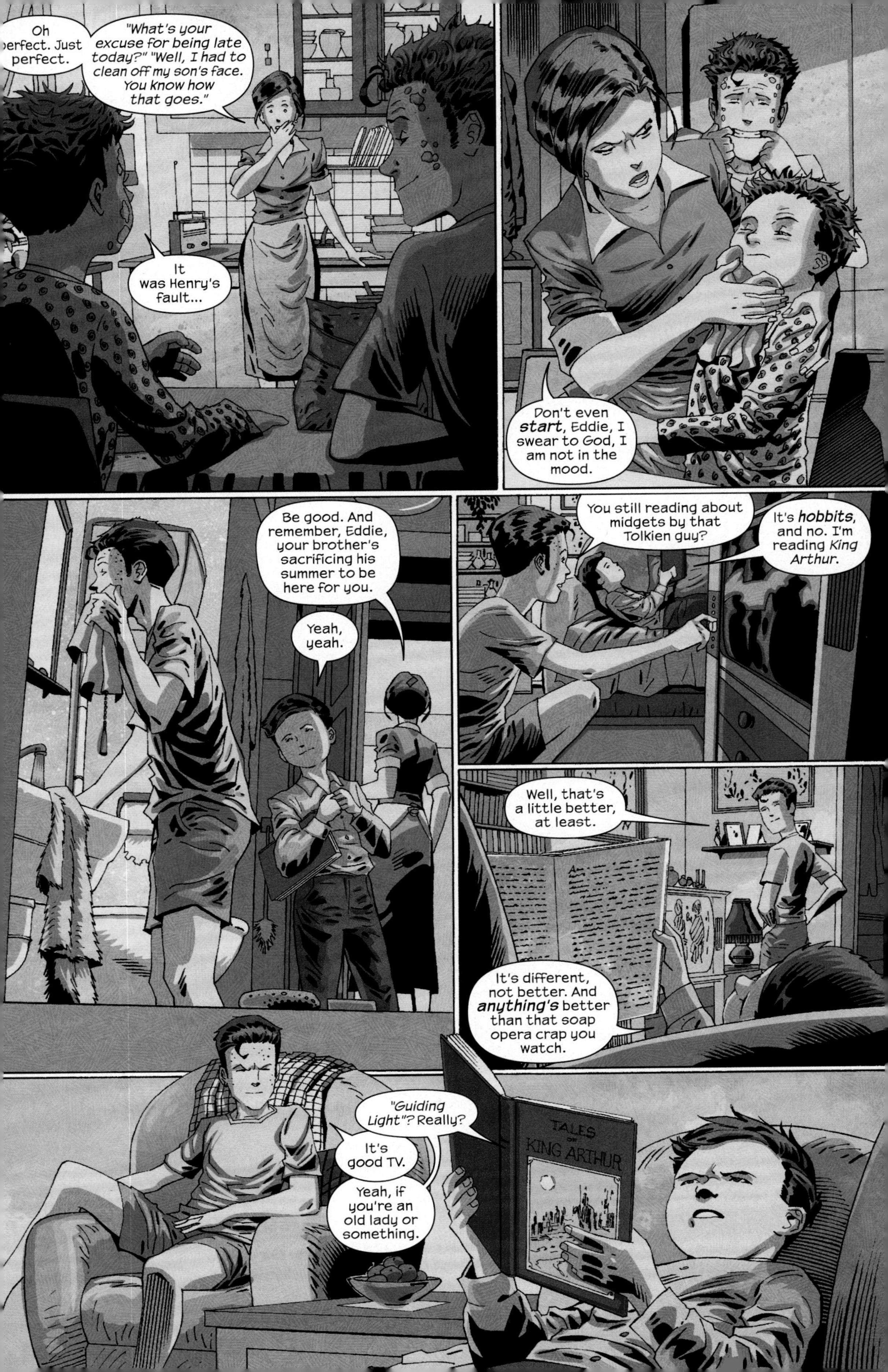
Oh perfect. Just perfect.
"What's your excuse for being late today?" "Well, I had to clean off my son's face. You know how that goes."
It was Henry's fault...
Don't even start, Eddie, I swear to God, I am not in the mood.
Be good. And remember, Eddie, your brother's sacrificing his summer to be here for you.
Yeah, yeah.
You still reading about midgets by that Tolkien guy?
It's hobbits, and no. I'm reading King Arthur.
Well, that's a little better, at least.
It's different, not better. And anything's better than that soap opera crap you watch.
"Guiding Light"? Really?
It's good TV.
Yeah, if you're an old lady or something.
TALES OF KING ARTHUR

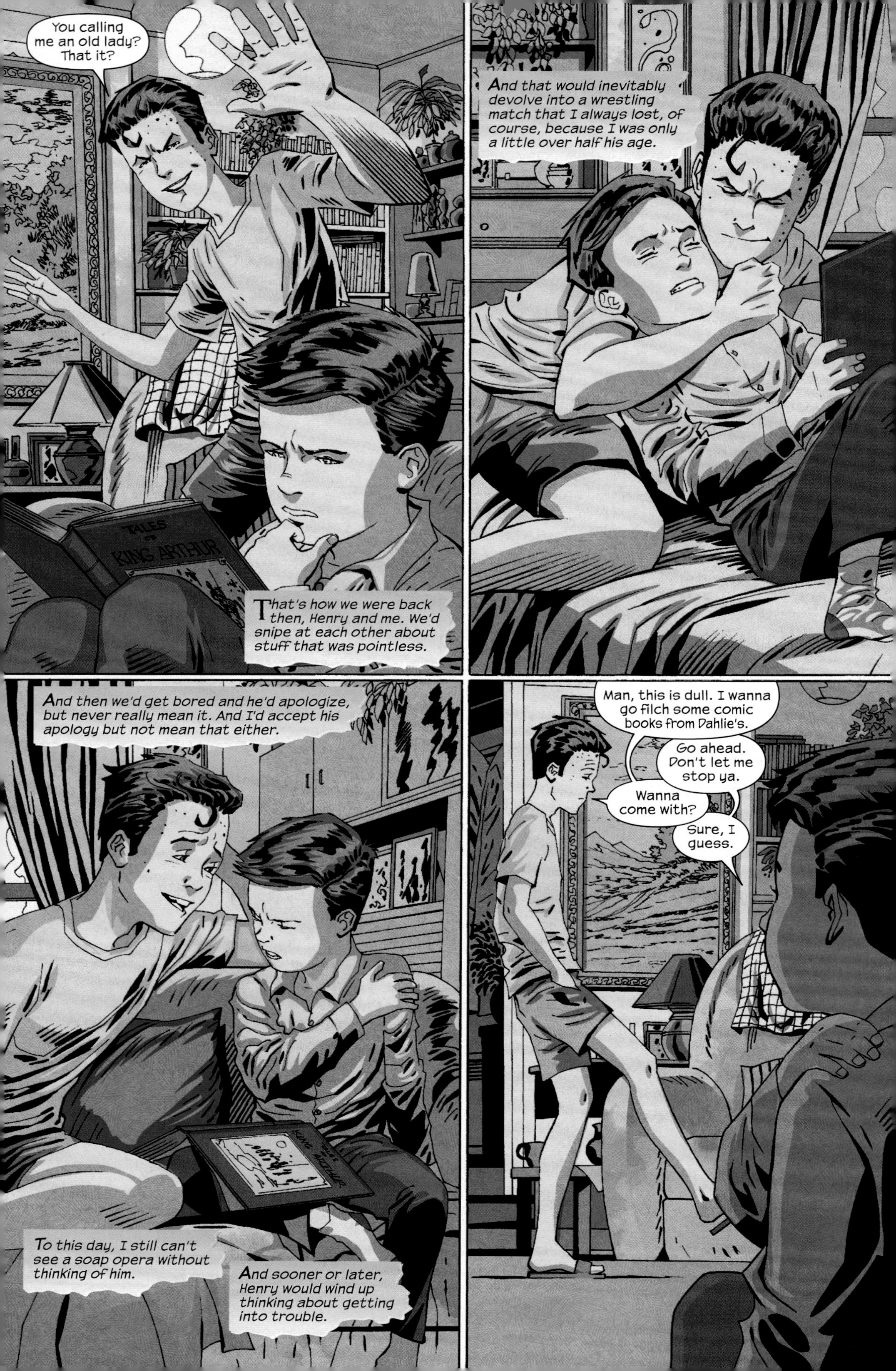
You calling me an old lady? That it?
That's how we were back then, Henry and me. We'd snipe at each other about stuff that was pointless.
And that would inevitably devolve into a wrestling match that I always lost, of course, because I was only a little over half his age.
And then we'd get bored and he'd apologize, but never really mean it. And I'd accept his apology but not mean that either.
To this day, I still can't see a soap opera without thinking of him.
And sooner or later, Henry would wind up thinking about getting into trouble.
Man, this is dull. I wanna go filch some comic books from Dahlie's.
Go ahead. Don't let me stop ya.
Wanna come with?
Sure, I guess.

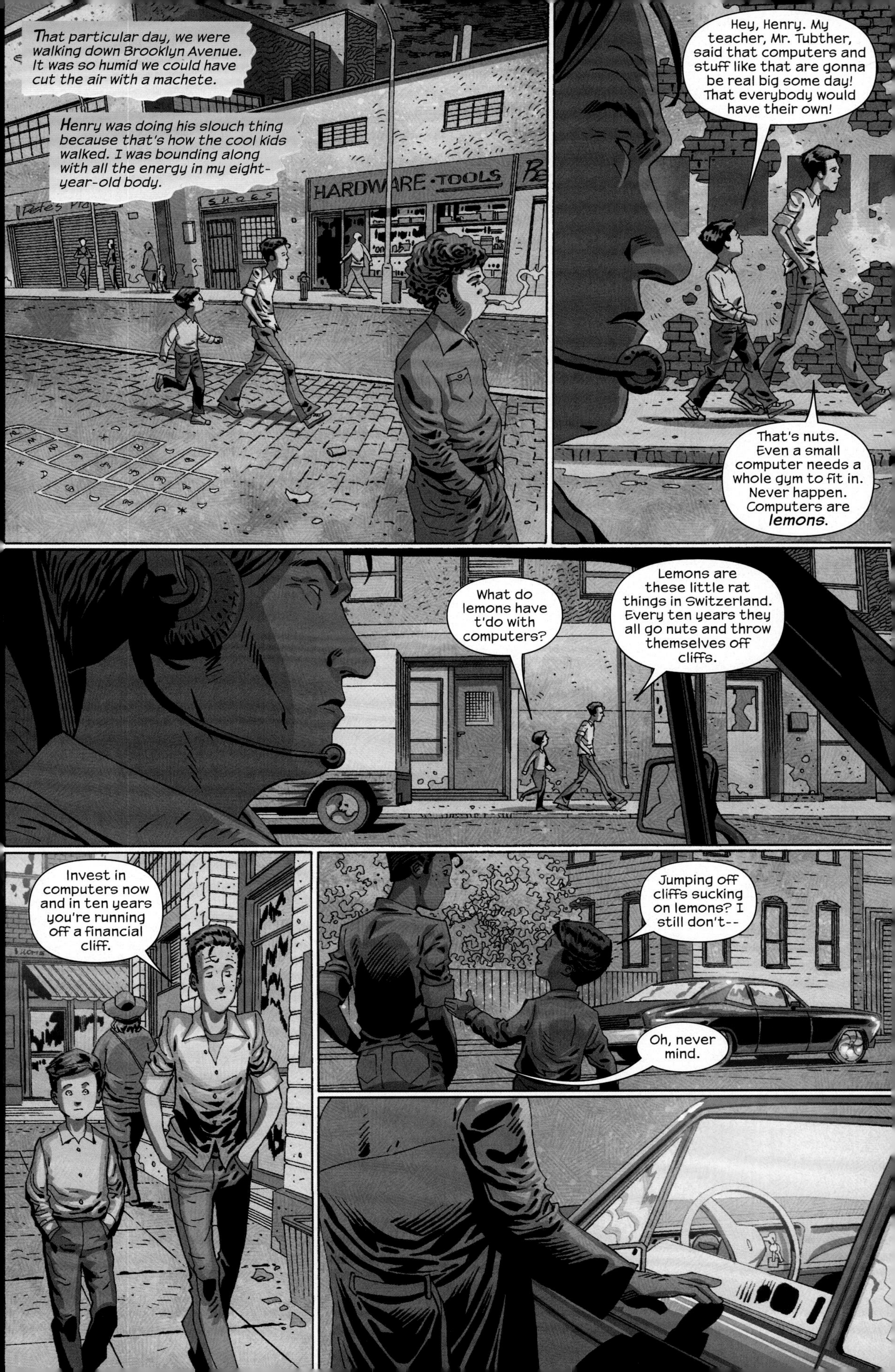
That particular day, we were walking down Brooklyn Avenue. It was so humid we could have cut the air with a machete.
Henry was doing his slouch thing because that's how the cool kids walked. I was bounding along with all the energy in my eight-year-old body.
HARDWARE · TOOLS
SHOES
Hey, Henry. My teacher, Mr. Tubther, said that computers and stuff like that are gonna be real big some day! That everybody would have their own!
That's nuts. Even a small computer needs a whole gym to fit in. Never happen. Computers are *lemons*.
What do lemons have t'do with computers?
Lemons are these little rat things in Switzerland. Every ten years they all go nuts and throw themselves off cliffs.
Invest in computers now and in ten years you're running off a financial cliff.
Jumping off cliffs sucking on lemons? I still don't--
Oh, never mind.

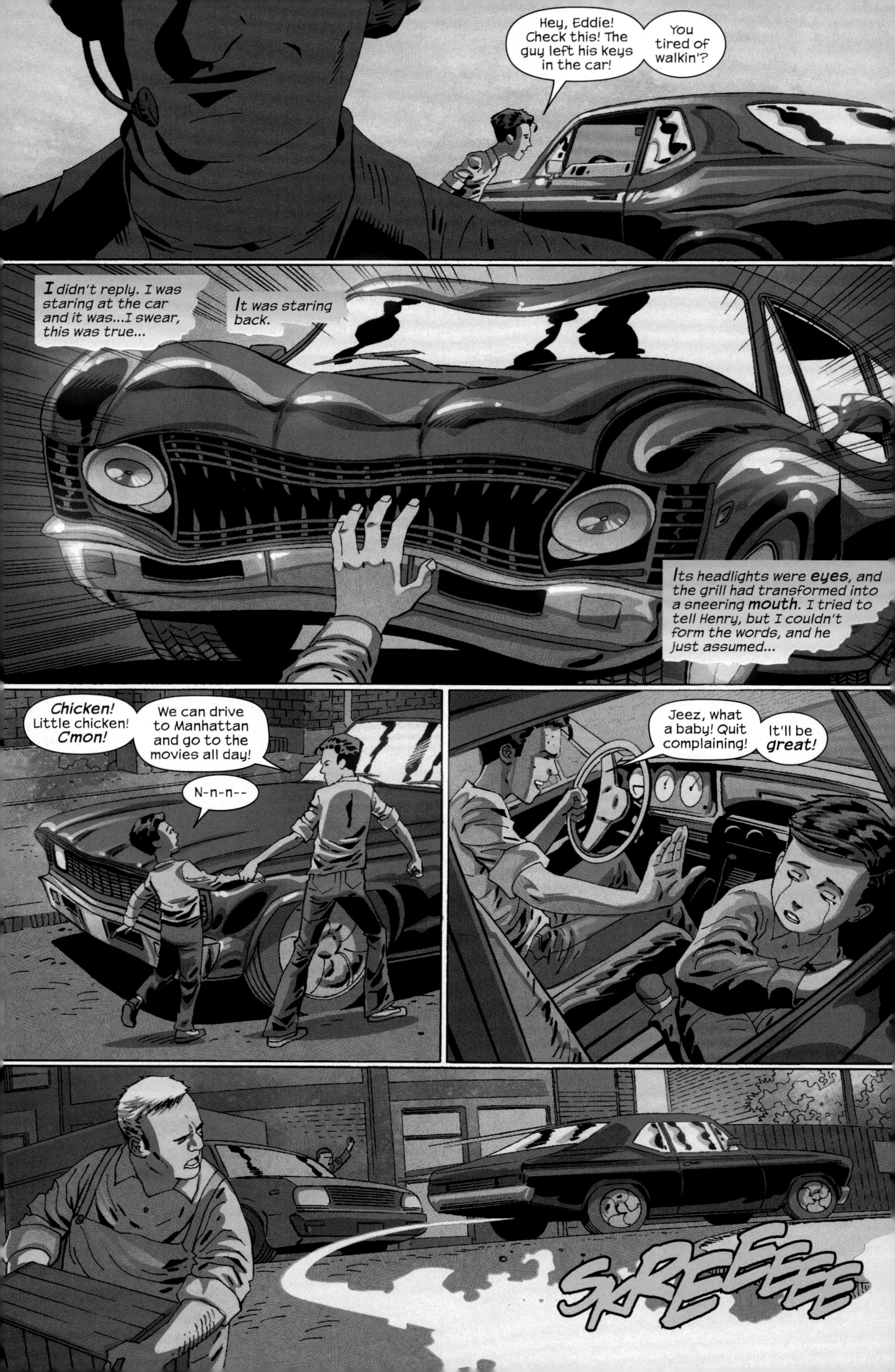
Hey, Eddie! Check this! The guy left his keys in the car!
You tired of walkin'?
I didn't reply. I was staring at the car and it was...I swear, this was true...
It was staring back.
Its headlights were eyes, and the grill had transformed into a sneering mouth. I tried to tell Henry, but I couldn't form the words, and he just assumed...
Chicken! Little chicken! Cmon!
We can drive to Manhattan and go to the movies all day!
N-n-n--
Jeez, what a baby! Quit complaining!
It'll be great!
SKREEEEEE

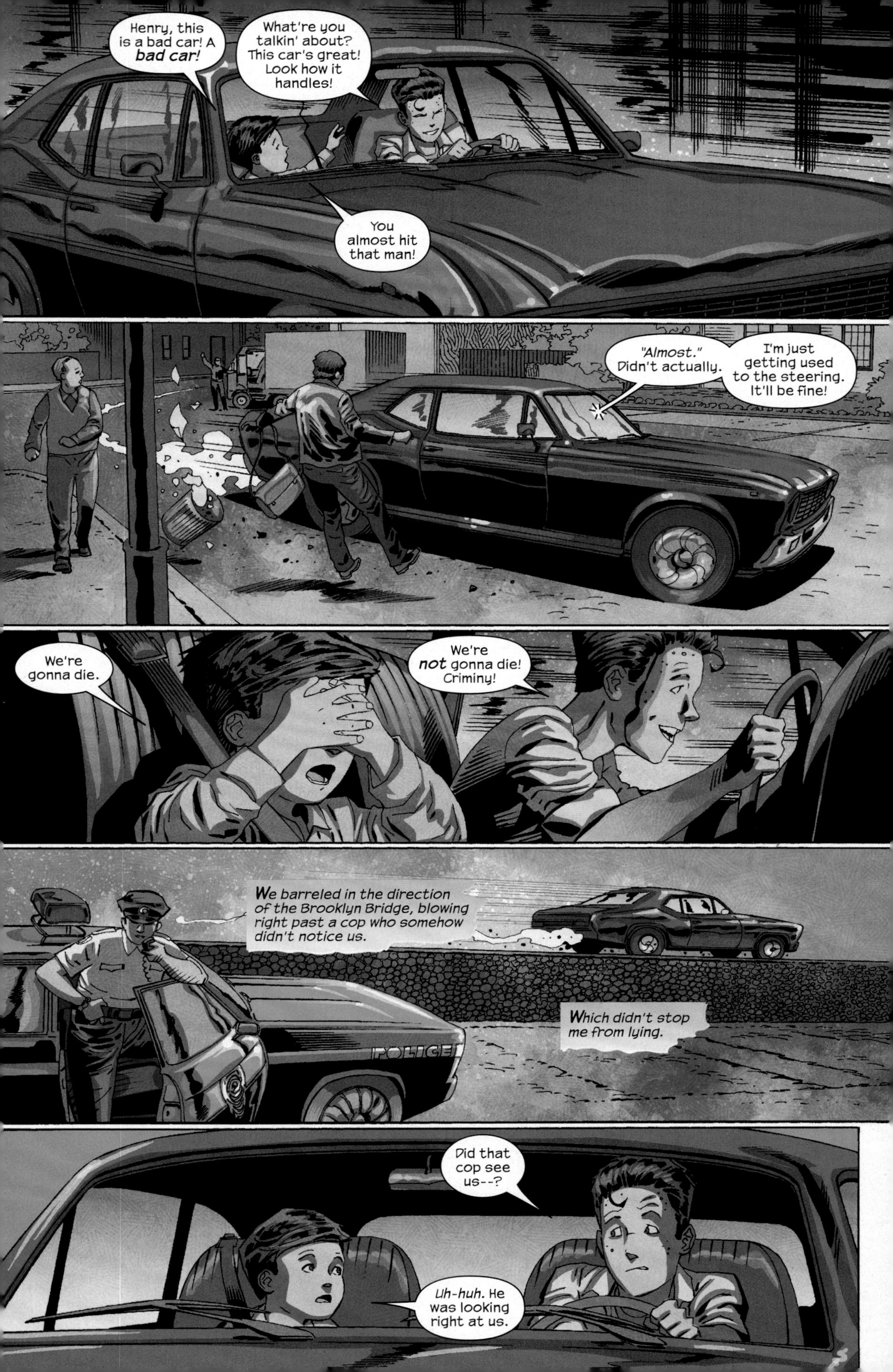
Henry, this is a bad car! A **bad car!**
What're you talkin' about? This car's great! Look how it handles!
You almost hit that man!
"Almost." Didn't actually.
I'm just getting used to the steering. It'll be fine!
We're gonna die.
We're **not** gonna die! Criminy!
We barreled in the direction of the Brooklyn Bridge, blowing right past a cop who somehow didn't notice us.
Which didn't stop me from lying.
POLICE
Did that cop see us--?
Uh-huh. He was looking right at us.

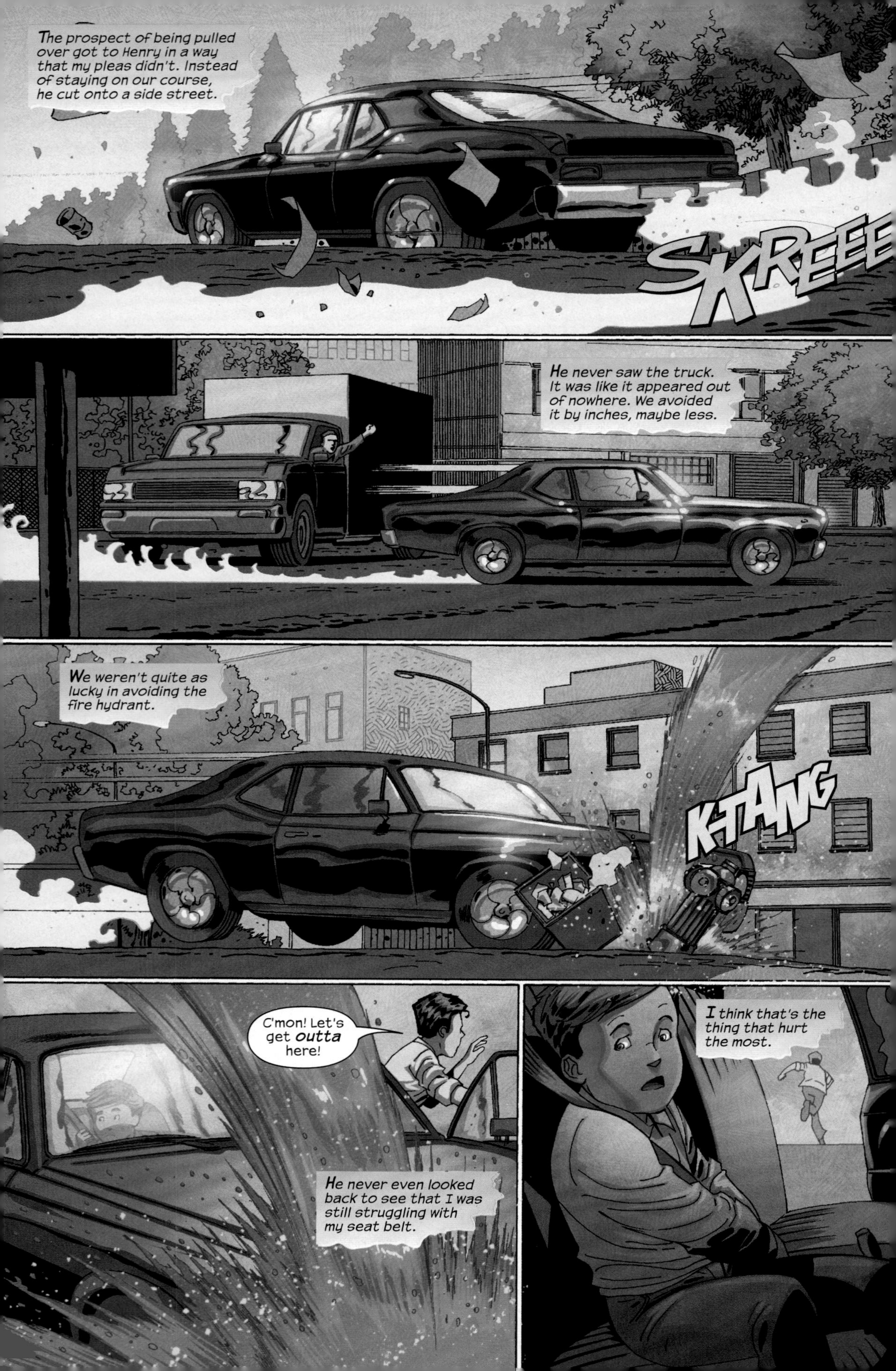
The prospect of being pulled over got to Henry in a way that my pleas didn't. Instead of staying on our course, he cut onto a side street.
SKREEE
He never saw the truck. It was like it appeared out of nowhere. We avoided it by inches, maybe less.
We weren't quite as lucky in avoiding the fire hydrant.
K-TANG
C'mon! Let's get outta here!
He never even looked back to see that I was still struggling with my seat belt.
I think that's the thing that hurt the most.

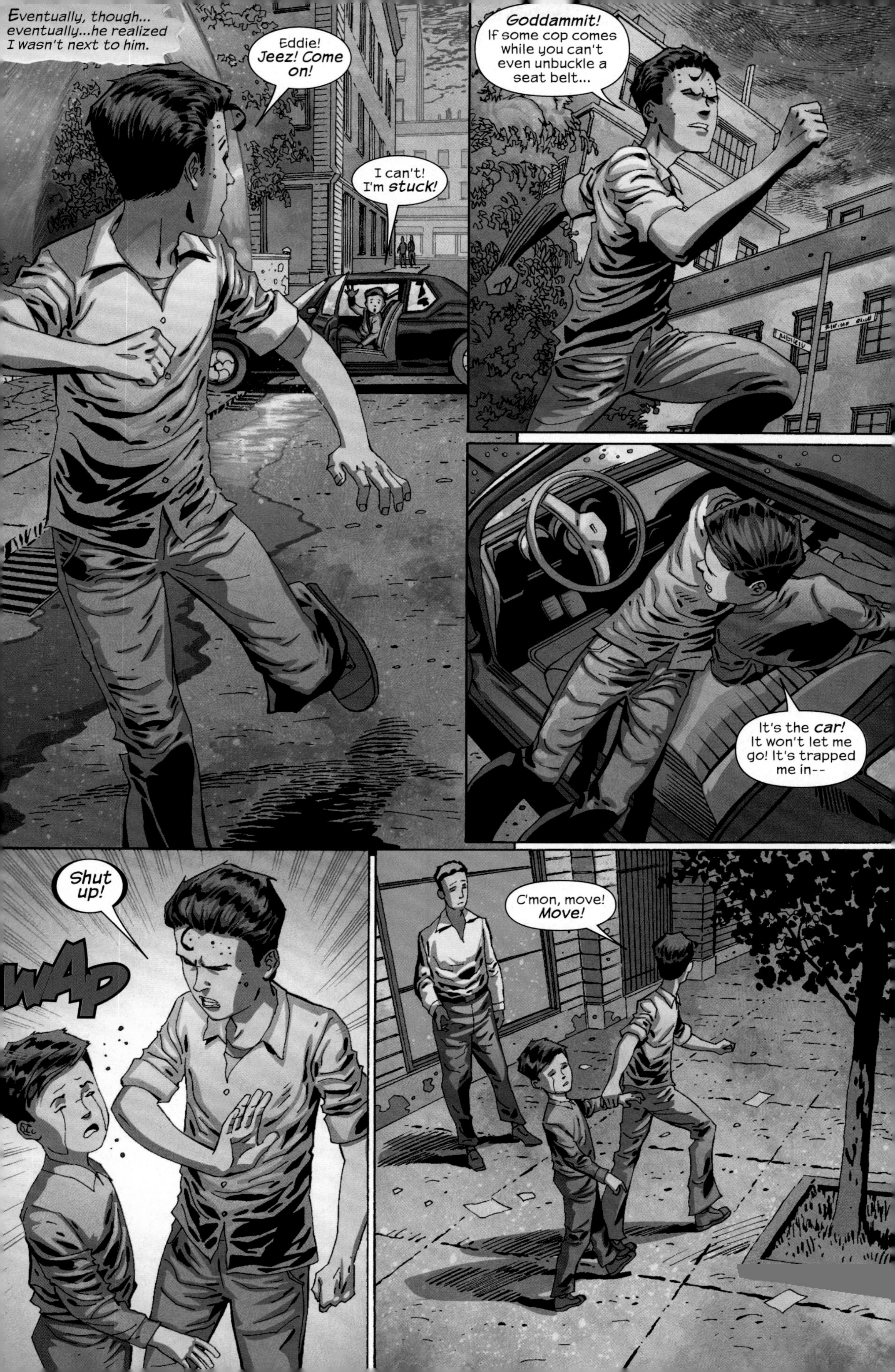
Eventually, though... eventually...he realized I wasn't next to him.
Eddie! Jeez! Come on!
I can't! I'm stuck!
Goddammit! If some cop comes while you can't even unbuckle a seat belt...
It's the car! It won't let me go! It's trapped me in--
Shut up!
WAP
C'mon, move! Move!

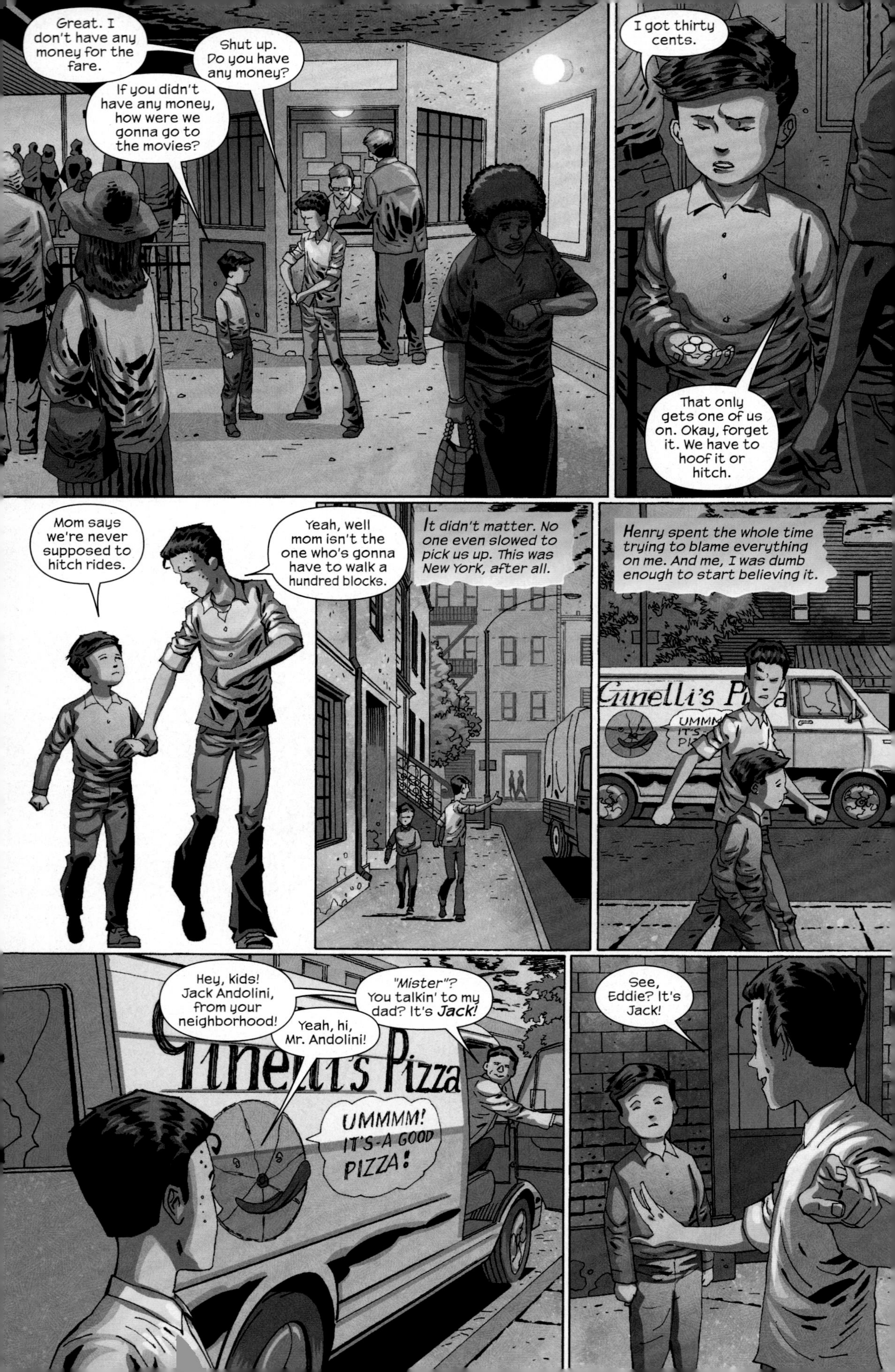
Great. I don't have any money for the fare.
Shut up. Do you have any money?
If you didn't have any money, how were we gonna go to the movies?
I got thirty cents.
That only gets one of us on. Okay, forget it. We have to hoof it or hitch.
Mom says we're never supposed to hitch rides.
Yeah, well mom isn't the one who's gonna have to walk a hundred blocks.
It didn't matter. No one even slowed to pick us up. This was New York, after all.
Henry spent the whole time trying to blame everything on me. And me, I was dumb enough to start believing it.
Hey, kids! Jack Andolini, from your neighborhood!
Yeah, hi, Mr. Andolini!
"Mister"? You talkin' to my dad? It's Jack!
Gunelli's Pizza
UMMMM! IT'S-A GOOD PIZZA!
See, Eddie? It's Jack!

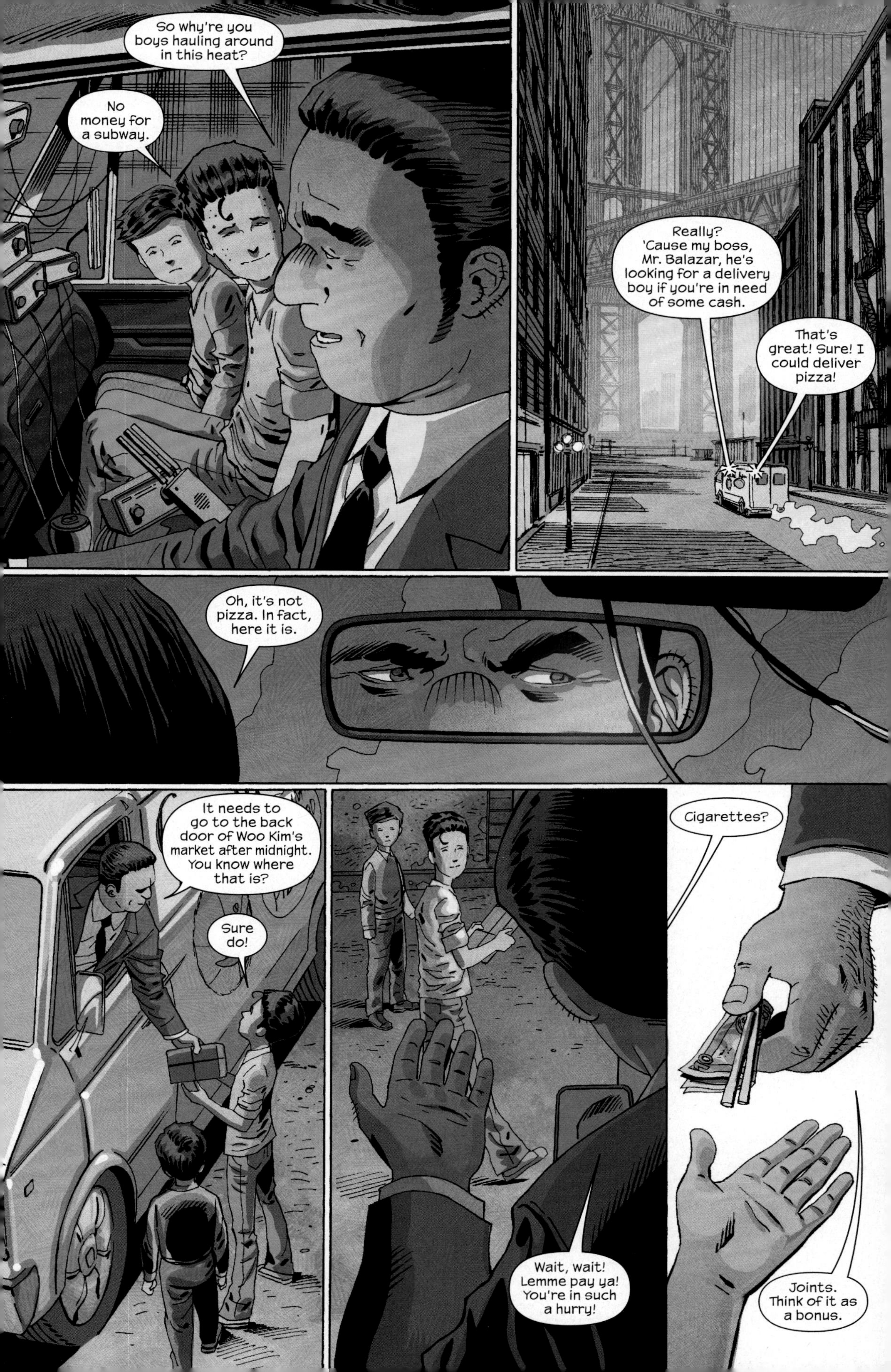

So why're you boys hauling around in this heat?
No money for a subway.
Really? 'Cause my boss, Mr. Balazar, he's looking for a delivery boy if you're in need of some cash.
That's great! Sure! I could deliver pizza!
Oh, it's not pizza. In fact, here it is.
It needs to go to the back door of Woo Kim's market after midnight. You know where that is?
Sure do!
Wait, wait! Lemme pay ya! You're in such a hurry!
Cigarettes?
Joints. Think of it as a bonus.

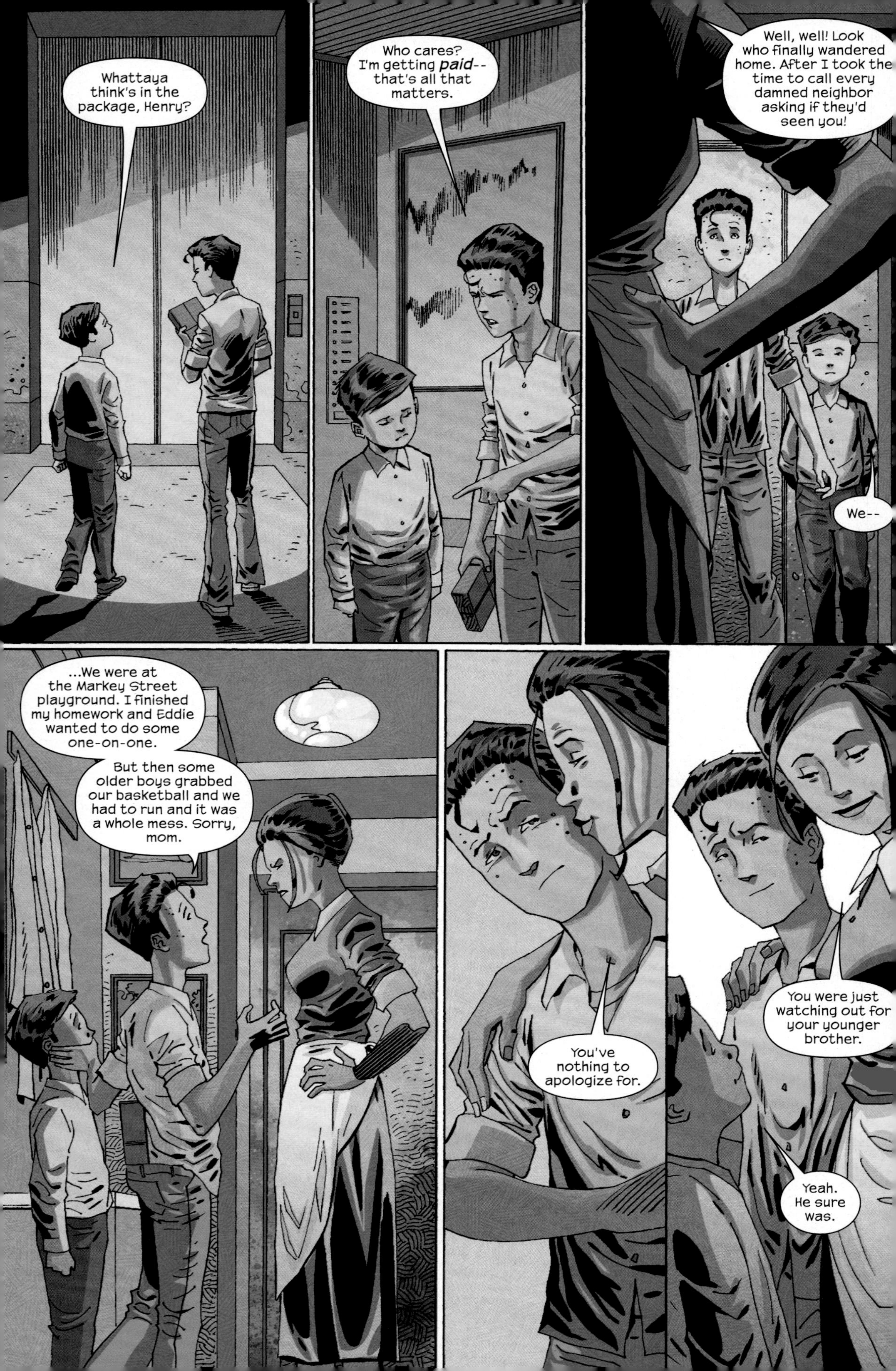
Whattaya think's in the package, Henry?
Who cares? I'm getting *paid*-- that's all that matters.
Well, well! Look who finally wandered home. After I took the time to call every damned neighbor asking if they'd seen you!
We--
...We were at the Markey Street playground. I finished my homework and Eddie wanted to do some one-on-one.
But then some older boys grabbed our basketball and we had to run and it was a whole mess. Sorry, mom.
You've nothing to apologize for.
You were just watching out for your younger brother.
Yeah. He sure was.

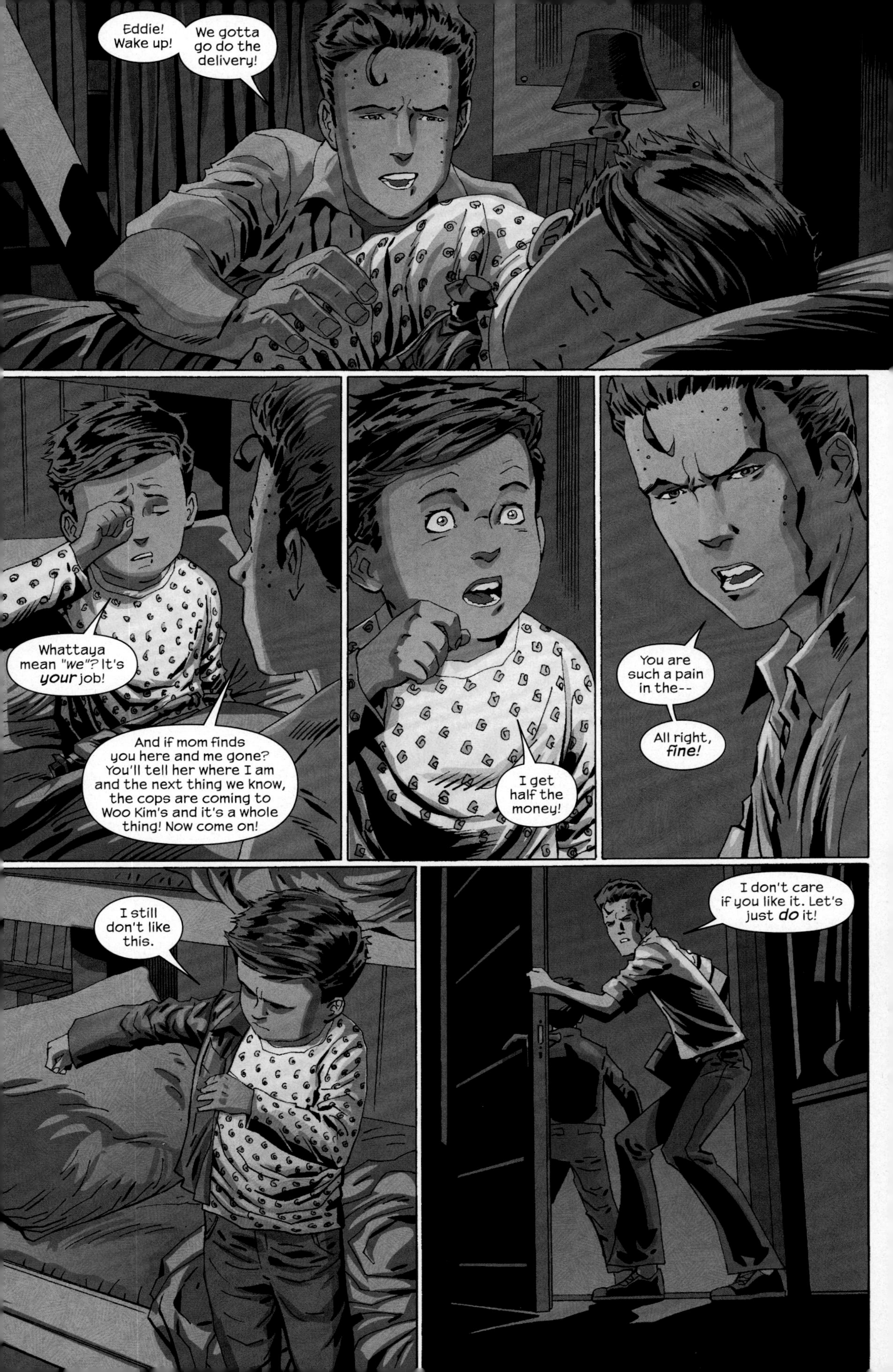
Eddie! Wake up!
We gotta go do the delivery!
Whattaya mean "we"? It's *your* job!
And if mom finds you here and me gone? You'll tell her where I am and the next thing we know, the cops are coming to Woo Kim's and it's a whole thing! Now come on!
I get half the money!
You are such a pain in the--
All right, *fine!*
I still don't like this.
I don't care if you like it. Let's just *do* it!

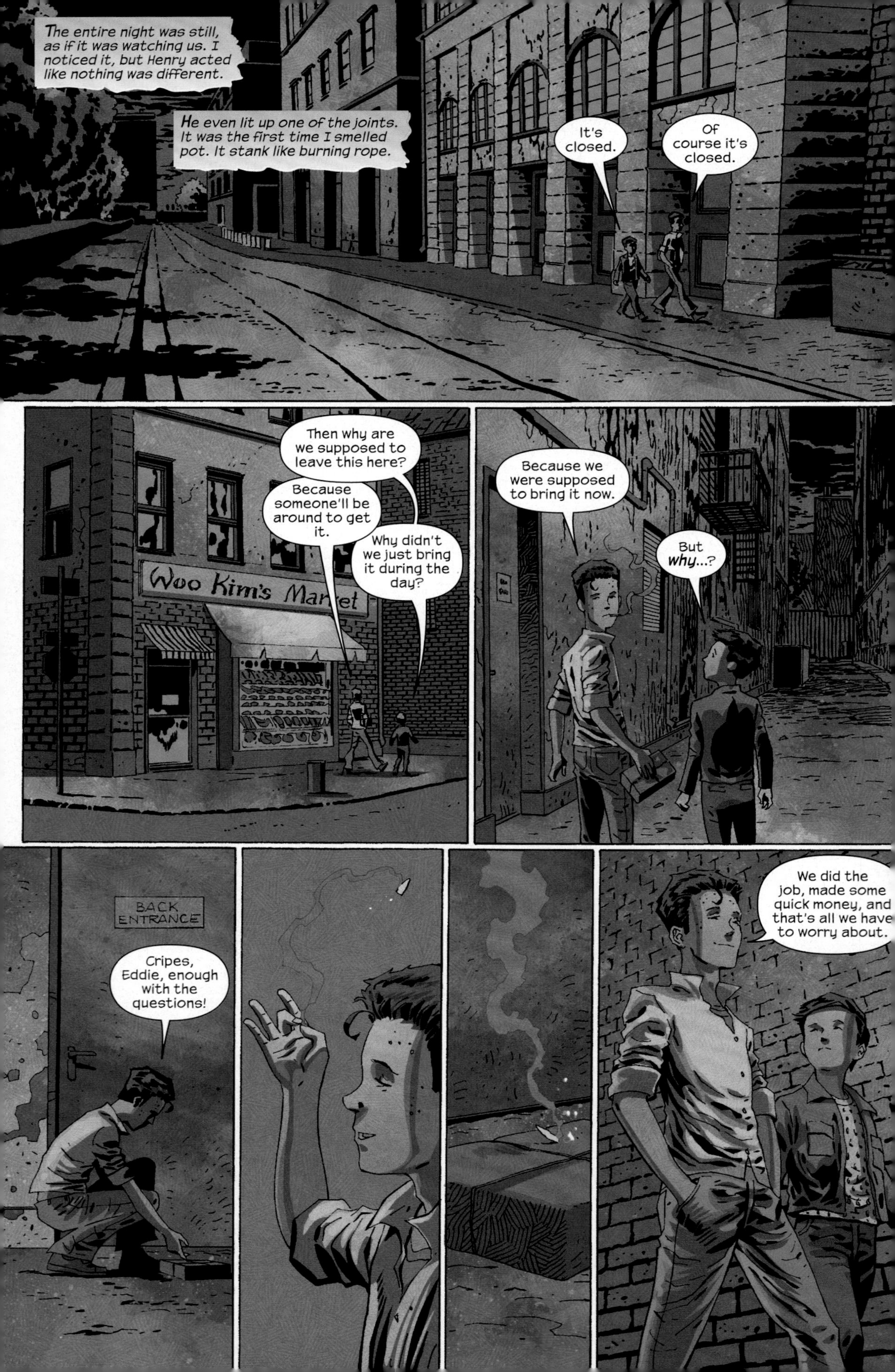
The entire night was still, as if it was watching us. I noticed it, but Henry acted like nothing was different.
He even lit up one of the joints. It was the first time I smelled pot. It stank like burning rope.
It's closed.
Of course it's closed.
Woo Kim's Market
Then why are we supposed to leave this here?
Because someone'll be around to get it.
Why didn't we just bring it during the day?
Because we were supposed to bring it now.
But *why*...?
BACK ENTRANCE
Cripes, Eddie, enough with the questions!
We did the job, made some quick money, and that's all we have to worry about.

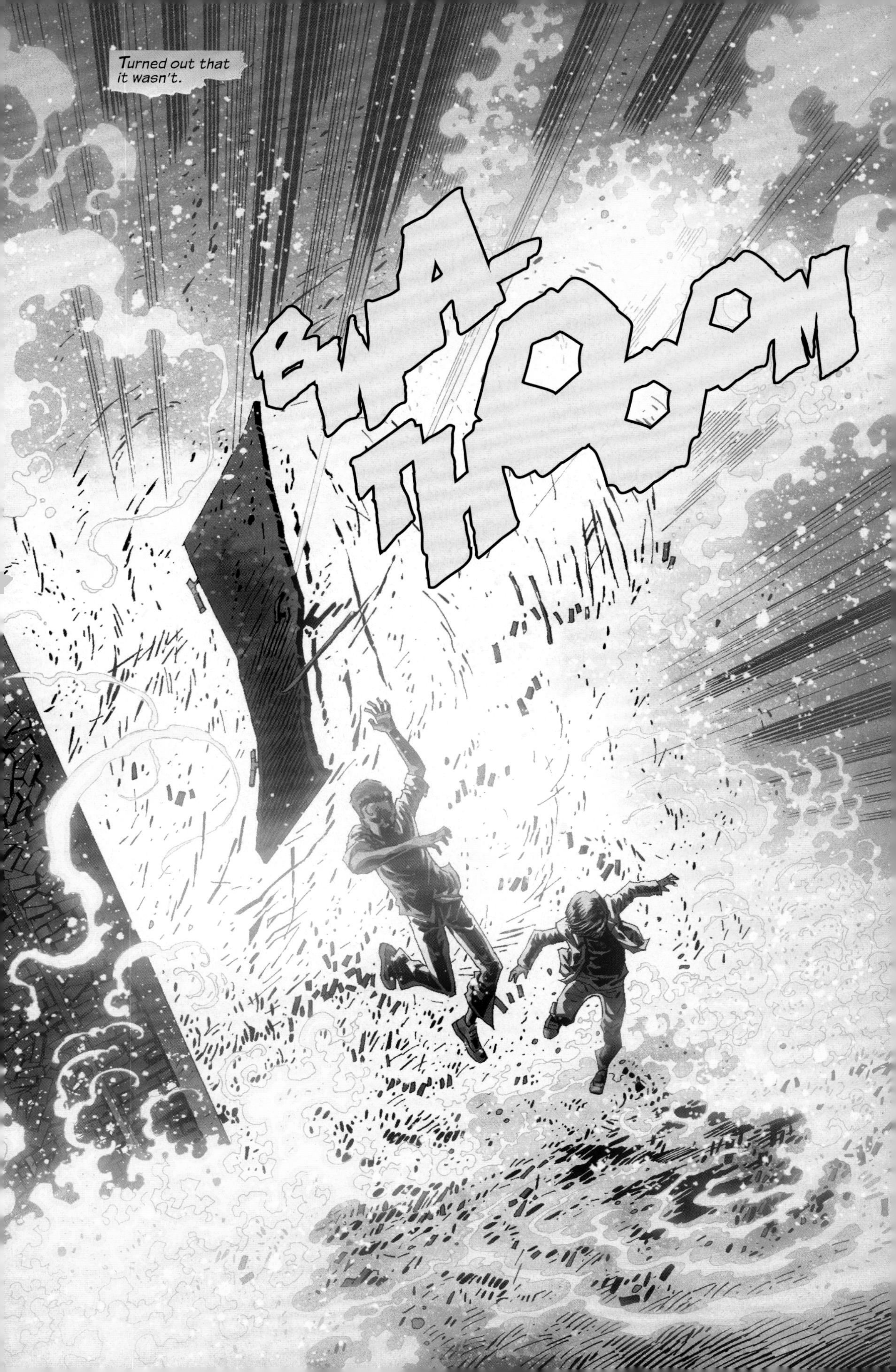
Turned out that it wasn't.
BWA-THOOM

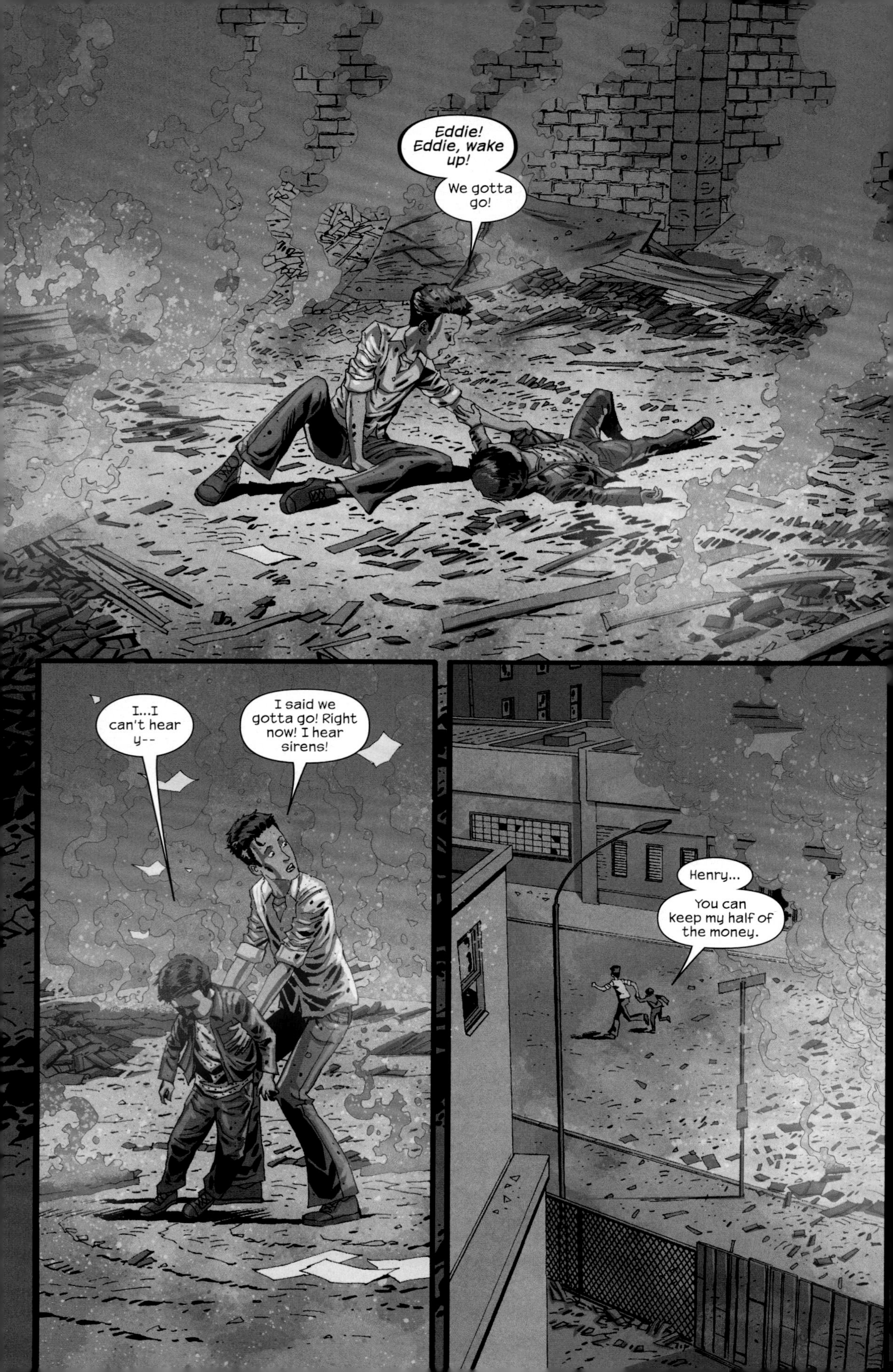
Eddie! Eddie, wake up!
We gotta go!
I...I can't hear y--
I said we gotta go! Right now! I hear sirens!
Henry...
You can keep my half of the money.

THE DARK TOWER
THE DRAWING OF THE THREE
STEPHEN KING

BY ORDER OF NYC
HOUSING AUTHORITY
THIS PROPERTY
CONDEMNED

ABSOLUTELY
NO TRESPASSING
UNDER PENALTY
OF LAW!

THE PRISONER
CHAPTER THREE

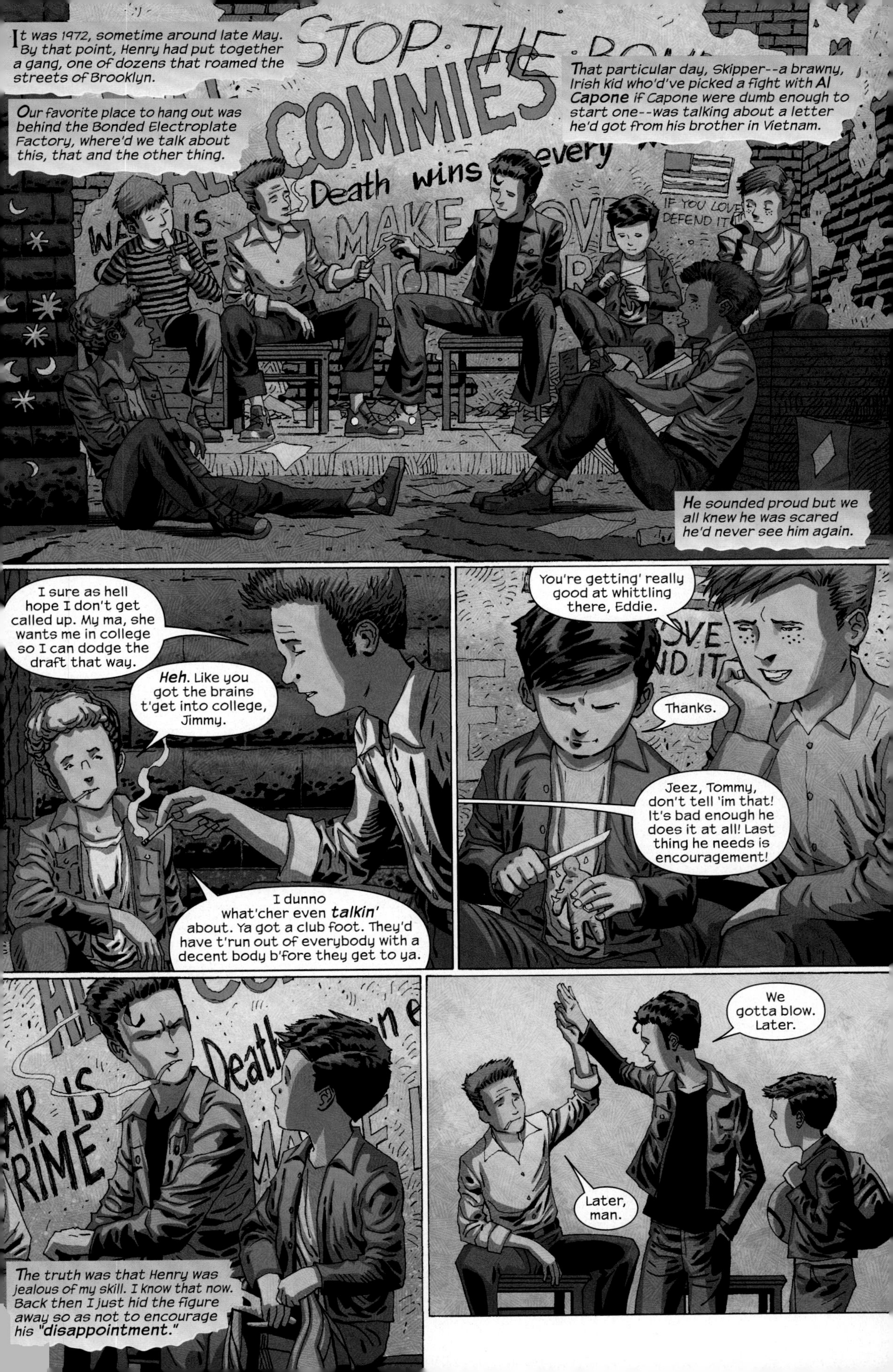
It was 1972, sometime around late May. By that point, Henry had put together a gang, one of dozens that roamed the streets of Brooklyn.
STOP THE
COMMIES
Our favorite place to hang out was behind the Bonded Electroplate Factory, where'd we talk about this, that and the other thing.
That particular day, Skipper--a brawny, Irish kid who'd've picked a fight with Al Capone if Capone were dumb enough to start one--was talking about a letter he'd got from his brother in Vietnam.
Death wins every
MAKE
IF YOU LOVE
DEFEND IT
He sounded proud but we all knew he was scared he'd never see him again.
I sure as hell hope I don't get called up. My ma, she wants me in college so I can dodge the draft that way.
Heh. Like you got the brains t'get into college, Jimmy.
I dunno what'cher even talkin' about. Ya got a club foot. They'd have t'run out of everybody with a decent body b'fore they get to ya.
You're getting' really good at whittling there, Eddie.
Thanks.
Jeez, Tommy, don't tell 'im that! It's bad enough he does it at all! Last thing he needs is encouragement!
Death
RIME
The truth was that Henry was jealous of my skill. I know that now. Back then I just hid the figure away so as not to encourage his "disappointment."
We gotta blow. Later.
Later, man.

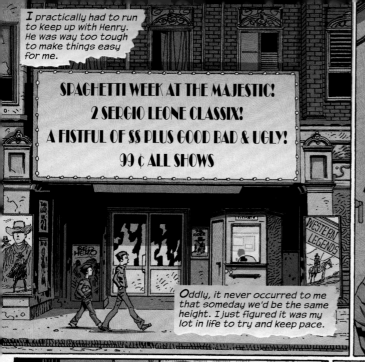

I practically had to run to keep up with Henry. He was way too tough to make things easy for me.

SPAGHETTI WEEK AT THE MAJESTIC!
2 SERGIO LEONE CLASSIX!
A FISTFUL OF $$ PLUS GOOD BAD & UGLY!
99¢ ALL SHOWS

Oddly, it never occurred to me that someday we'd be the same height. I just figured it was my lot in life to try and keep pace.

Watch this.

Aw jeez, you're not gonna ask Maryanne out again, are you?

I never asked her out, and no, and *shut up.*

So! *Maryanne!* How's it going?

It was going fine until about three seconds ago. Buy a ticket or scram, Henry.

I just wanted to read the newspaper.

Henry! That's *mine!*

It *was.*

Jump for it, Maryanne! Jump, girl, *jump!*

Give it back!

Quit fooling around and give it back! *Bastard!*

Ooo! Bad wang-gwidge!

Using bad wang-gwidge around my kid brother? For shame!

He's gonna hear a lot *worse!*

WAP

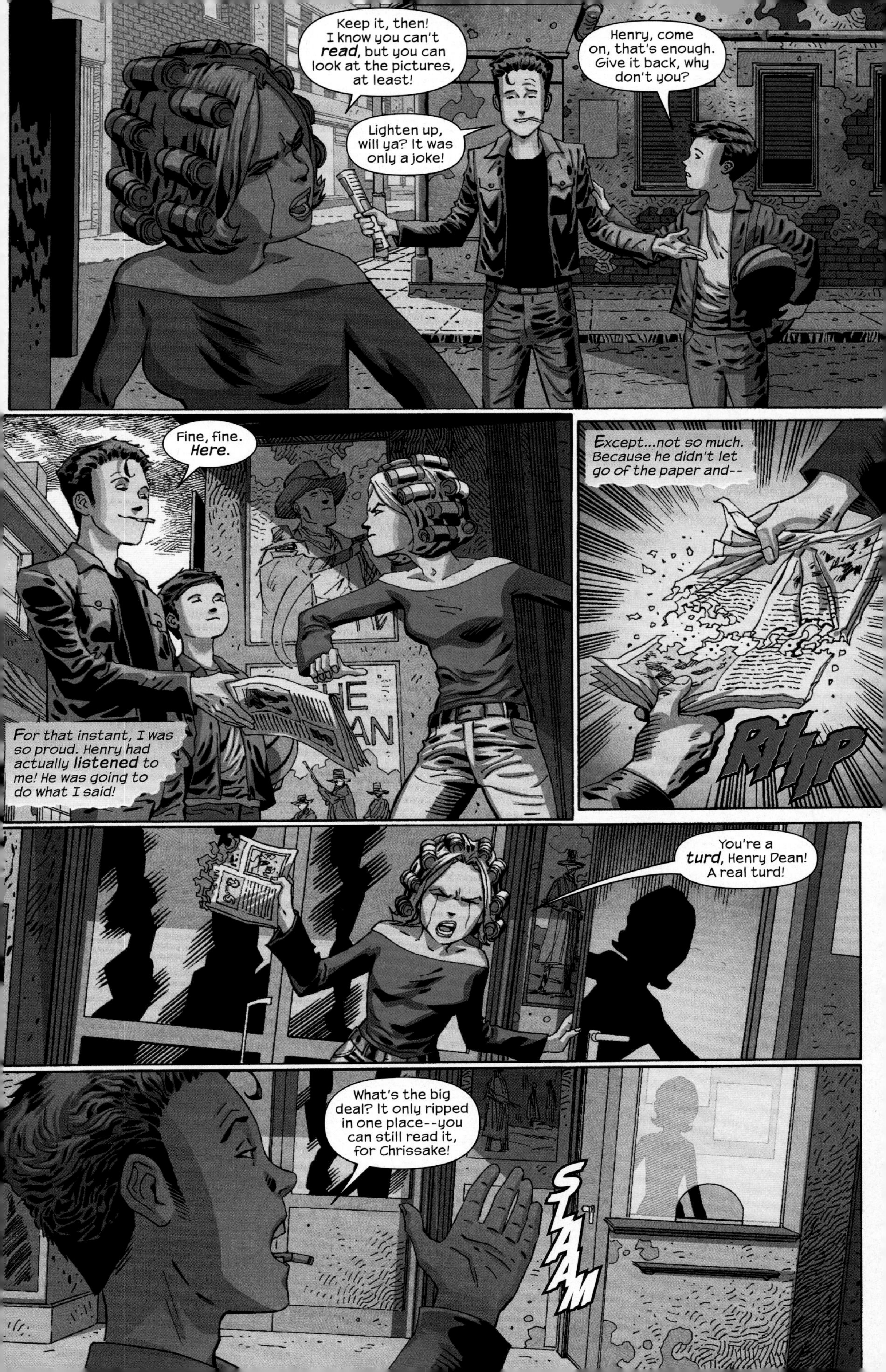

Keep it, then! I know you can't **read**, but you can look at the pictures, at least!
Lighten up, will ya? It was only a joke!
Henry, come on, that's enough. Give it back, why don't you?
Fine, fine. **Here.**
For that instant, I was so proud. Henry had actually **listened** to me! He was going to do what I said!
Except...not so much. Because he didn't let go of the paper and--
RRIIP
You're a **turd**, Henry Dean! A real turd!
What's the big deal? It only ripped in one place--you can still read it, for Chrissake!
SLAAM

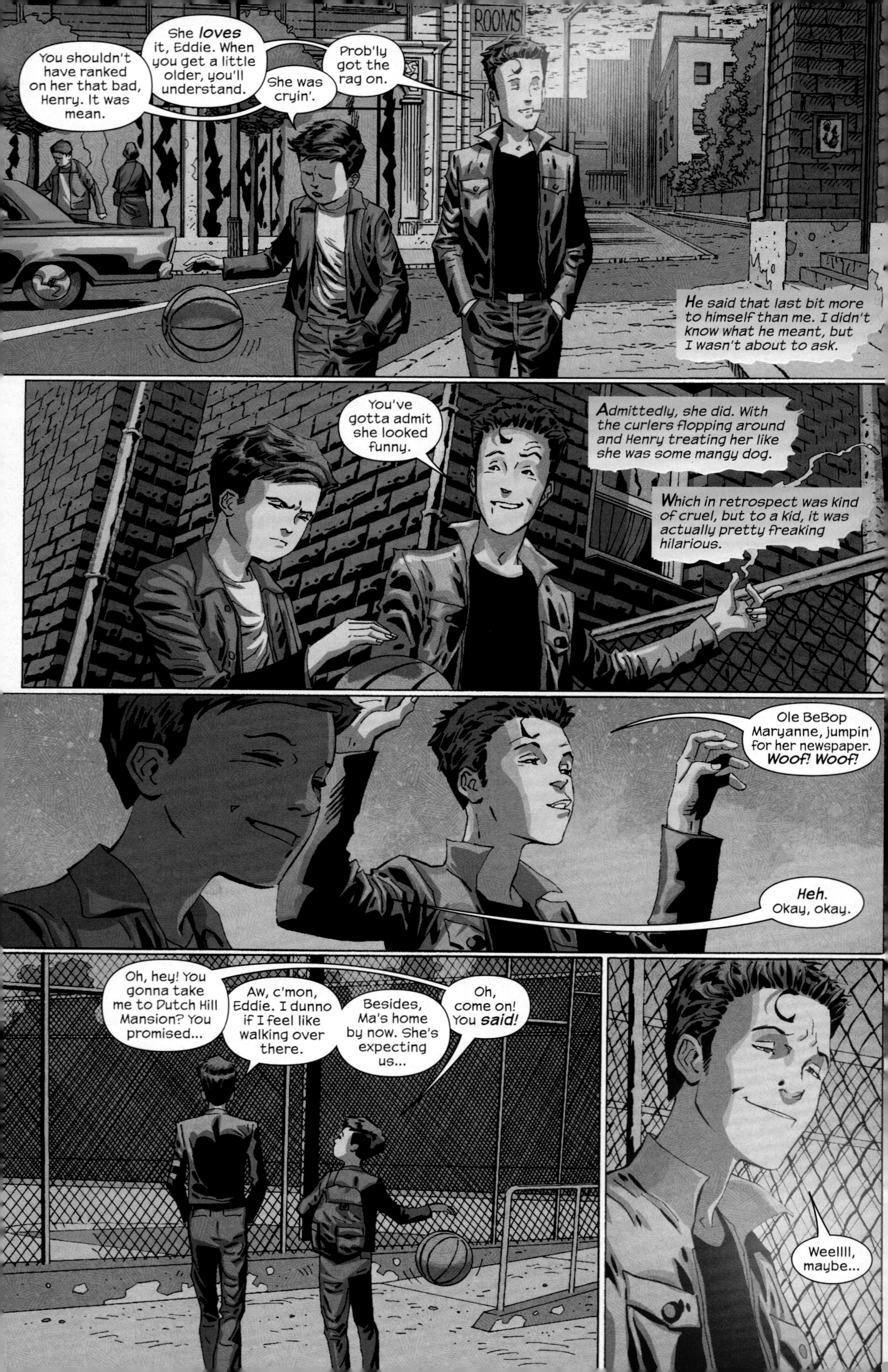
ROOMS
You shouldn't have ranked on her that bad, Henry. It was mean.
She *loves* it, Eddie. When you get a little older, you'll understand.
She was cryin'.
Prob'ly got the rag on.
He said that last bit more to himself than me. I didn't know what he meant, but I wasn't about to ask.
You've gotta admit she looked funny.
Admittedly, she did. With the curlers flopping around and Henry treating her like she was some mangy dog.
Which in retrospect was kind of cruel, but to a kid, it was actually pretty freaking hilarious.
Ole BeBop Maryanne, jumpin' for her newspaper. *Woof! Woof!*
Heh. Okay, okay.
Oh, hey! You gonna take me to Dutch Hill Mansion? You promised...
Aw, c'mon, Eddie. I dunno if I feel like walking over there.
Besides, Ma's home by now. She's expecting us...
Oh, come on! You *said!*
Weellll, maybe...

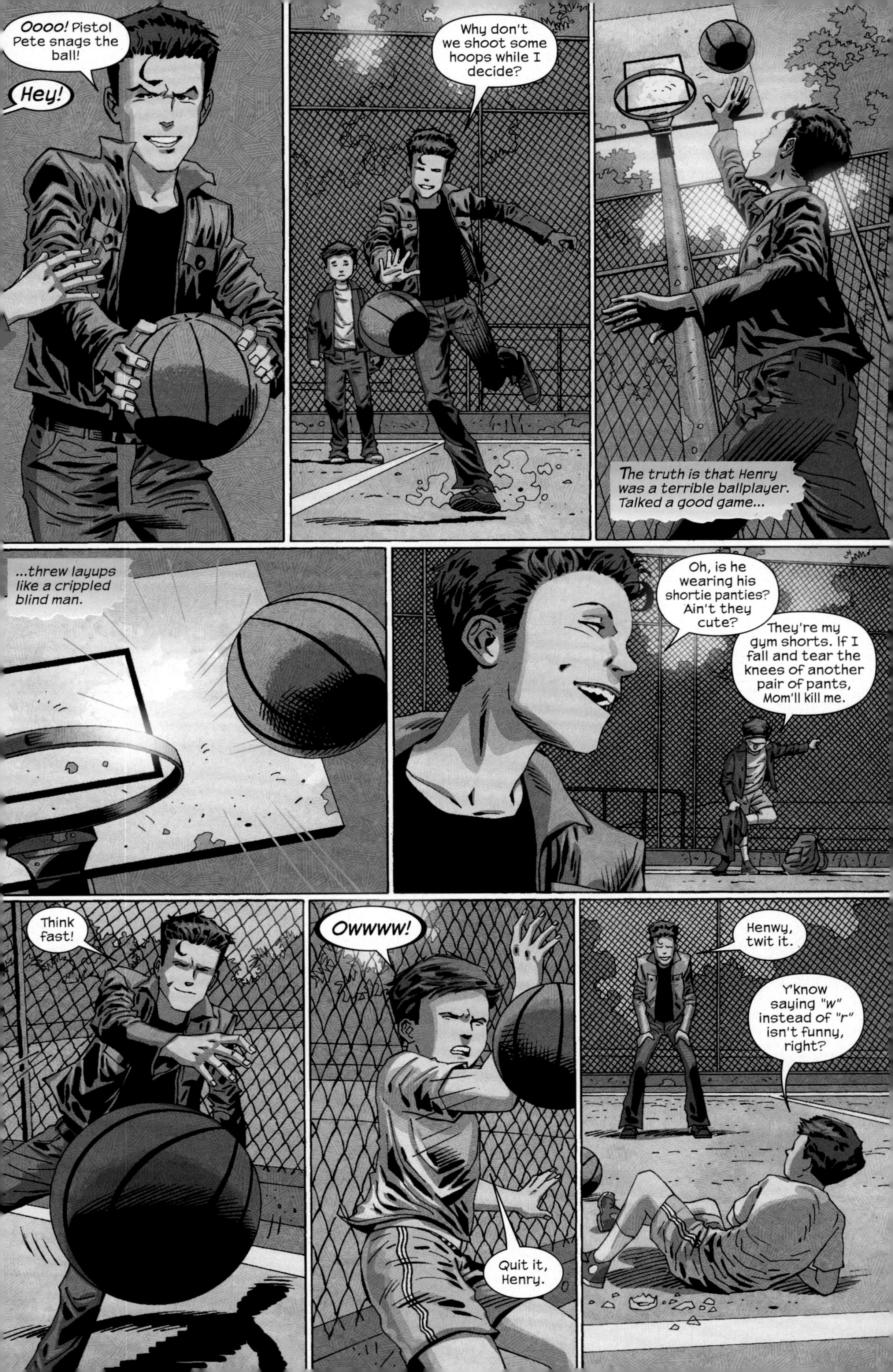
Oooo! Pistol Pete snags the ball!
Hey!
Why don't we shoot some hoops while I decide?
The truth is that Henry was a terrible ballplayer. Talked a good game...
...threw layups like a crippled blind man.
Oh, is he wearing his shortie panties? Ain't they cute?
They're my gym shorts. If I fall and tear the knees of another pair of pants, Mom'll kill me.
Think fast!
Owwww!
Quit it, Henry.
Henwy, twit it.
Y'know saying "w" instead of "r" isn't funny, right?

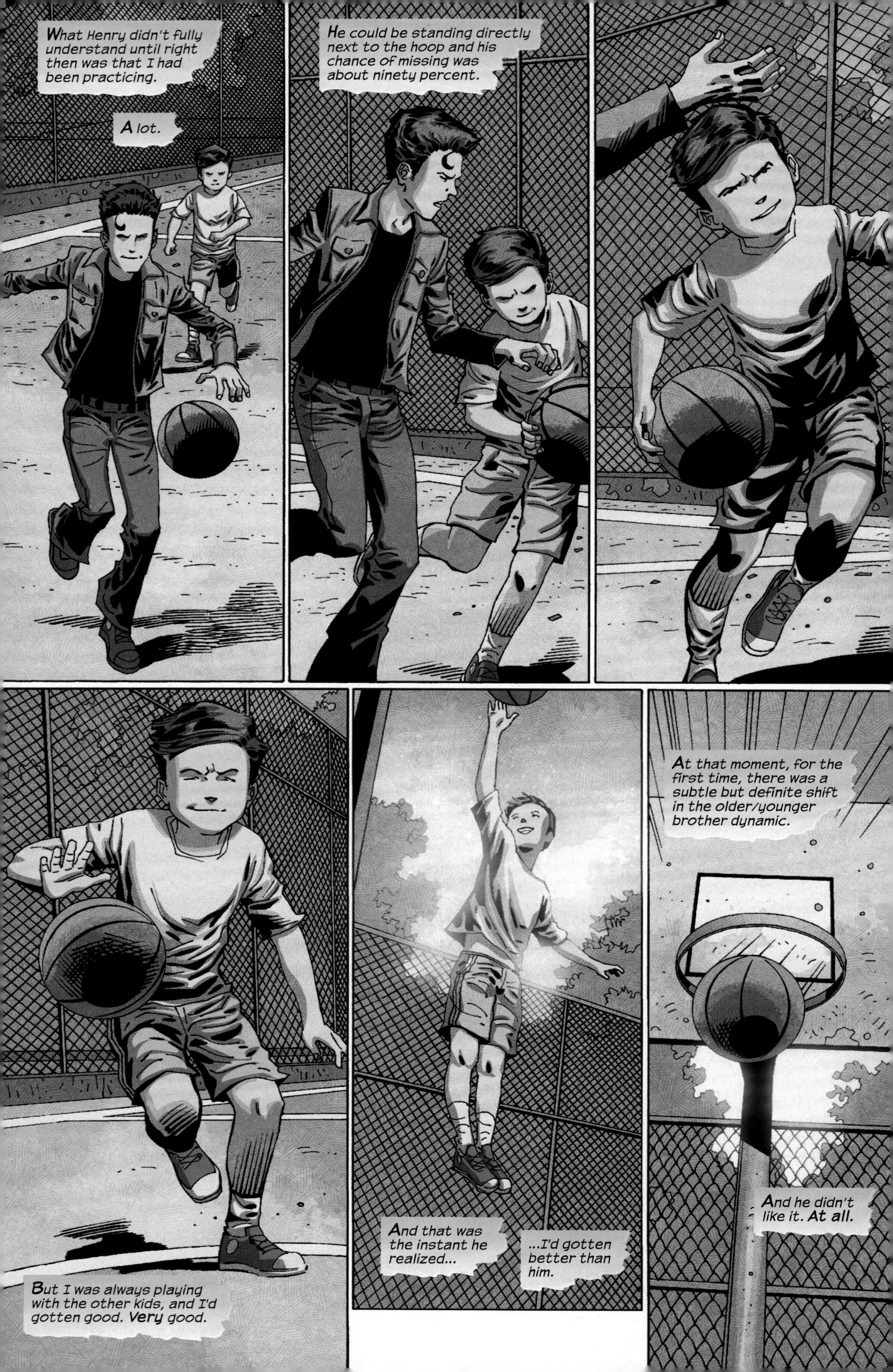
What Henry didn't fully understand until right then was that I had been practicing.
A lot.
He could be standing directly next to the hoop and his chance of missing was about ninety percent.
But I was always playing with the other kids, and I'd gotten good. **Very** good.
And that was the instant he realized...
...I'd gotten better than him.
At that moment, for the first time, there was a subtle but definite shift in the older/younger brother dynamic.
And he didn't like it. **At all.**

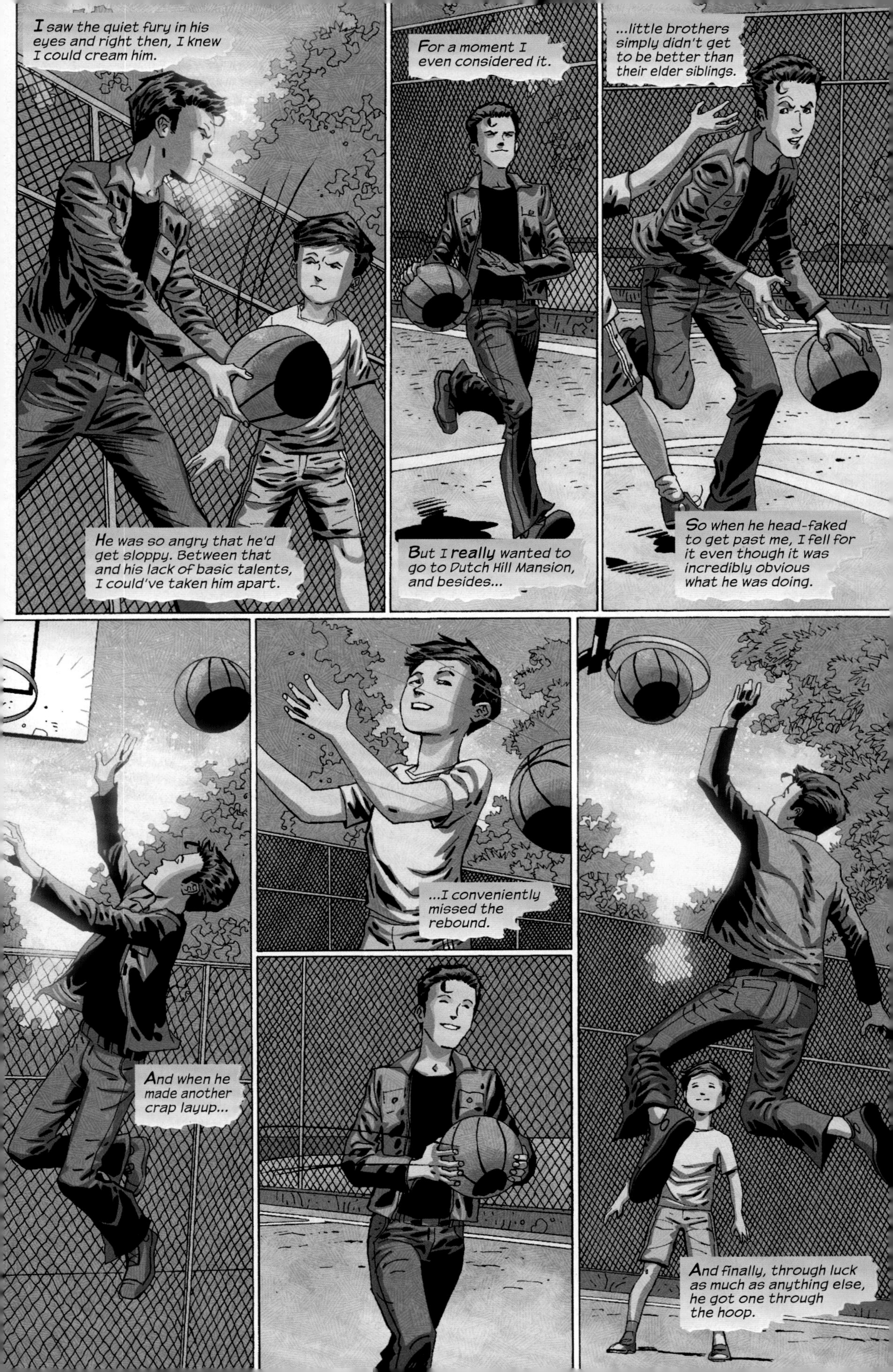
I saw the quiet fury in his eyes and right then, I knew I could cream him.
He was so angry that he'd get sloppy. Between that and his lack of basic talents, I could've taken him apart.
For a moment I even considered it.
But I really wanted to go to Dutch Hill Mansion, and besides...
...little brothers simply didn't get to be better than their elder siblings.
So when he head-faked to get past me, I fell for it even though it was incredibly obvious what he was doing.
And when he made another crap layup...
...I conveniently missed the rebound.
And finally, through luck as much as anything else, he got one through the hoop.

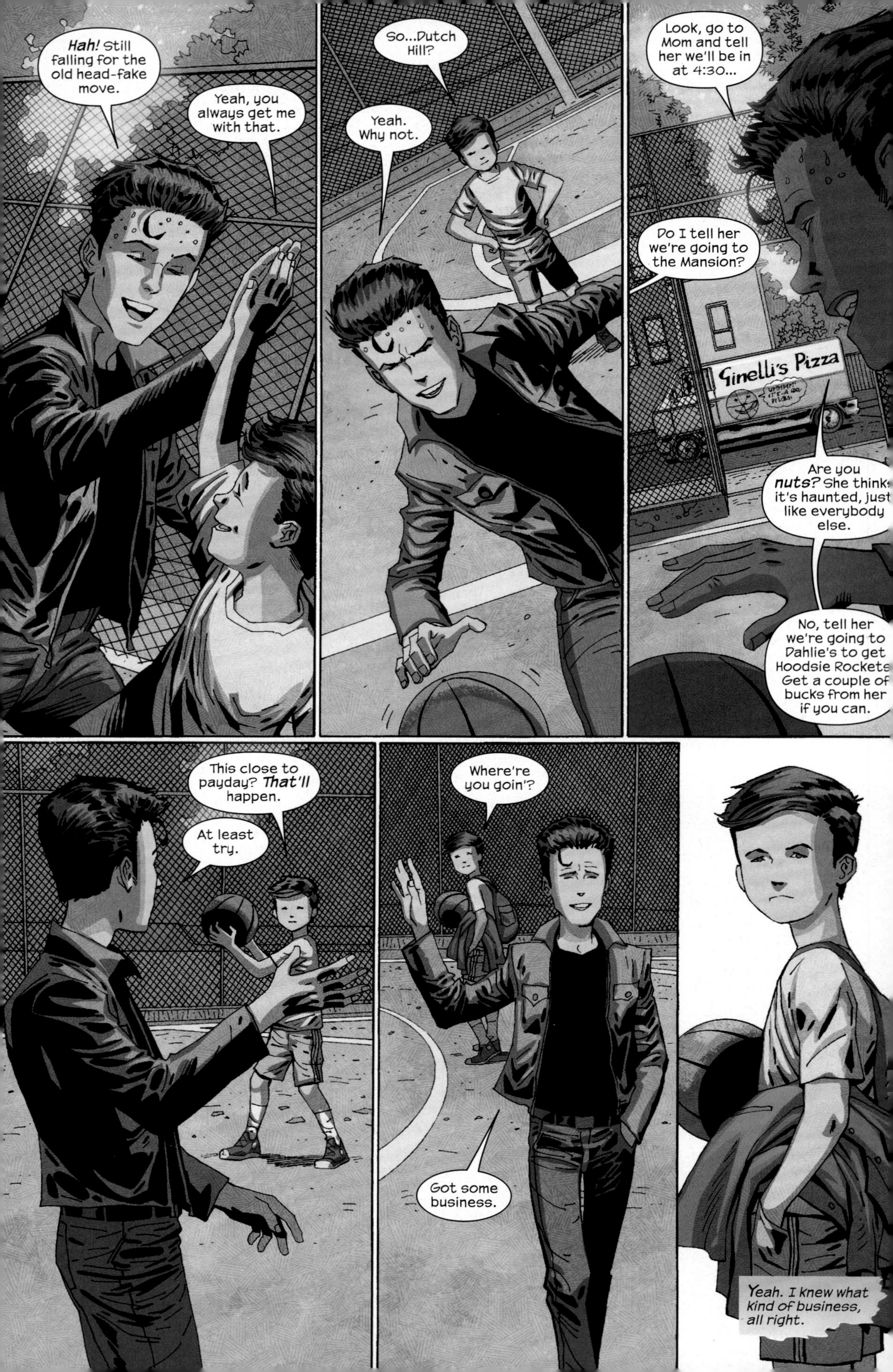

Hah! Still falling for the old head-fake move.
Yeah, you always get me with that.
So...Dutch Hill?
Yeah. Why not.
Look, go to Mom and tell her we'll be in at 4:30...
Do I tell her we're going to the Mansion?
Ginelli's Pizza
Are you ***nuts?*** She thinks it's haunted, just like everybody else.
No, tell her we're going to Dahlie's to get Hoodsie Rockets. Get a couple of bucks from her if you can.
This close to payday? ***That'll*** happen.
At least try.
Where're you goin'?
Got some business.
Yeah. I knew what kind of business, all right.

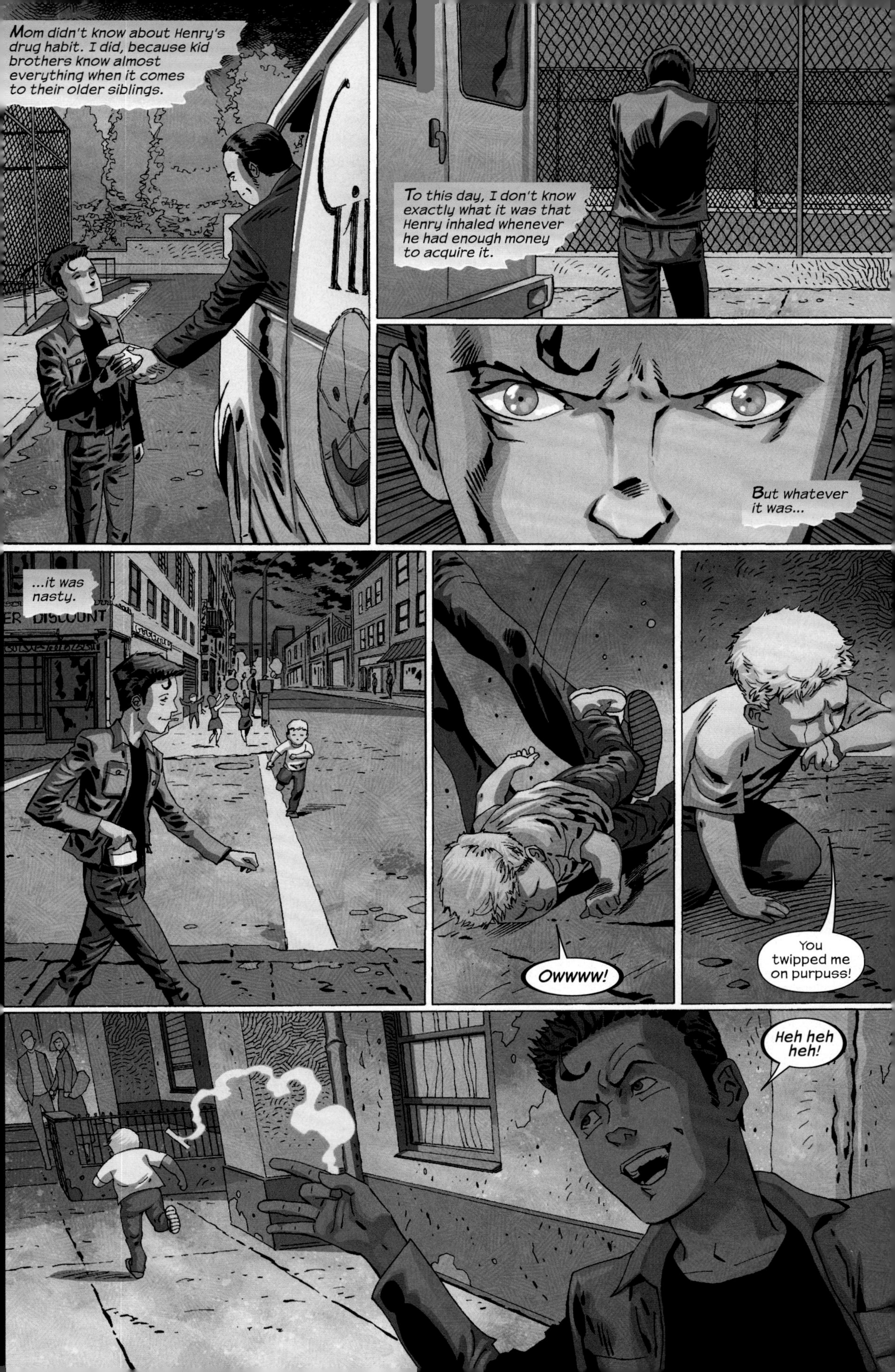
Mom didn't know about Henry's drug habit. I did, because kid brothers know almost everything when it comes to their older siblings.
To this day, I don't know exactly what it was that Henry inhaled whenever he had enough money to acquire it.
But whatever it was...
...it was nasty.
DISCOUNT
Owwww!
You twipped me on purpuss!
Heh heh heh!

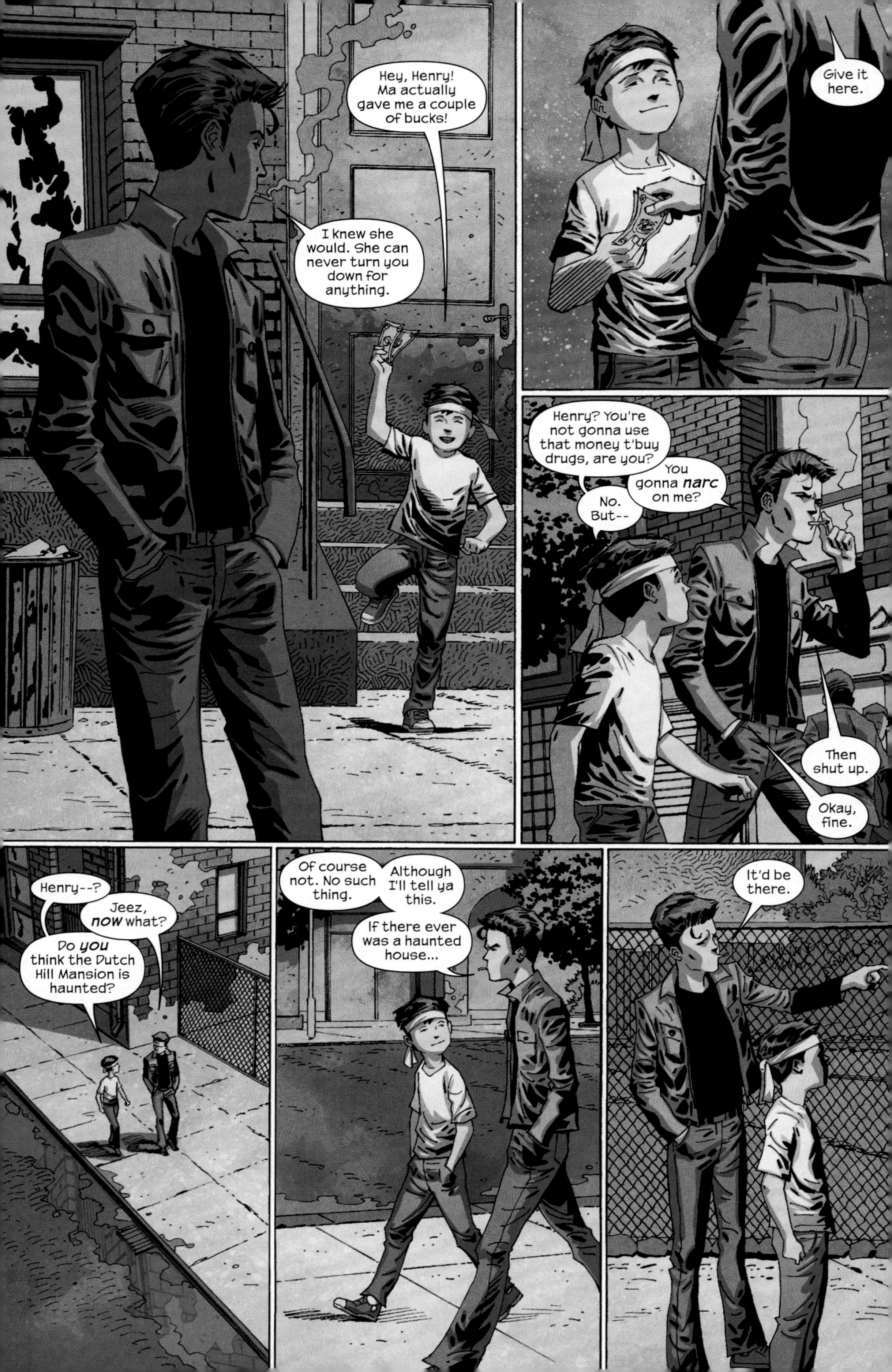

Hey, Henry! Ma actually gave me a couple of bucks!
I knew she would. She can never turn you down for anything.
Give it here.
Henry? You're not gonna use that money t'buy drugs, are you?
You gonna **narc** on me?
No. But--
Then shut up.
Okay, fine.
Henry--?
Jeez, **NOW** what?
Do **YOU** think the Dutch Hill Mansion is haunted?
Of course not. No such thing.
Although I'll tell ya this.
If there ever was a haunted house...
It'd be there.

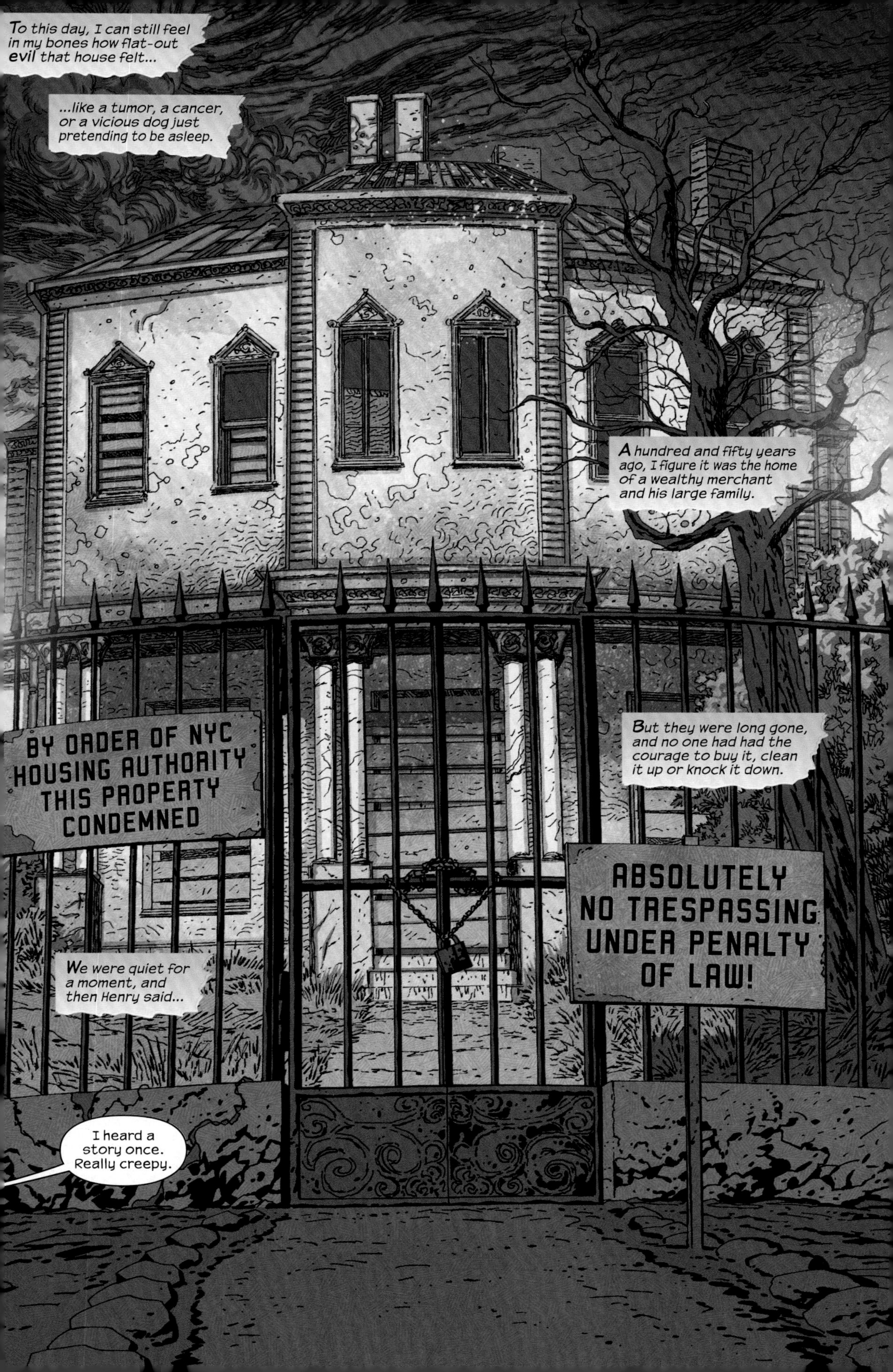
To this day, I can still feel in my bones how flat-out **evil** that house felt...
...like a tumor, a cancer, or a vicious dog just pretending to be asleep.
A hundred and fifty years ago, I figure it was the home of a wealthy merchant and his large family.
BY ORDER OF NYC HOUSING AUTHORITY THIS PROPERTY CONDEMNED
But they were long gone, and no one had had the courage to buy it, clean it up or knock it down.
ABSOLUTELY NO TRESPASSING UNDER PENALTY OF LAW!
We were quiet for a moment, and then Henry said...
I heard a story once. Really creepy.

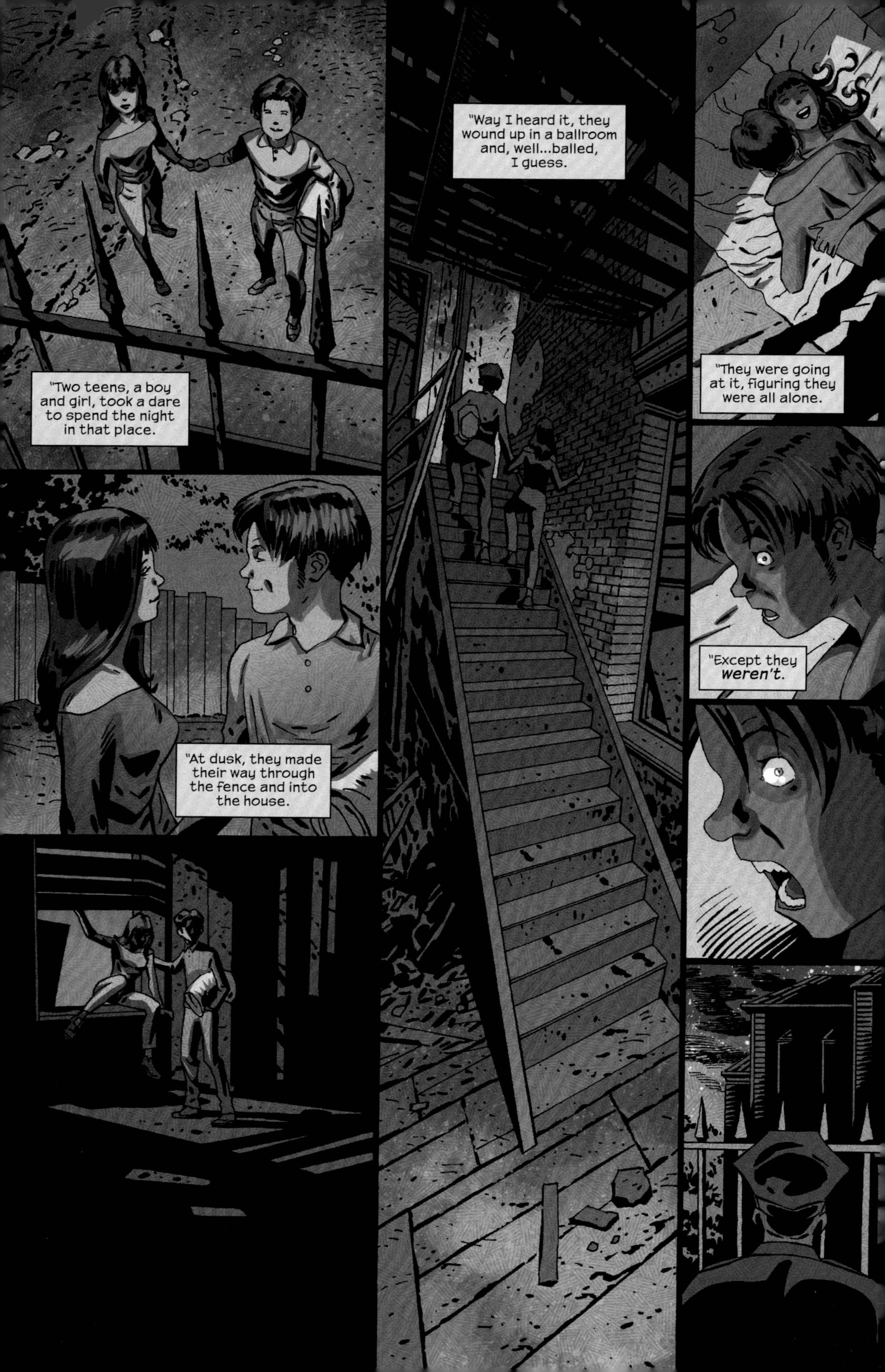
"Two teens, a boy and girl, took a dare to spend the night in that place.
"At dusk, they made their way through the fence and into the house.
"Way I heard it, they wound up in a ballroom and, well...balled, I guess.
"They were going at it, figuring they were all alone.
"Except they *weren't*.

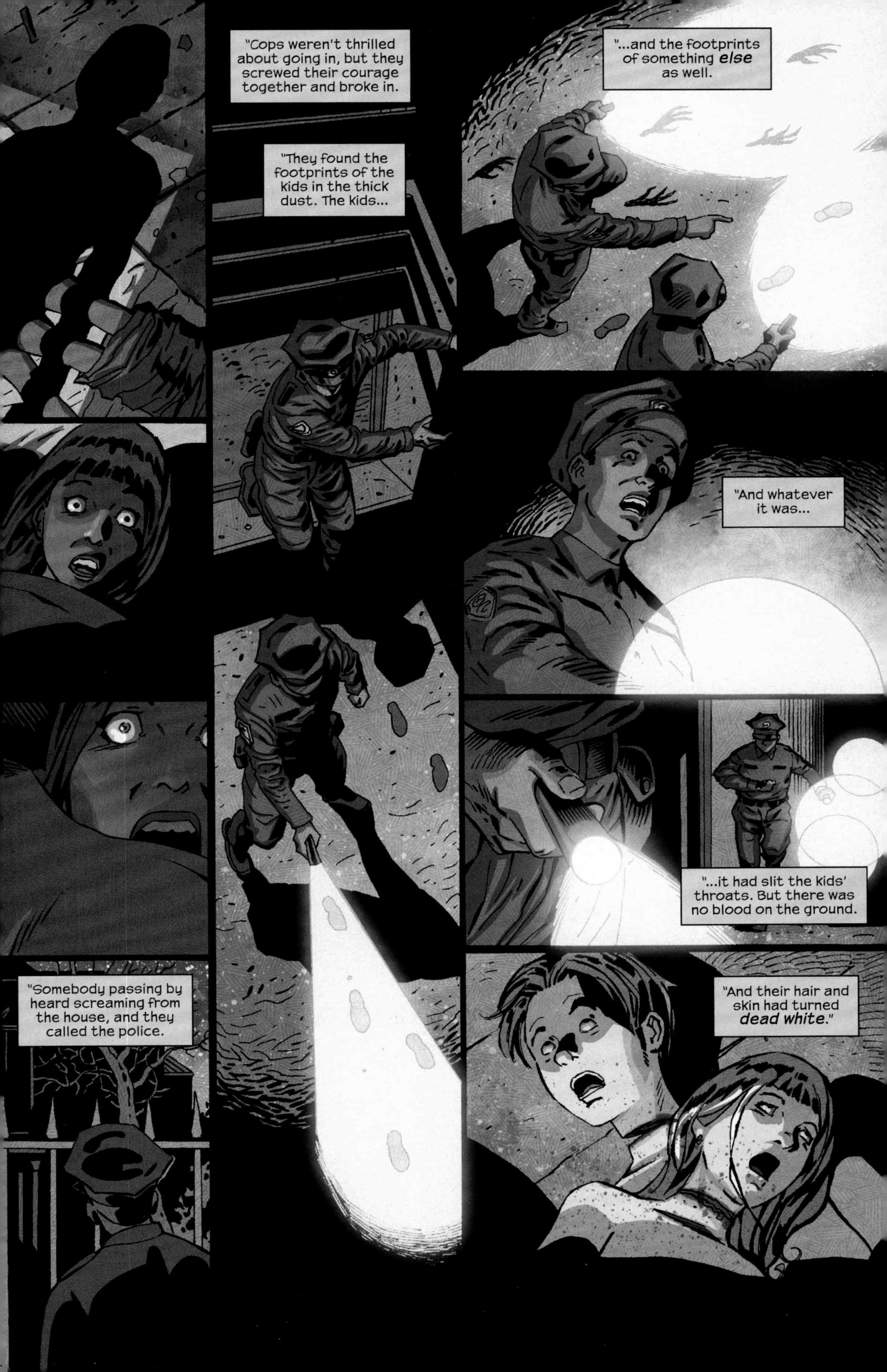
"Cops weren't thrilled about going in, but they screwed their courage together and broke in.
"They found the footprints of the kids in the thick dust. The kids...
"...and the footprints of something *else* as well.
"And whatever it was...
"Somebody passing by heard screaming from the house, and they called the police.
"...it had slit the kids' throats. But there was no blood on the ground.
"And their hair and skin had turned *dead white*."

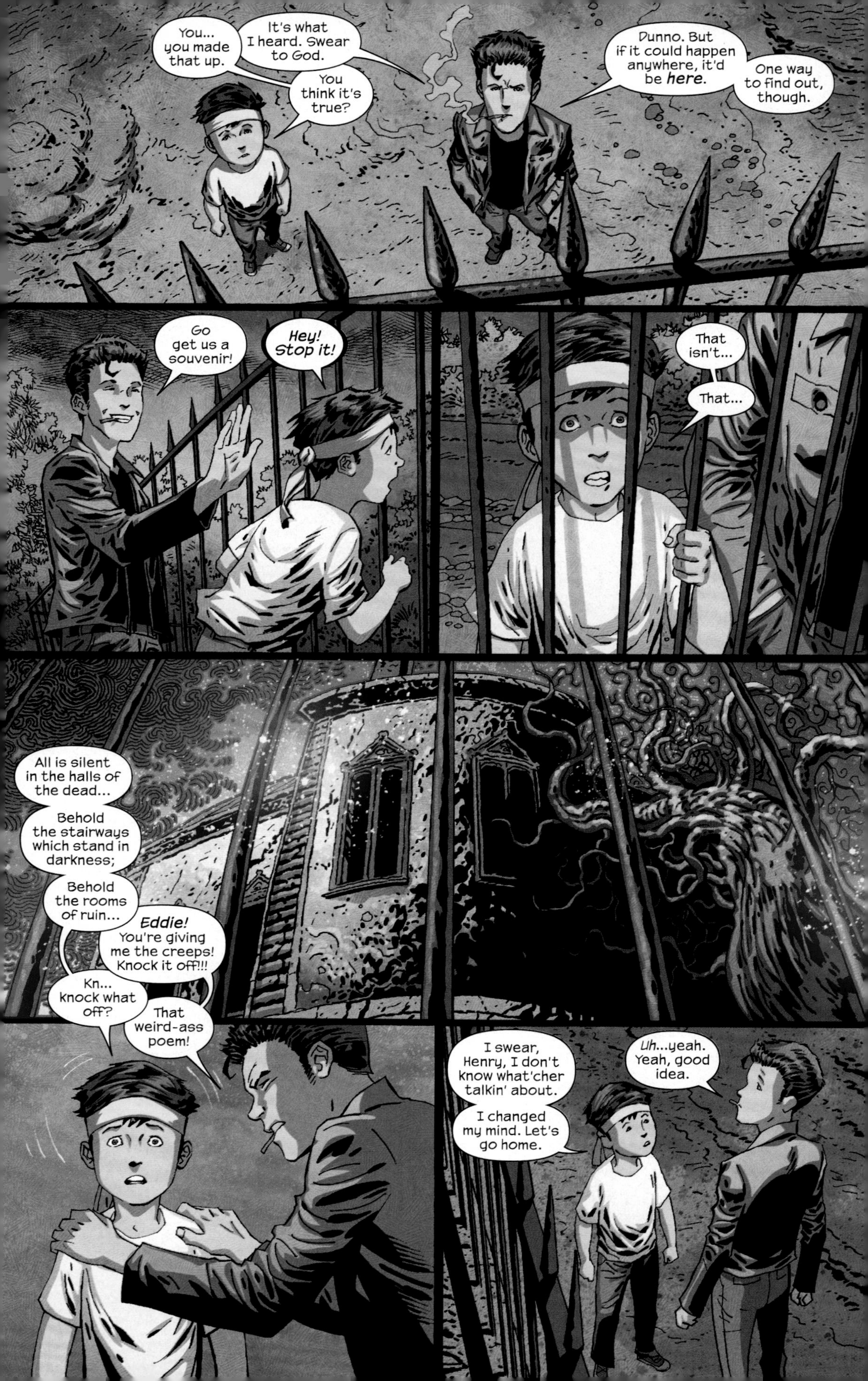
You... you made that up.
It's what I heard. Swear to God.
You think it's true?
Dunno. But if it could happen anywhere, it'd be *here*.
One way to find out, though.
Go get us a souvenir!
Hey! Stop it!
That isn't...
That...
All is silent in the halls of the dead...
Behold the stairways which stand in darkness;
Behold the rooms of ruin...
Eddie! You're giving me the creeps! Knock it off!!!
Kn... knock what off?
That weird-ass poem!
I swear, Henry, I don't know what'cher talkin' about.
I changed my mind. Let's go home.
Uh...yeah. Yeah, good idea.

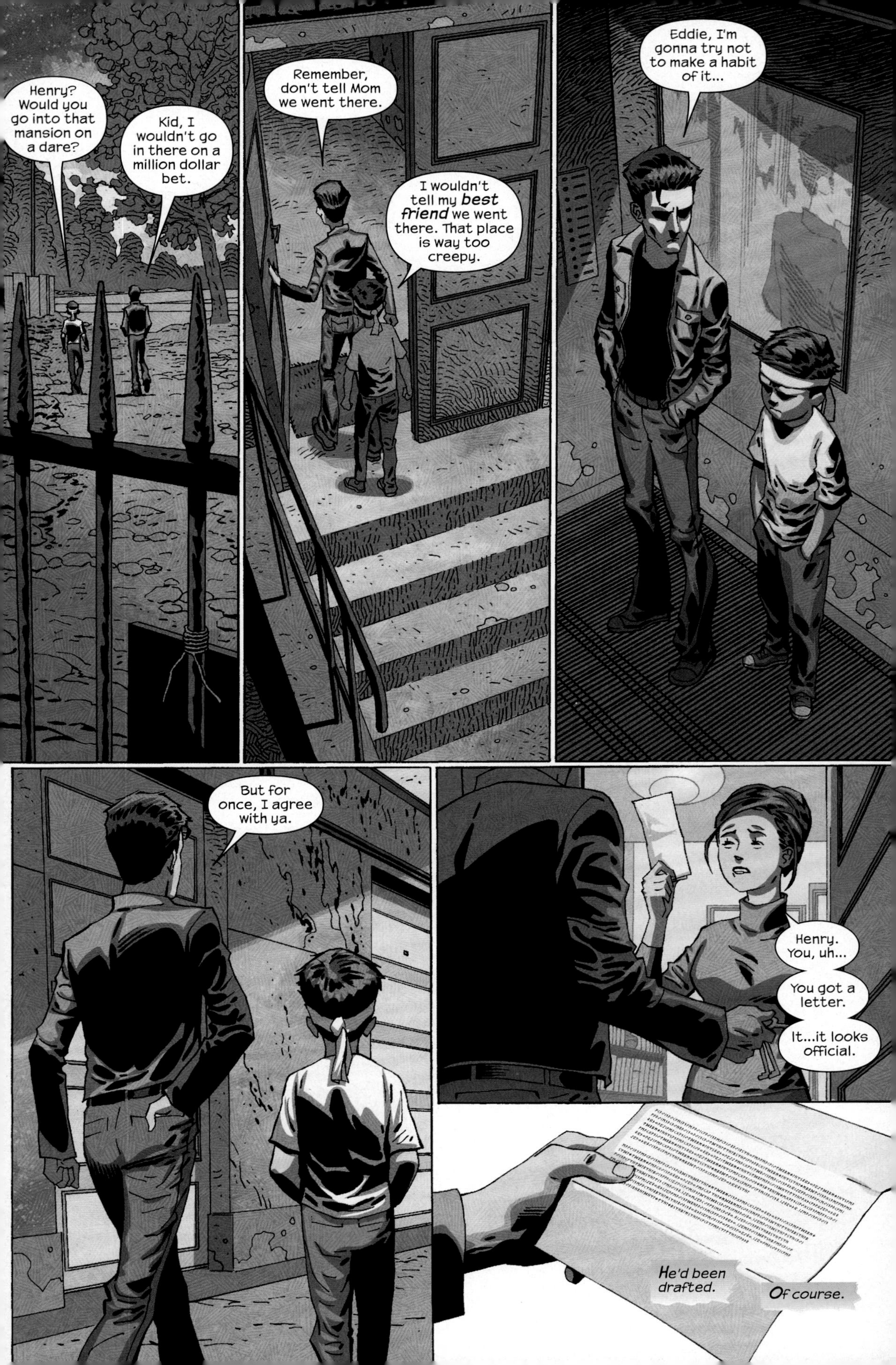
Henry? Would you go into that mansion on a dare?
Kid, I wouldn't go in there on a million dollar bet.
Remember, don't tell Mom we went there.
I wouldn't tell my **best friend** we went there. That place is way too creepy.
Eddie, I'm gonna try not to make a habit of it...
But for once, I agree with ya.
Henry. You, uh...
You got a letter.
It...it looks official.
He'd been drafted.
Of course.

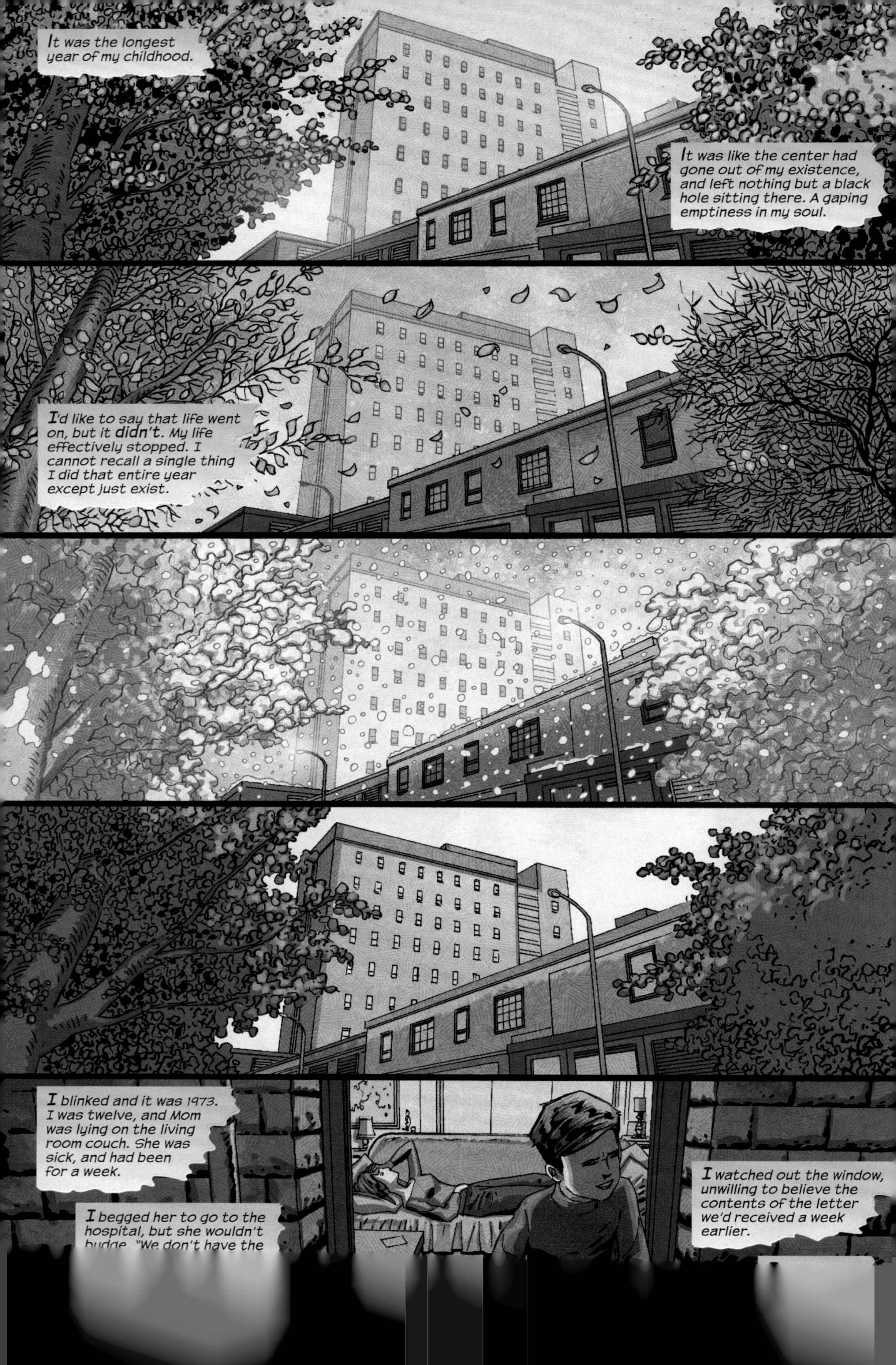
It was the longest year of my childhood.
It was like the center had gone out of my existence, and left nothing but a black hole sitting there. A gaping emptiness in my soul.
I'd like to say that life went on, but it didn't. My life effectively stopped. I cannot recall a single thing I did that entire year except just exist.
I blinked and it was 1973. I was twelve, and Mom was lying on the living room couch. She was sick, and had been for a week.
I begged her to go to the hospital, but she wouldn't budge. "We don't have the
I watched out the window, unwilling to believe the contents of the letter we'd received a week earlier.

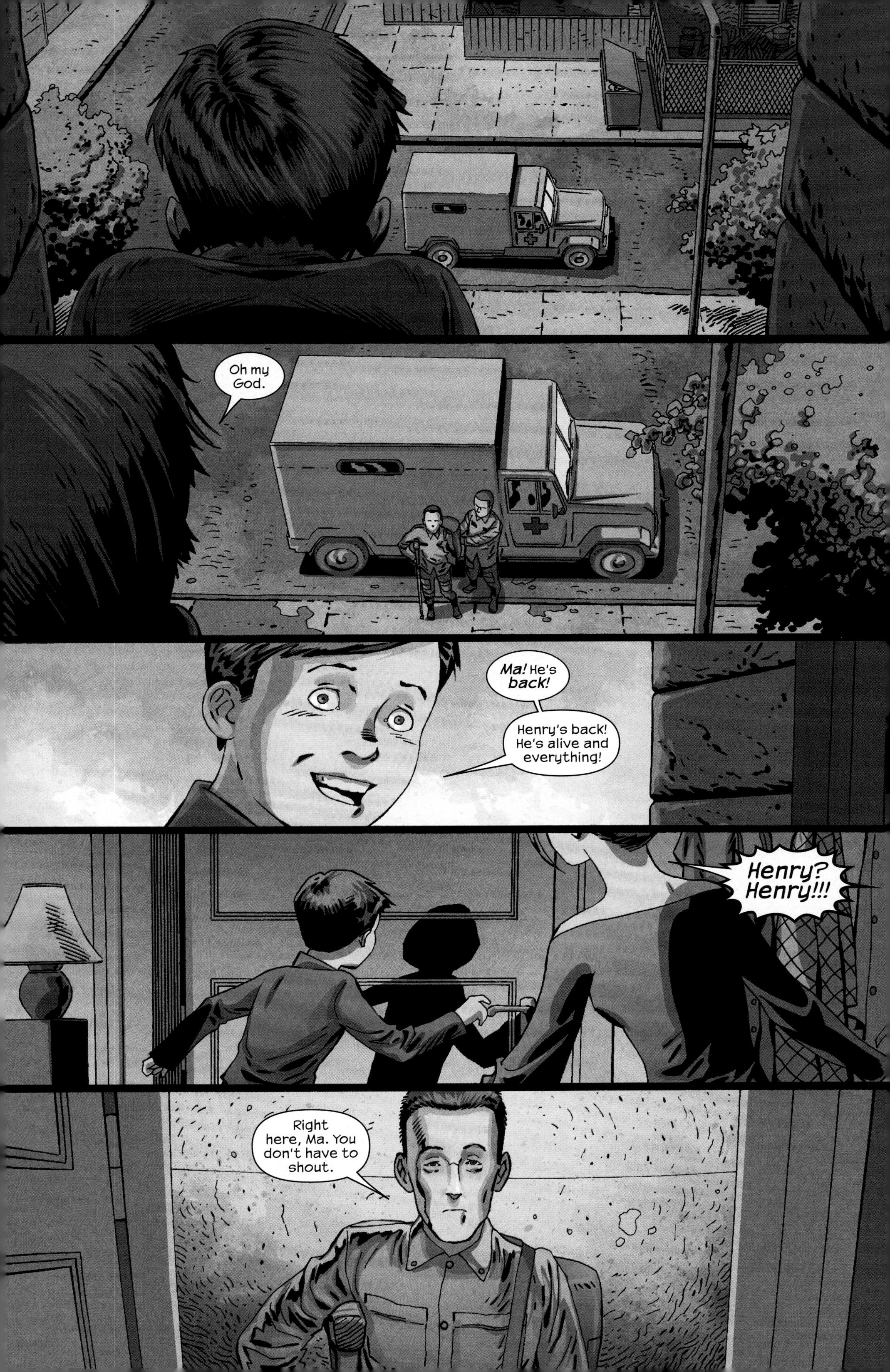
Oh my God.
Ma! He's back!
Henry's back! He's alive and everything!
Henry? Henry!!!
Right here, Ma. You don't have to shout.

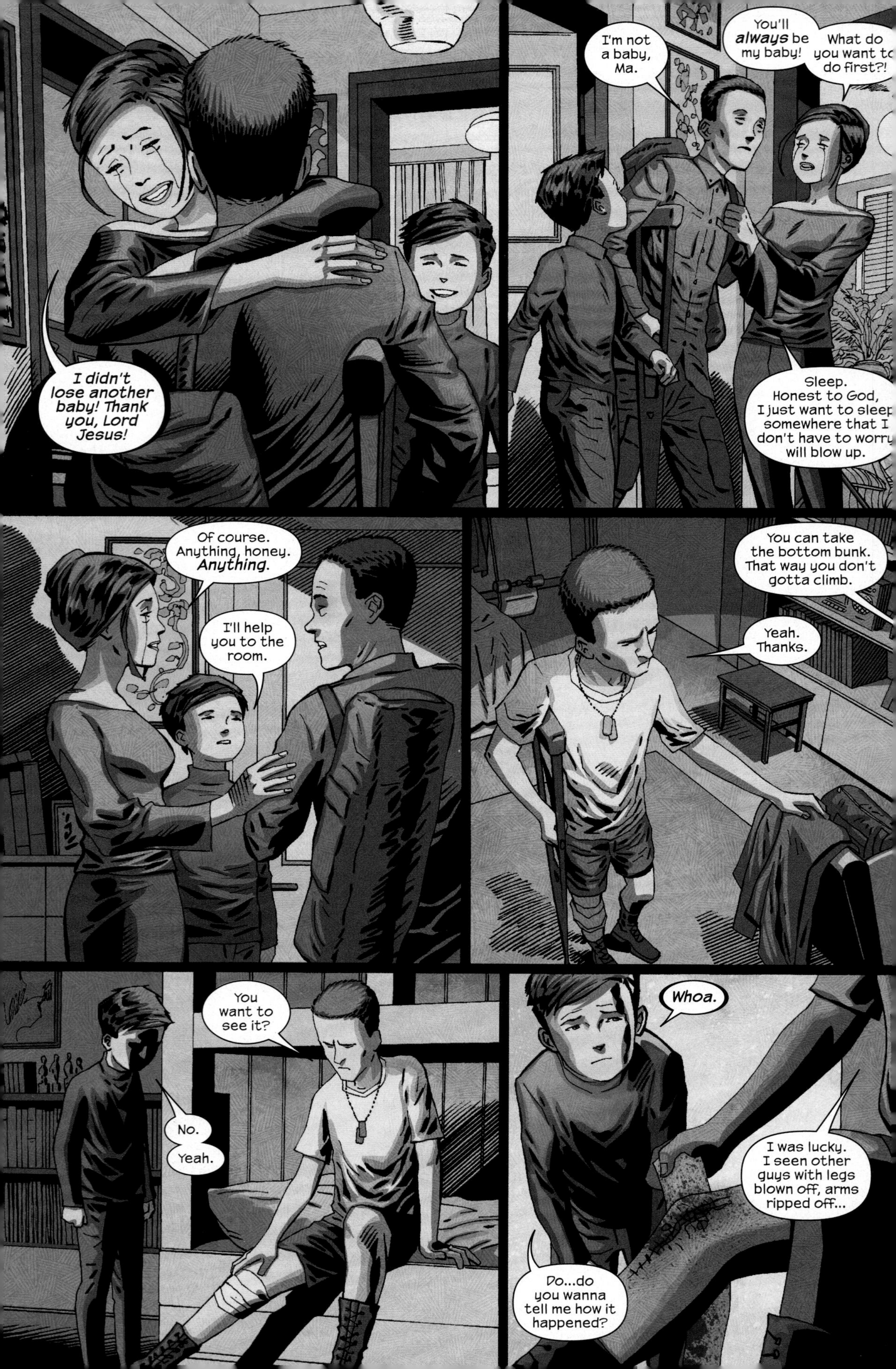
I didn't lose another baby! Thank you, Lord Jesus!
I'm not a baby, Ma.
You'll *always* be my baby!
What do you want to do first?!
Sleep. Honest to God, I just want to sleep somewhere that I don't have to worry will blow up.
Of course. Anything, honey. *Anything*.
I'll help you to the room.
You can take the bottom bunk. That way you don't gotta climb.
Yeah. Thanks.
You want to see it?
No.
Yeah.
Whoa.
I was lucky. I seen other guys with legs blown off, arms ripped off...
Do...do you wanna tell me how it happened?

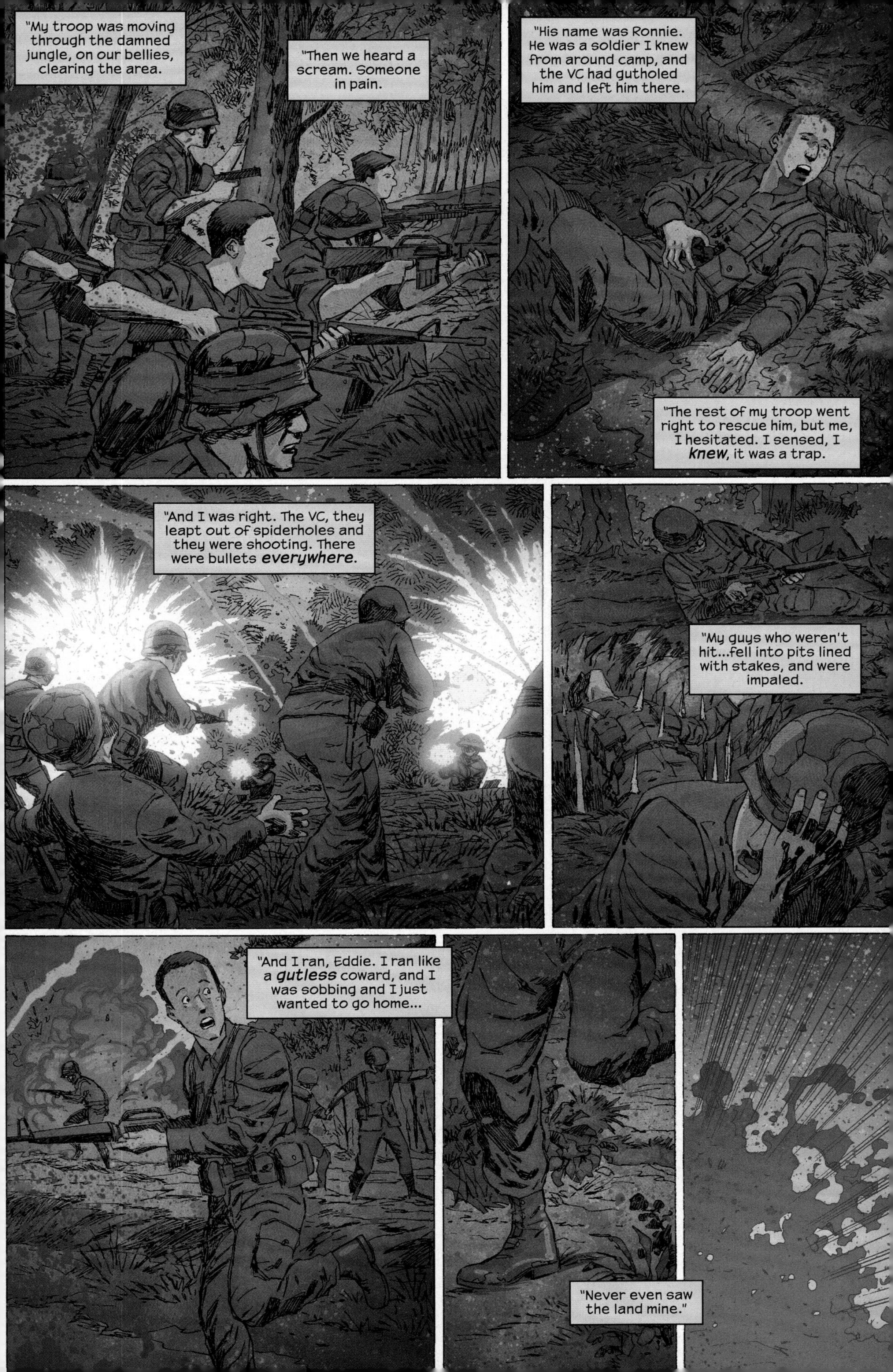
"My troop was moving through the damned jungle, on our bellies, clearing the area.
"Then we heard a scream. Someone in pain.
"His name was Ronnie. He was a soldier I knew from around camp, and the VC had gutholed him and left him there.
"The rest of my troop went right to rescue him, but me, I hesitated. I sensed, I *knew*, it was a trap.
"And I was right. The VC, they leapt out of spiderholes and they were shooting. There were bullets *everywhere*.
"My guys who weren't hit...fell into pits lined with stakes, and were impaled.
"And I ran, Eddie. I ran like a *gutless* coward, and I was sobbing and I just wanted to go home...
"Never even saw the land mine."

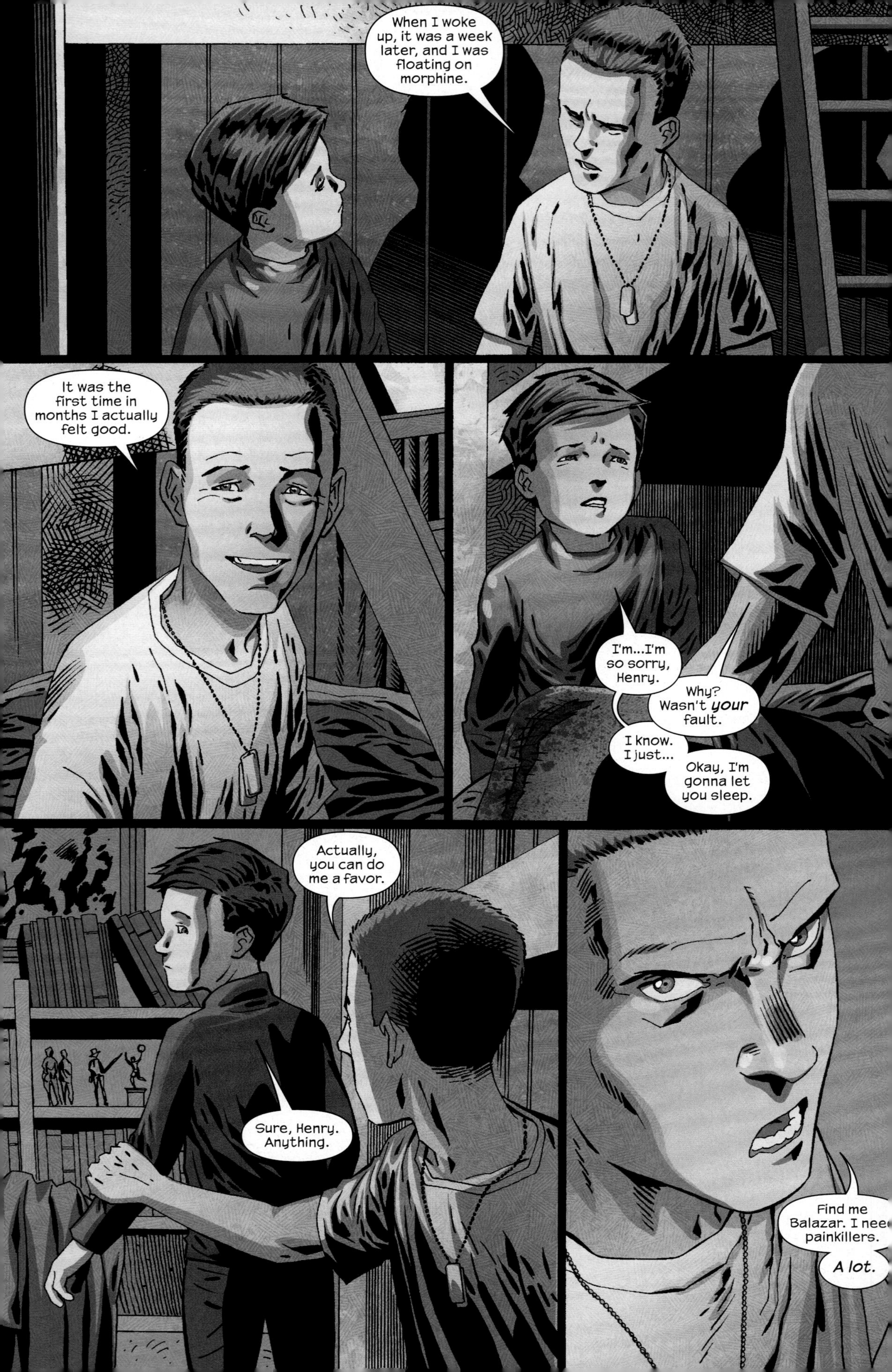
When I woke up, it was a week later, and I was floating on morphine.
It was the first time in months I actually felt good.
I'm...I'm so sorry, Henry.
Why? Wasn't *your* fault.
I know. I just...
Okay, I'm gonna let you sleep.
Actually, you can do me a favor.
Sure, Henry. Anything.
Find me Balazar. I nee painkillers.
A lot.

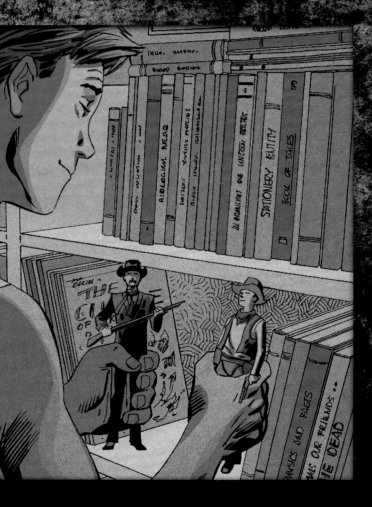

HE DARK TOWER

THE DRAWING OF THE THREE

STEPHEN KING

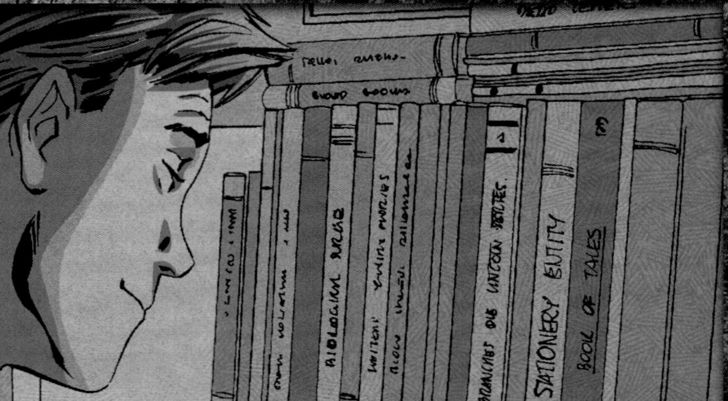
STATIONERY
BOOK OF TALES

HE PRISONER

CHAPTER FOUR

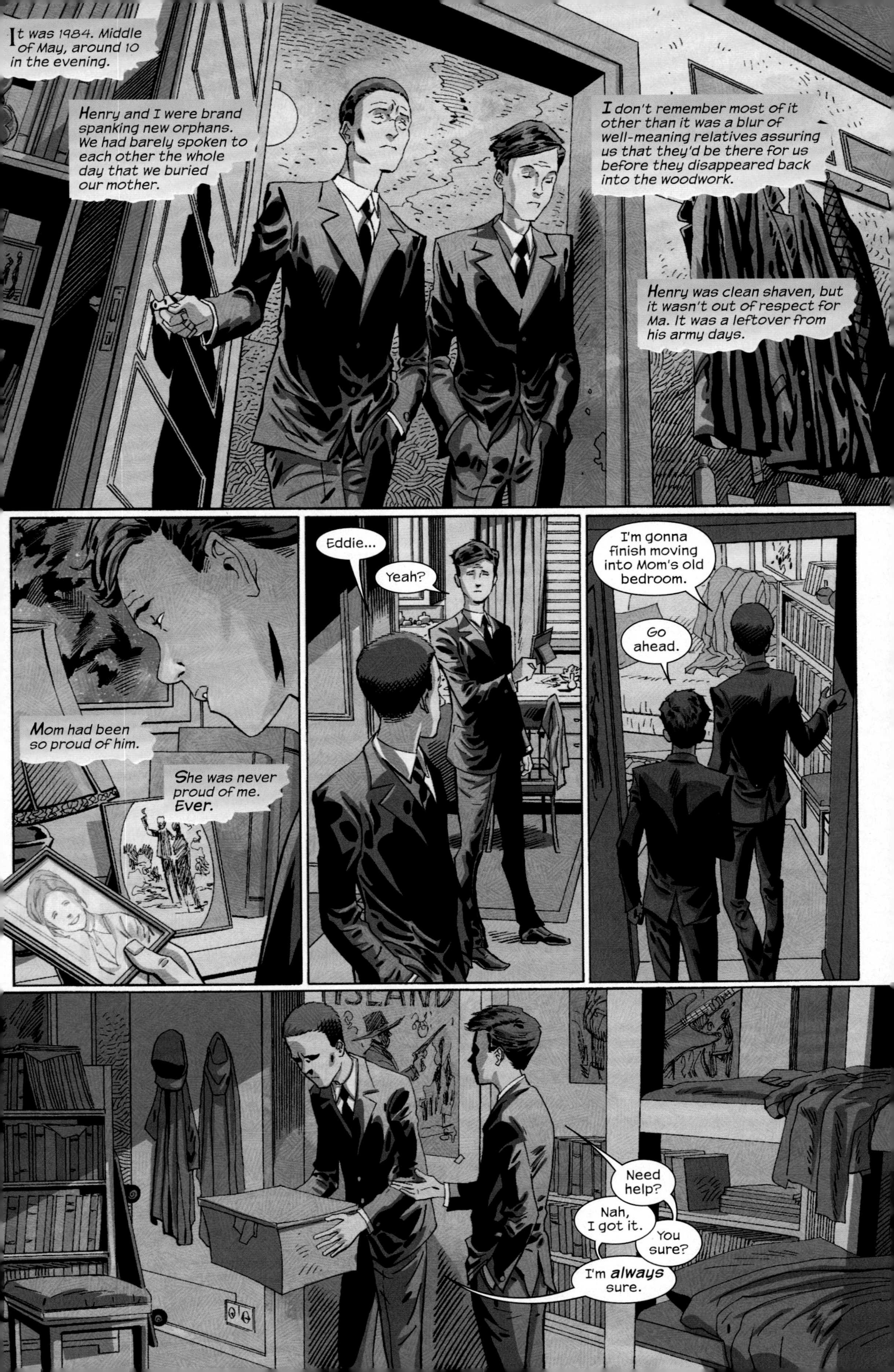
It was 1984. Middle of May, around 10 in the evening.
Henry and I were brand spanking new orphans. We had barely spoken to each other the whole day that we buried our mother.
I don't remember most of it other than it was a blur of well-meaning relatives assuring us that they'd be there for us before they disappeared back into the woodwork.
Henry was clean shaven, but it wasn't out of respect for Ma. It was a leftover from his army days.
Mom had been so proud of him.
She was never proud of me. Ever.
Eddie...
Yeah?
I'm gonna finish moving into Mom's old bedroom.
Go ahead.
Need help?
Nah, I got it.
You sure?
I'm always sure.

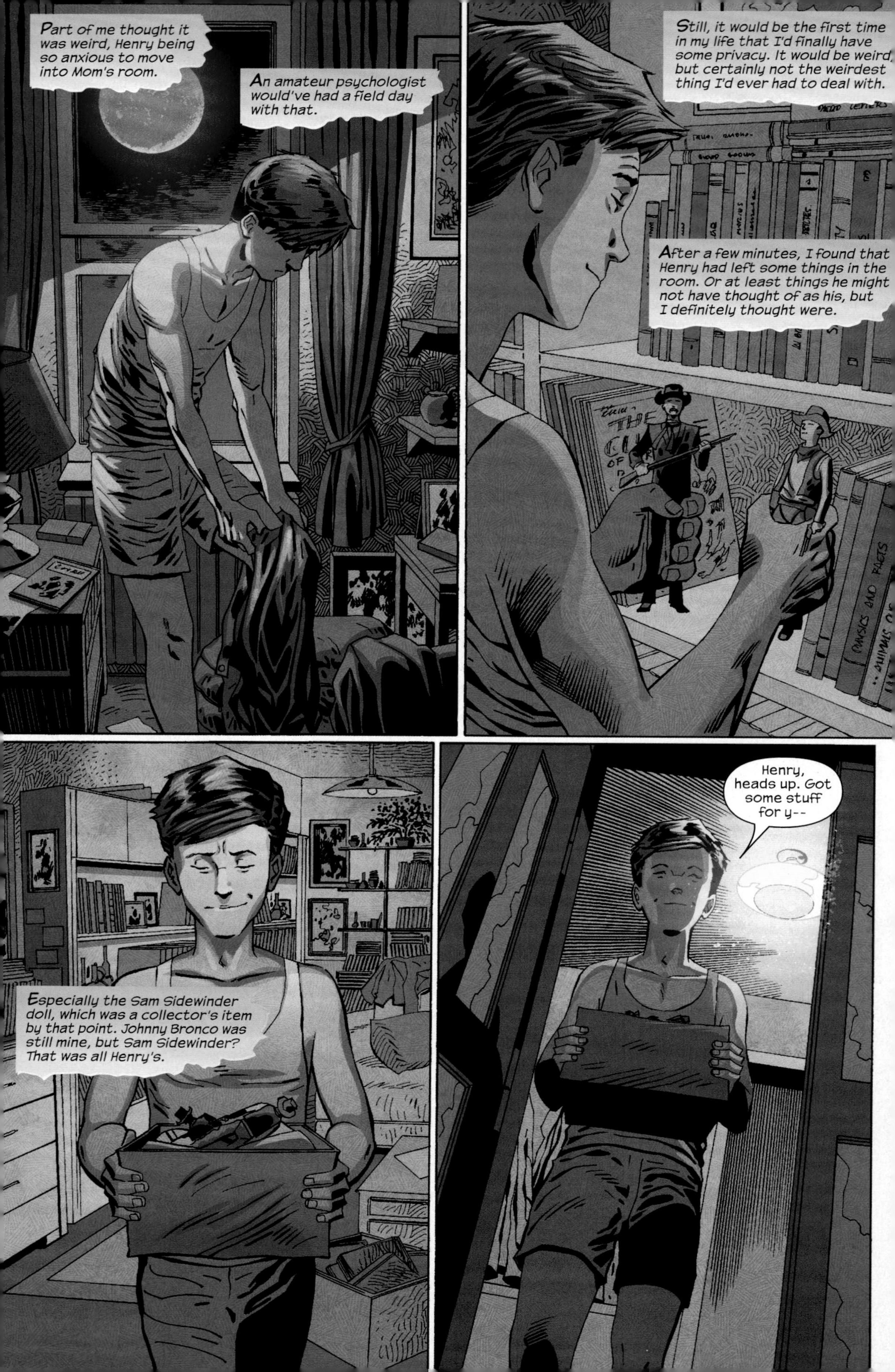
Part of me thought it was weird, Henry being so anxious to move into Mom's room.
An amateur psychologist would've had a field day with that.
Still, it would be the first time in my life that I'd finally have some privacy. It would be weird, but certainly not the weirdest thing I'd ever had to deal with.
After a few minutes, I found that Henry had left some things in the room. Or at least things he might not have thought of as his, but I definitely thought were.
Especially the Sam Sidewinder doll, which was a collector's item by that point. Johnny Bronco was still mine, but Sam Sidewinder? That was all Henry's.
Henry, heads up. Got some stuff for y--

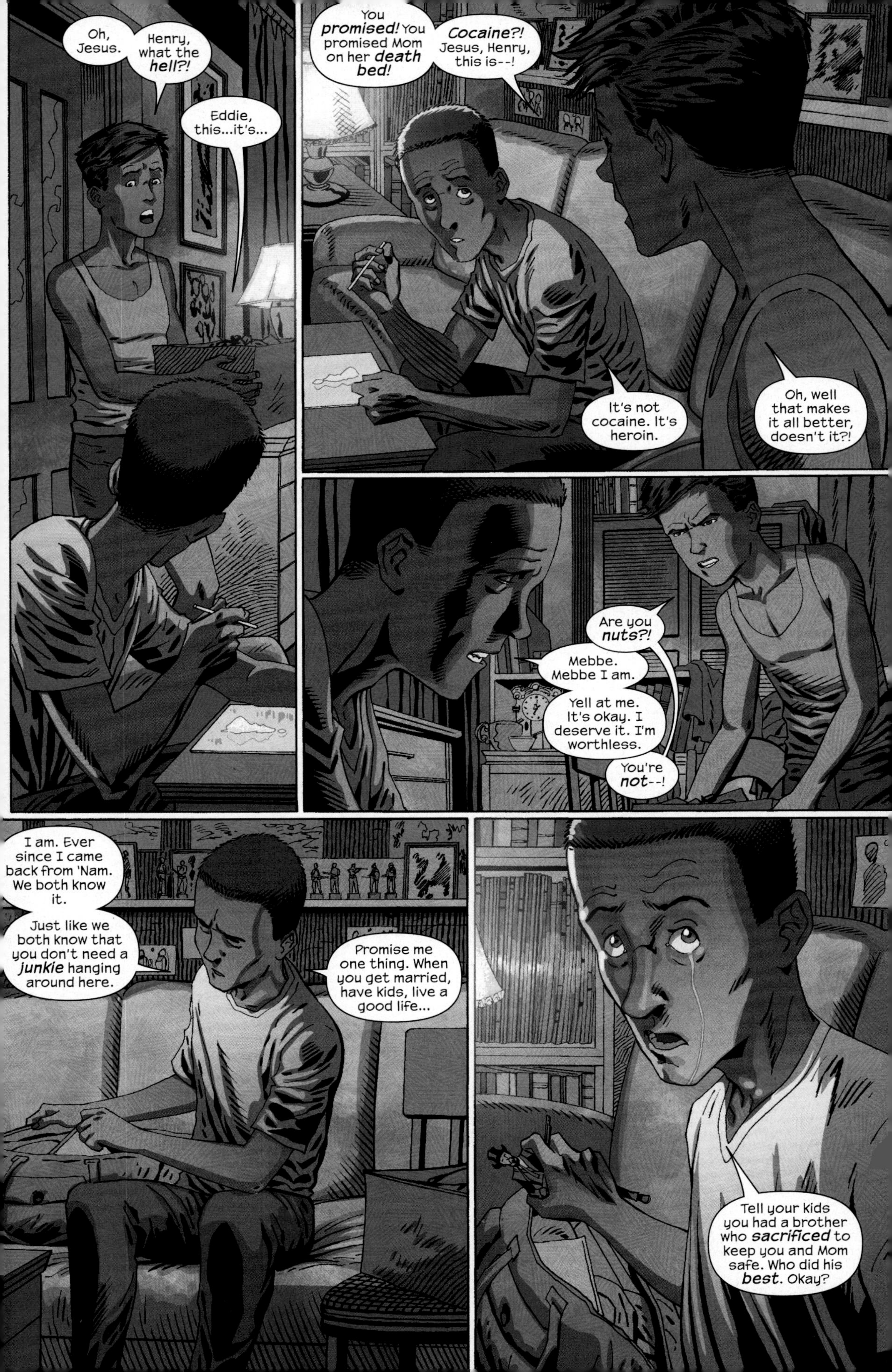
Oh, Jesus.
Henry, what the *hell?!*
Eddie, this...it's...
You *promised!* You promised Mom on her *death bed!*
Cocaine?! Jesus, Henry, this is--!
It's not cocaine. It's heroin.
Oh, well that makes it all better, doesn't it?!
Are you *nuts?!*
Mebbe. Mebbe I am.
Yell at me. It's okay. I deserve it. I'm worthless.
You're *not*--!
I am. Ever since I came back from 'Nam. We both know it.
Just like we both know that you don't need a *junkie* hanging around here.
Promise me one thing. When you get married, have kids, live a good life...
Tell your kids you had a brother who *sacrificed* to keep you and Mom safe. Who did his *best*. Okay?

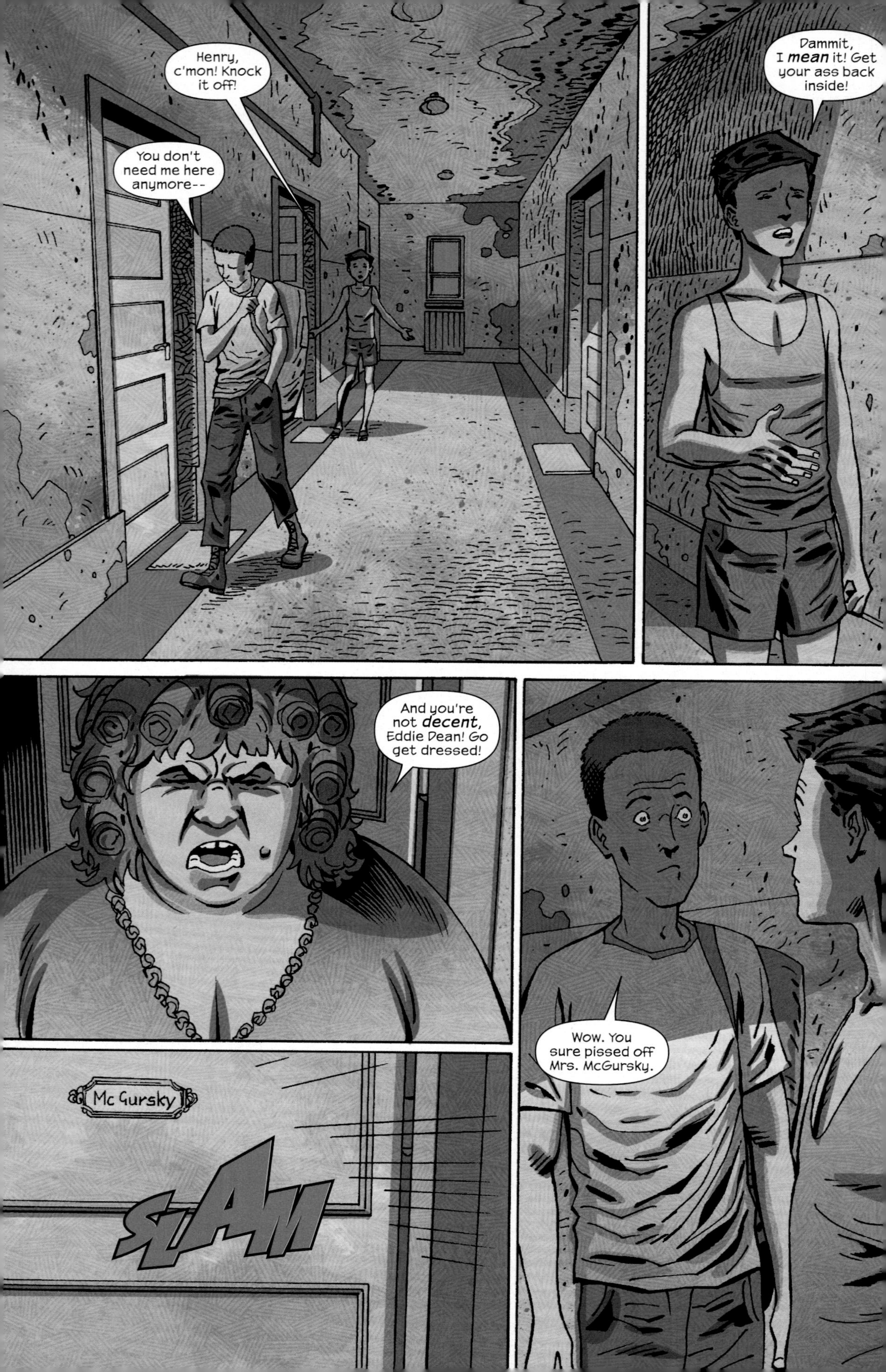

Henry, c'mon! Knock it off!
You don't need me here anymore--
Dammit, I *mean* it! Get your ass back inside!
And you're not *decent*, Eddie Dean! Go get dressed!
McGursky
SLAM
Wow. You sure pissed off Mrs. McGursky.

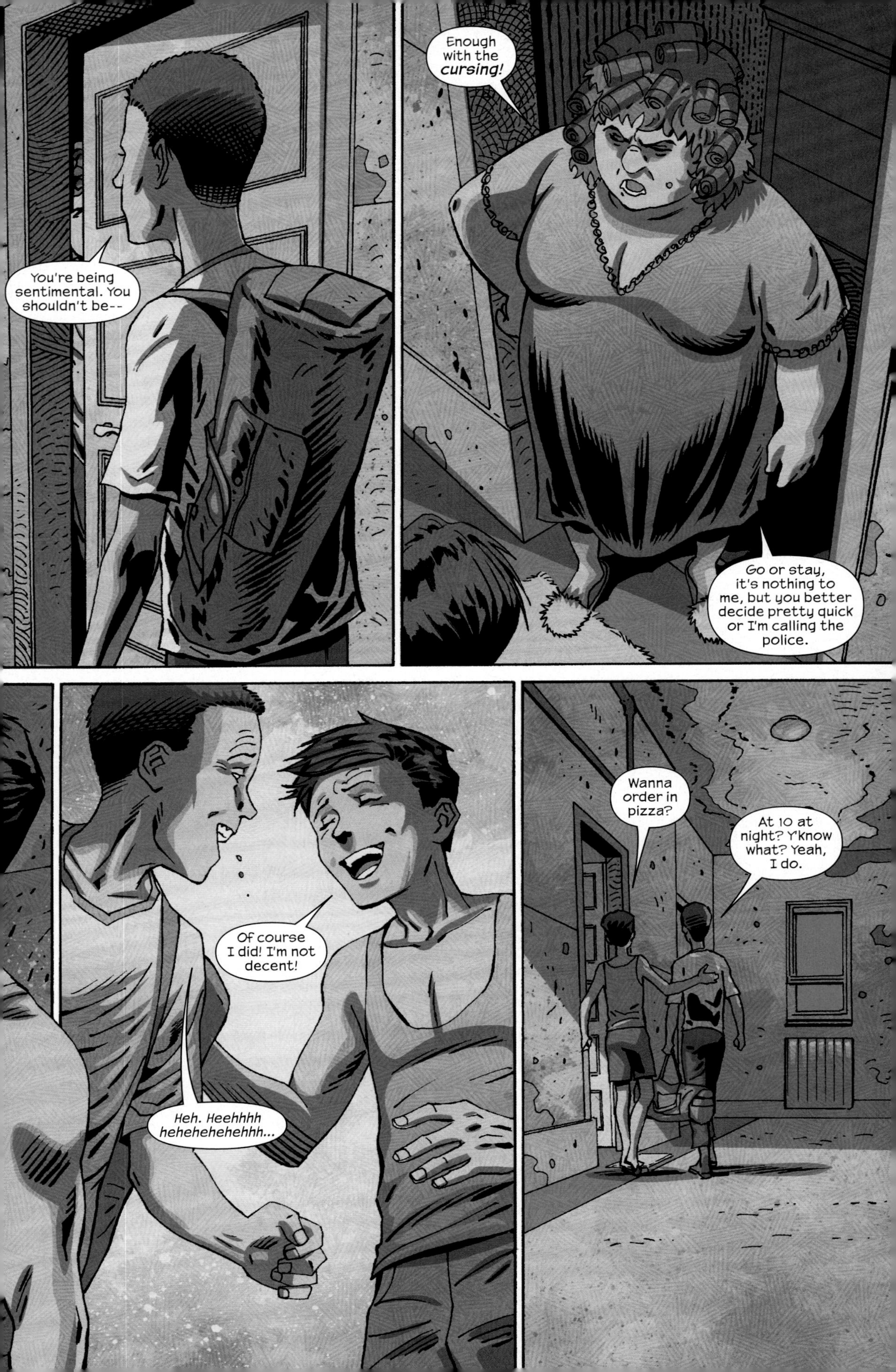
You're being sentimental. You shouldn't be--
Enough with the *cursing!*
Go or stay, it's nothing to me, but you better decide pretty quick or I'm calling the police.
Of course I did! I'm not decent!
Heh. Heehhhh hehehehehehhh...
Wanna order in pizza?
At 10 at night? Y'know what? Yeah, I do.

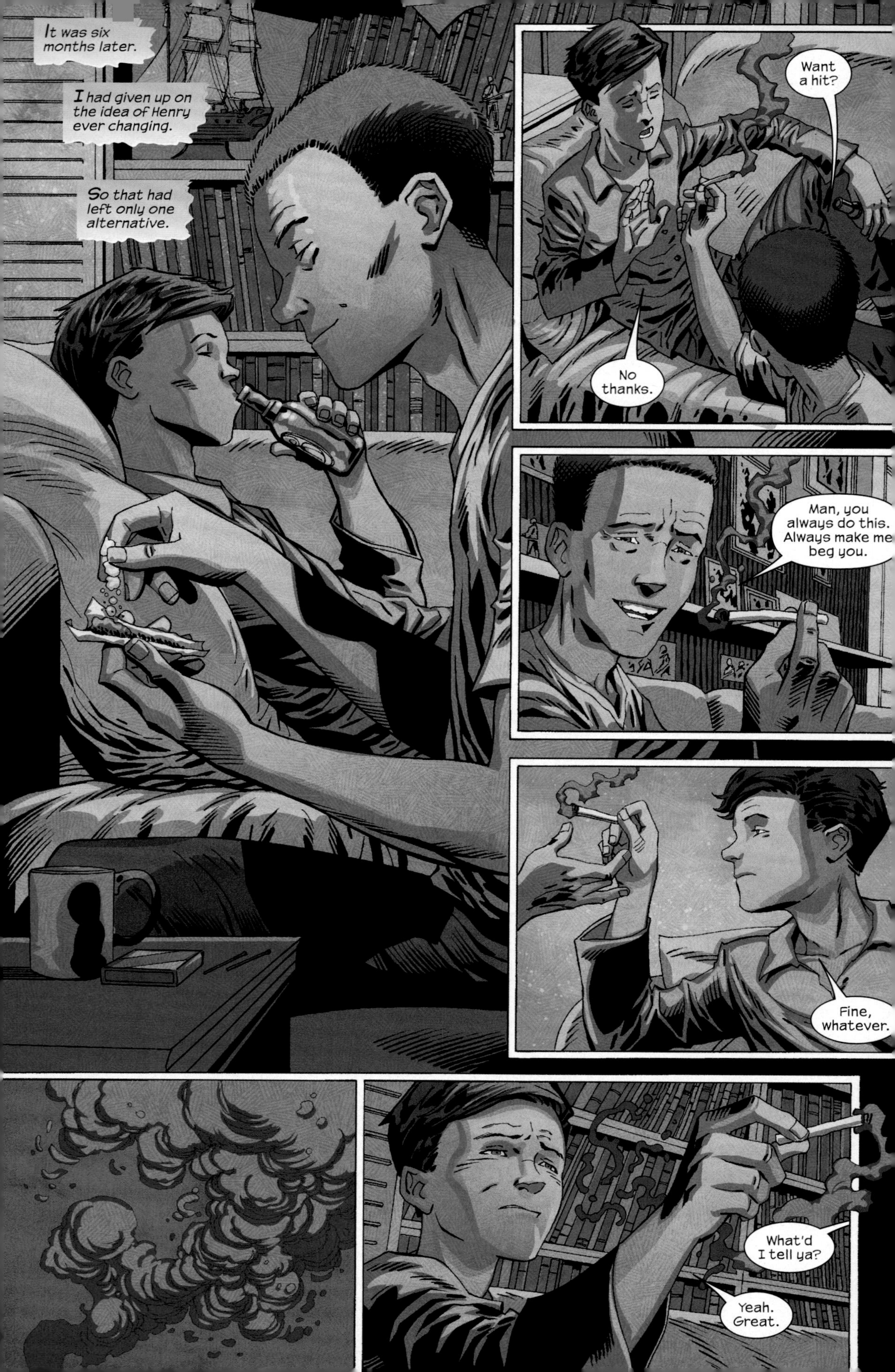
It was six months later.
I had given up on the idea of Henry ever changing.
So that had left only one alternative.
Want a hit?
No thanks.
Man, you always do this. Always make me beg you.
Fine, whatever.
What'd I tell ya?
Yeah. Great.

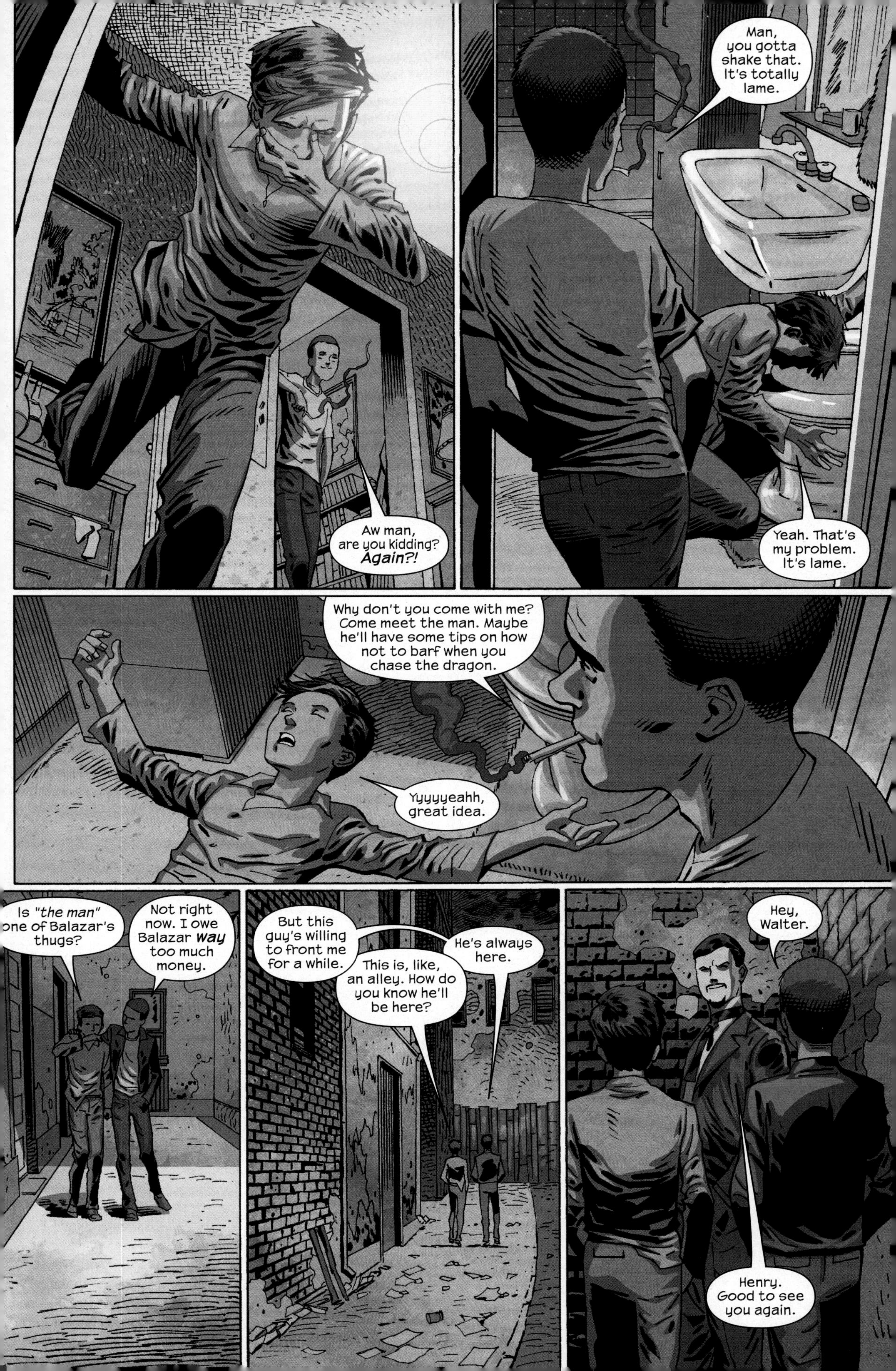
Aw man, are you kidding? Again?!
Man, you gotta shake that. It's totally lame.
Yeah. That's my problem. It's lame.
Why don't you come with me? Come meet the man. Maybe he'll have some tips on how not to barf when you chase the dragon.
Yyyyyeahh, great idea.
Is "the man" one of Balazar's thugs?
Not right now. I owe Balazar way too much money.
But this guy's willing to front me for a while.
This is, like, an alley. How do you know he'll be here?
He's always here.
Hey, Walter.
Henry. Good to see you again.

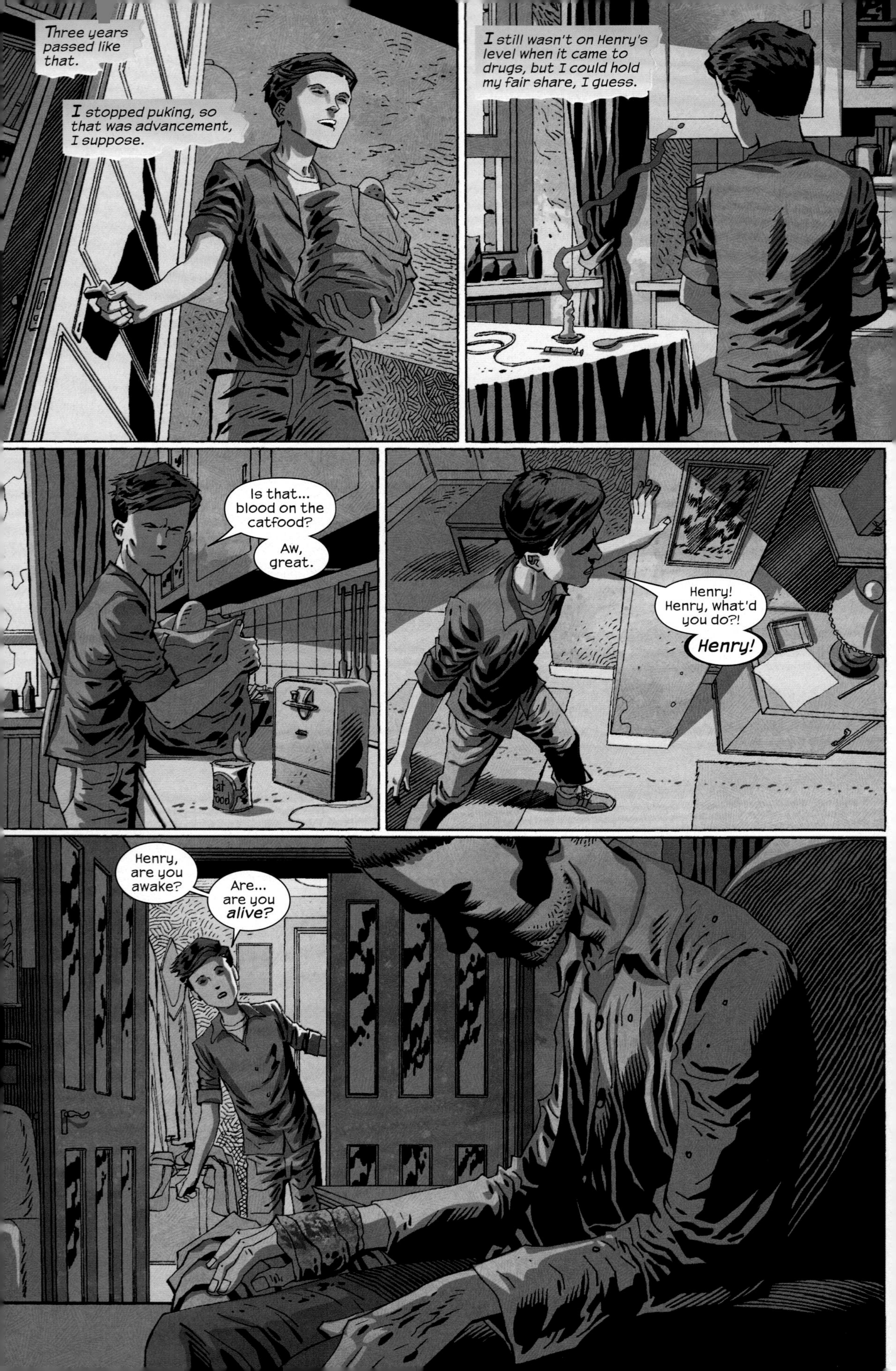
Three years passed like that.
I stopped puking, so that was advancement, I suppose.
I still wasn't on Henry's level when it came to drugs, but I could hold my fair share, I guess.
Is that... blood on the catfood?
Aw, great.
Cat Food
Henry! Henry, what'd you do?!
Henry!
Henry, are you awake?
Are... are you alive?

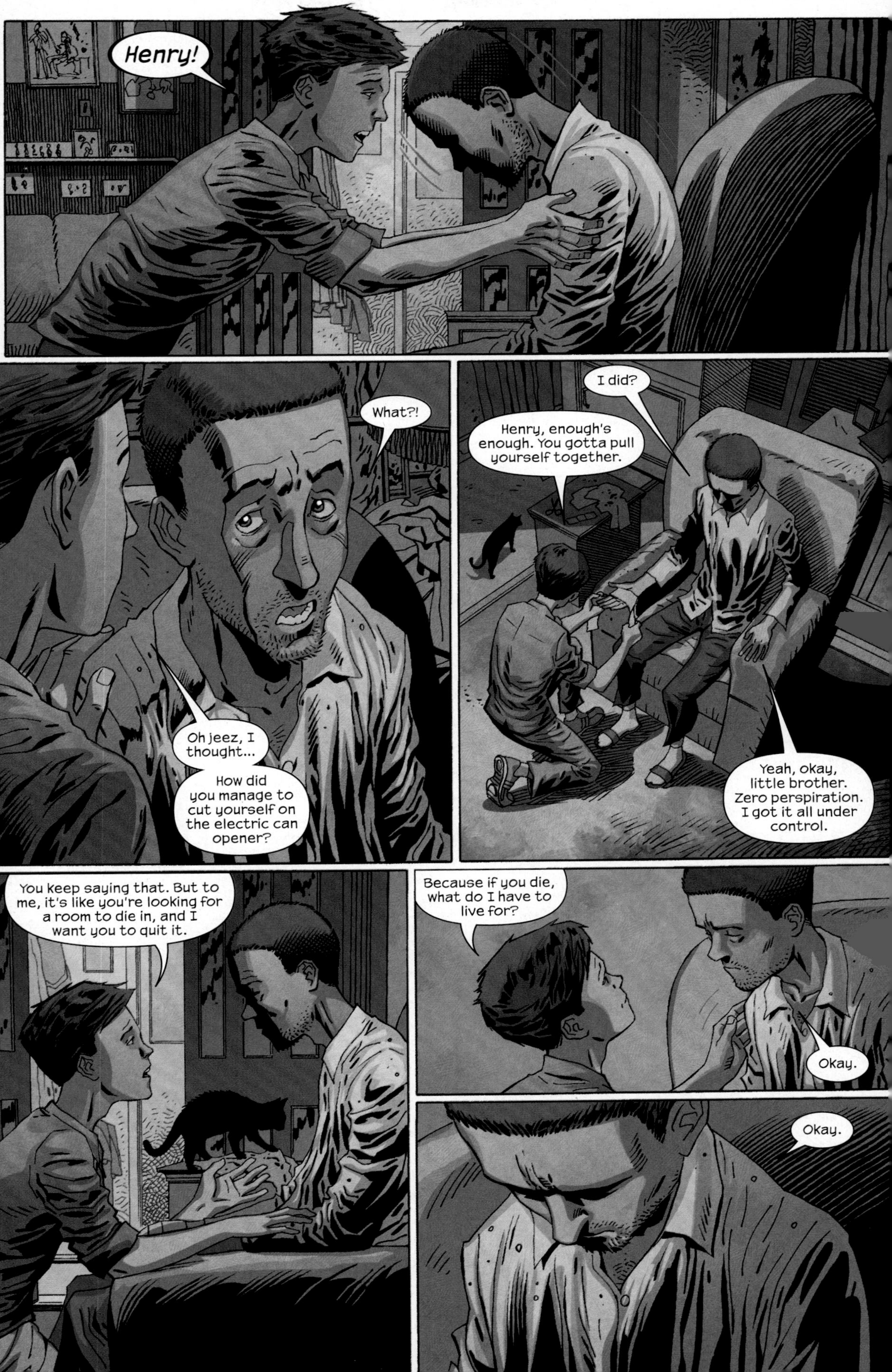

Henry!
What?!
Oh jeez, I thought...
How did you manage to cut yourself on the electric can opener?
I did?
Henry, enough's enough. You gotta pull yourself together.
Yeah, okay, little brother. Zero perspiration. I got it all under control.
You keep saying that. But to me, it's like you're looking for a room to die in, and I want you to quit it.
Because if you die, what do I have to live for?
Okay.
Okay.

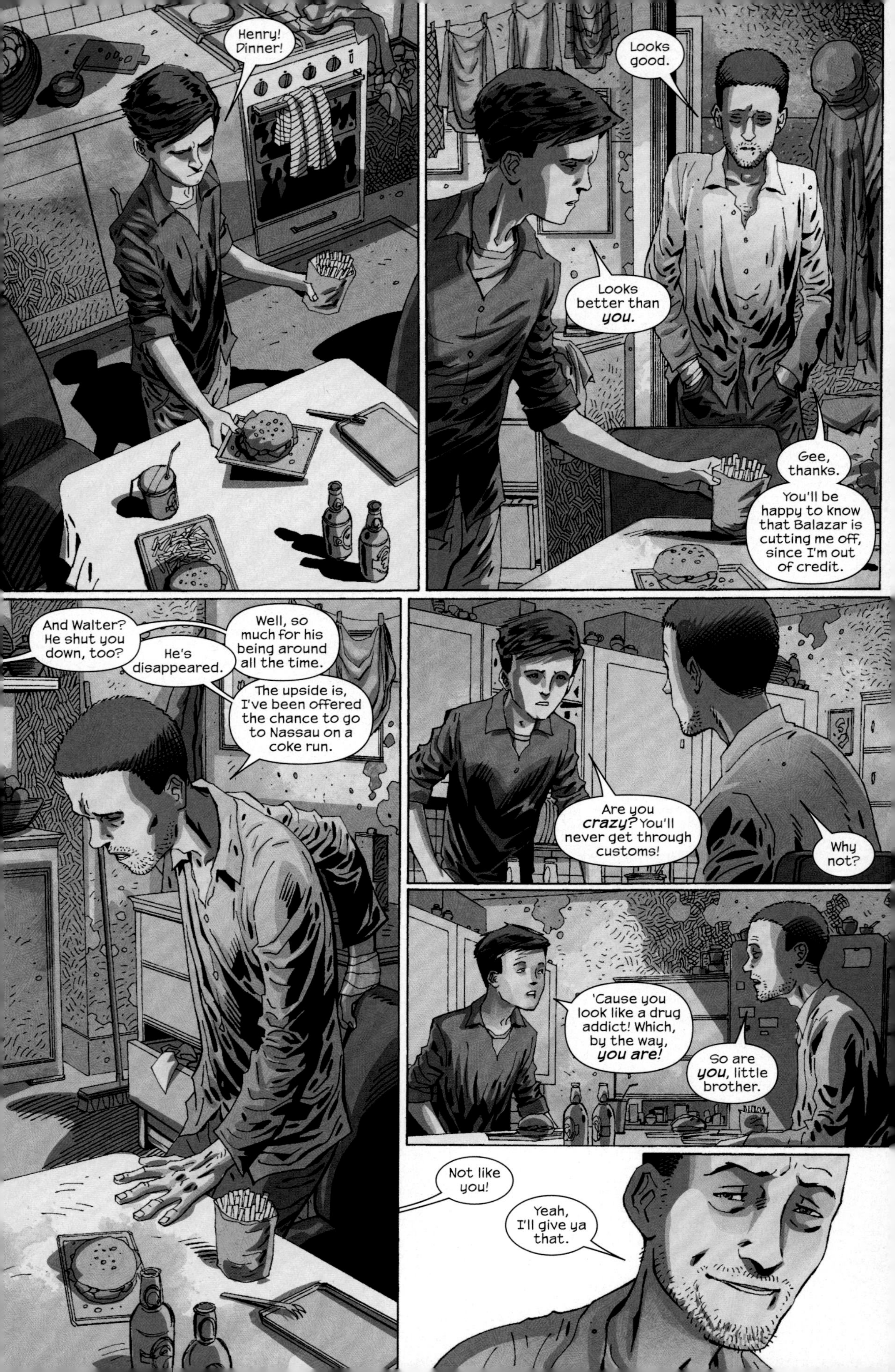
Henry! Dinner!
Looks good.
Looks better than *you.*
Gee, thanks.
You'll be happy to know that Balazar is cutting me off, since I'm out of credit.
And Walter? He shut you down, too?
He's disappeared.
Well, so much for his being around all the time.
The upside is, I've been offered the chance to go to Nassau on a coke run.
Are you *crazy?* You'll never get through customs!
Why not?
'Cause you look like a drug addict! Which, by the way, *you are!*
So are *you,* little brother.
Not like you!
Yeah, I'll give ya that.

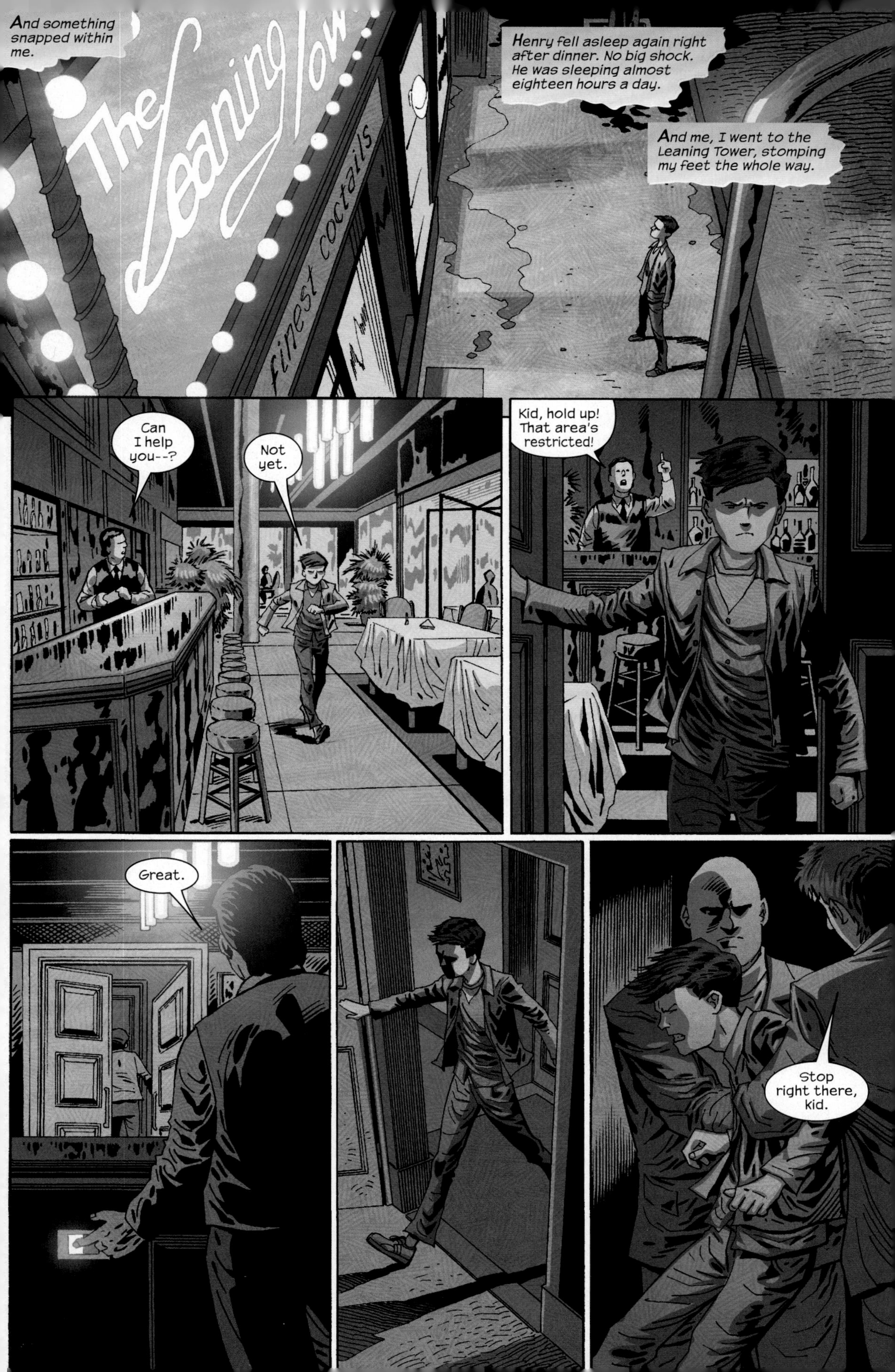
And something snapped within me.
The Leaning Tow
finest coctails
Henry fell asleep again right after dinner. No big shock. He was sleeping almost eighteen hours a day.
And me, I went to the Leaning Tower, stomping my feet the whole way.
Can I help you--?
Not yet.
Kid, hold up! That area's restricted!
Great.
Stop right there, kid.

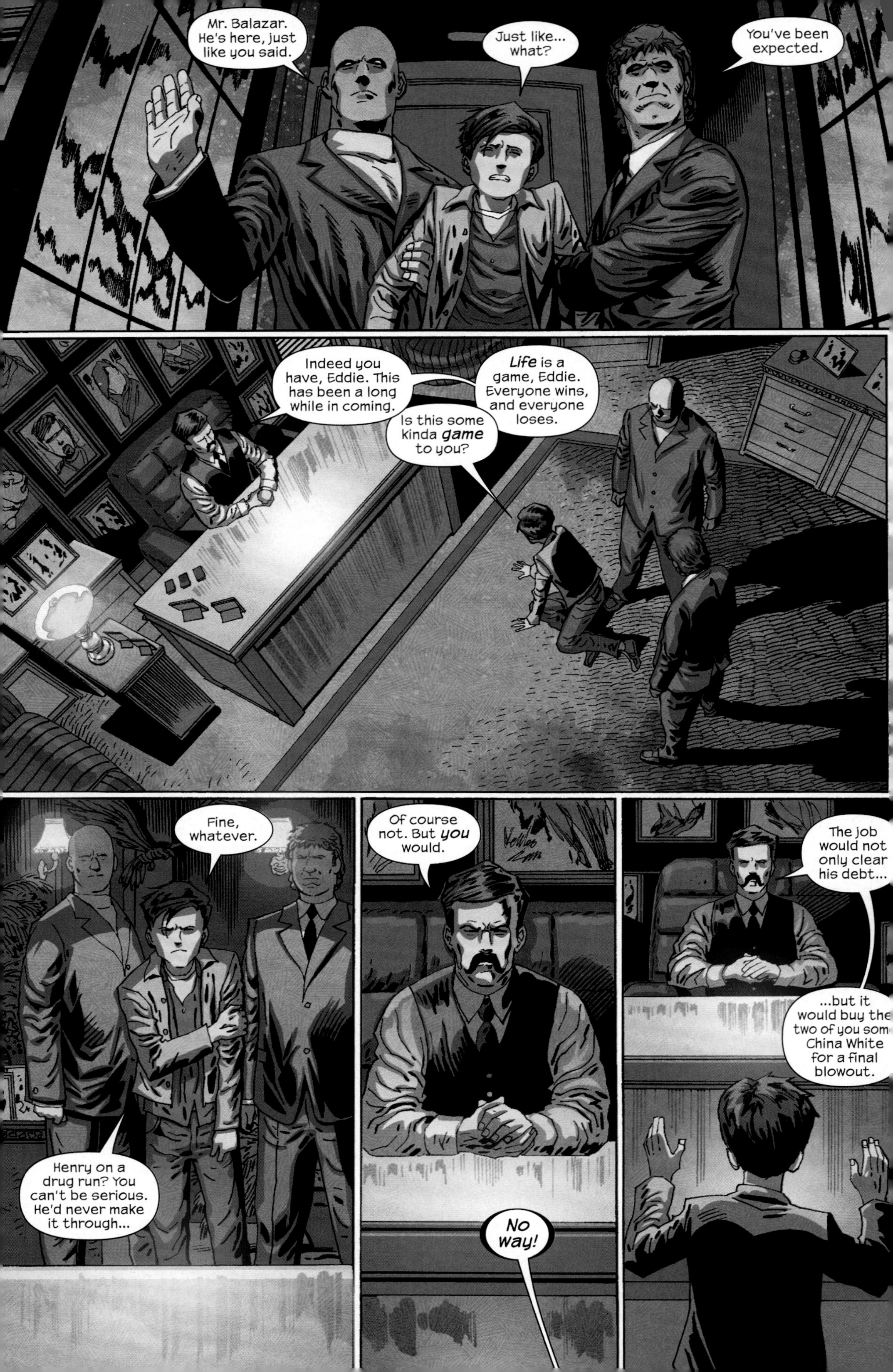

Mr. Balazar. He's here, just like you said.
Just like... what?
You've been expected.
Indeed you have, Eddie. This has been a long while in coming.
Is this some kinda *game* to you?
Life is a game, Eddie. Everyone wins, and everyone loses.
Fine, whatever.
Henry on a drug run? You can't be serious. He'd never make it through...
Of course not. But *you* would.
No way!
The job would not only clear his debt...
...but it would buy the two of you som China White for a final blowout.

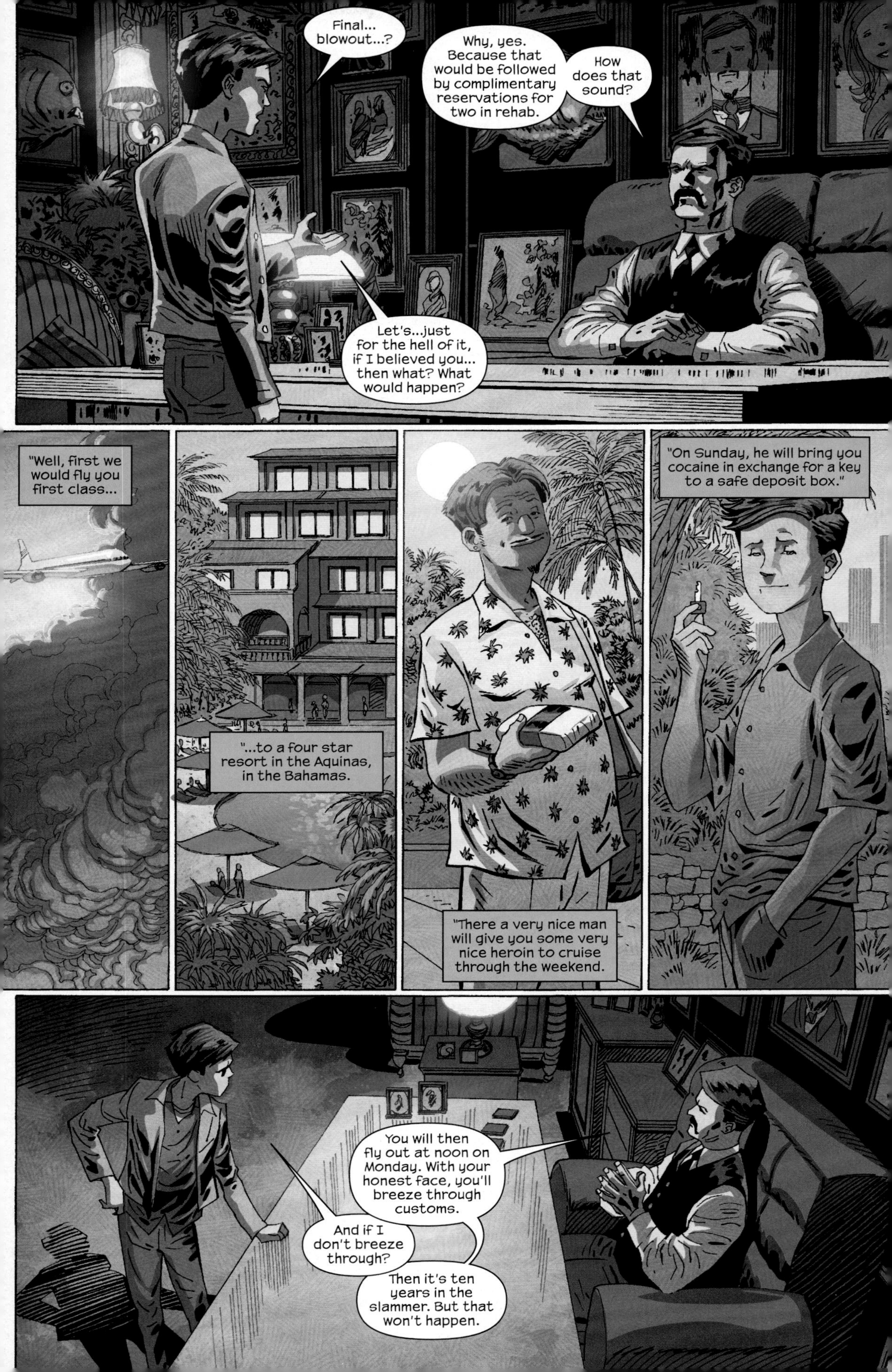
Final... blowout...?
Why, yes. Because that would be followed by complimentary reservations for two in rehab.
How does that sound?
Let's...just for the hell of it, if I believed you... then what? What would happen?
"Well, first we would fly you first class...
"...to a four star resort in the Aquinas, in the Bahamas.
"There a very nice man will give you some very nice heroin to cruise through the weekend.
"On Sunday, he will bring you cocaine in exchange for a key to a safe deposit box."
You will then fly out at noon on Monday. With your honest face, you'll breeze through customs.
And if I don't breeze through?
Then it's ten years in the slammer. But that won't happen.

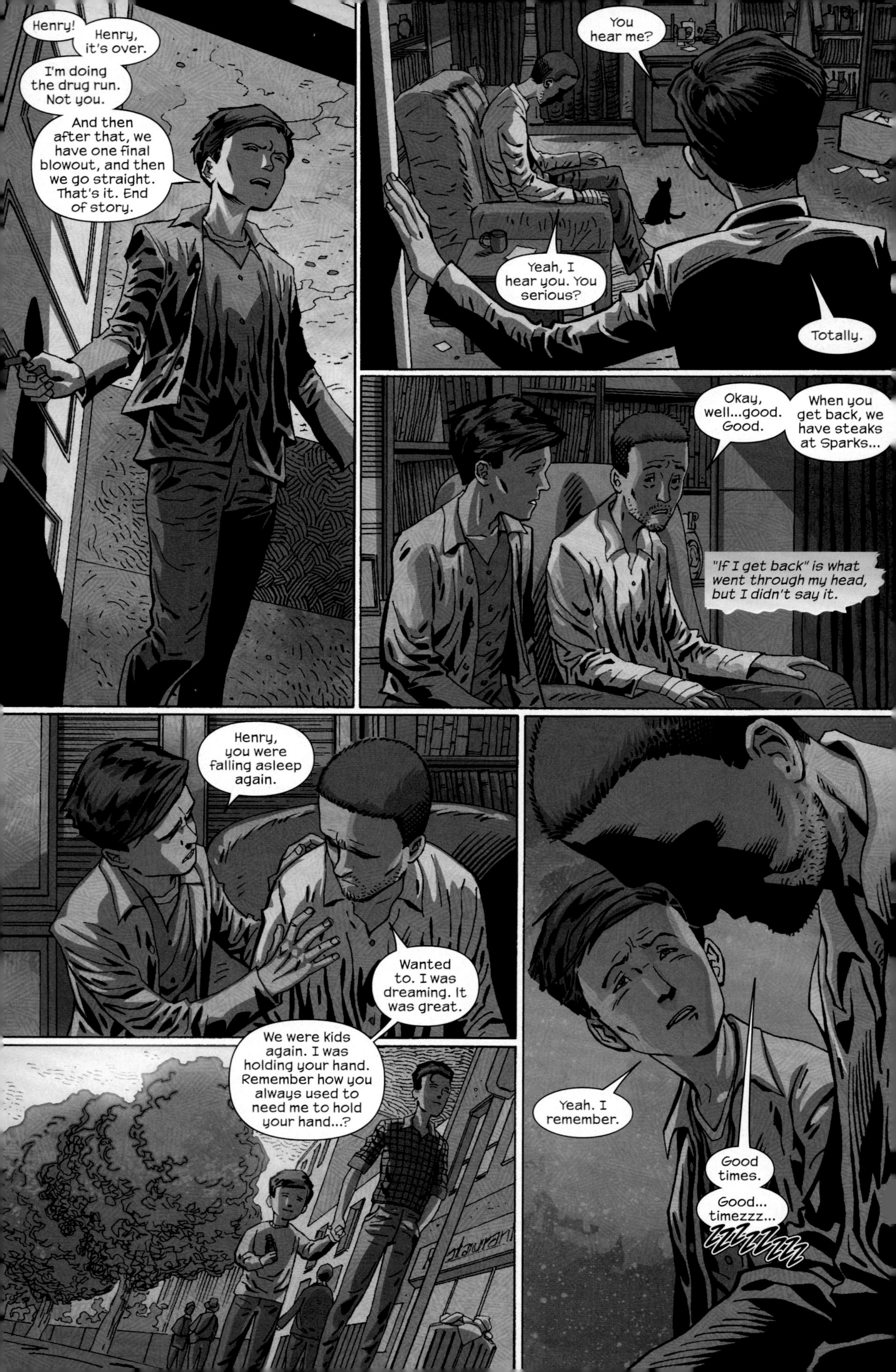
Henry!
Henry, it's over.
I'm doing the drug run. Not you.
And then after that, we have one final blowout, and then we go straight. That's it. End of story.
You hear me?
Yeah, I hear you. You serious?
Totally.
Okay, well...good. Good.
When you get back, we have steaks at Sparks...
"If I get back" is what went through my head, but I didn't say it.
Henry, you were falling asleep again.
Wanted to. I was dreaming. It was great.
We were kids again. I was holding your hand. Remember how you always used to need me to hold your hand...?
Yeah. I remember.
Good times.
Good... timezzz...
ZZZZZZZ

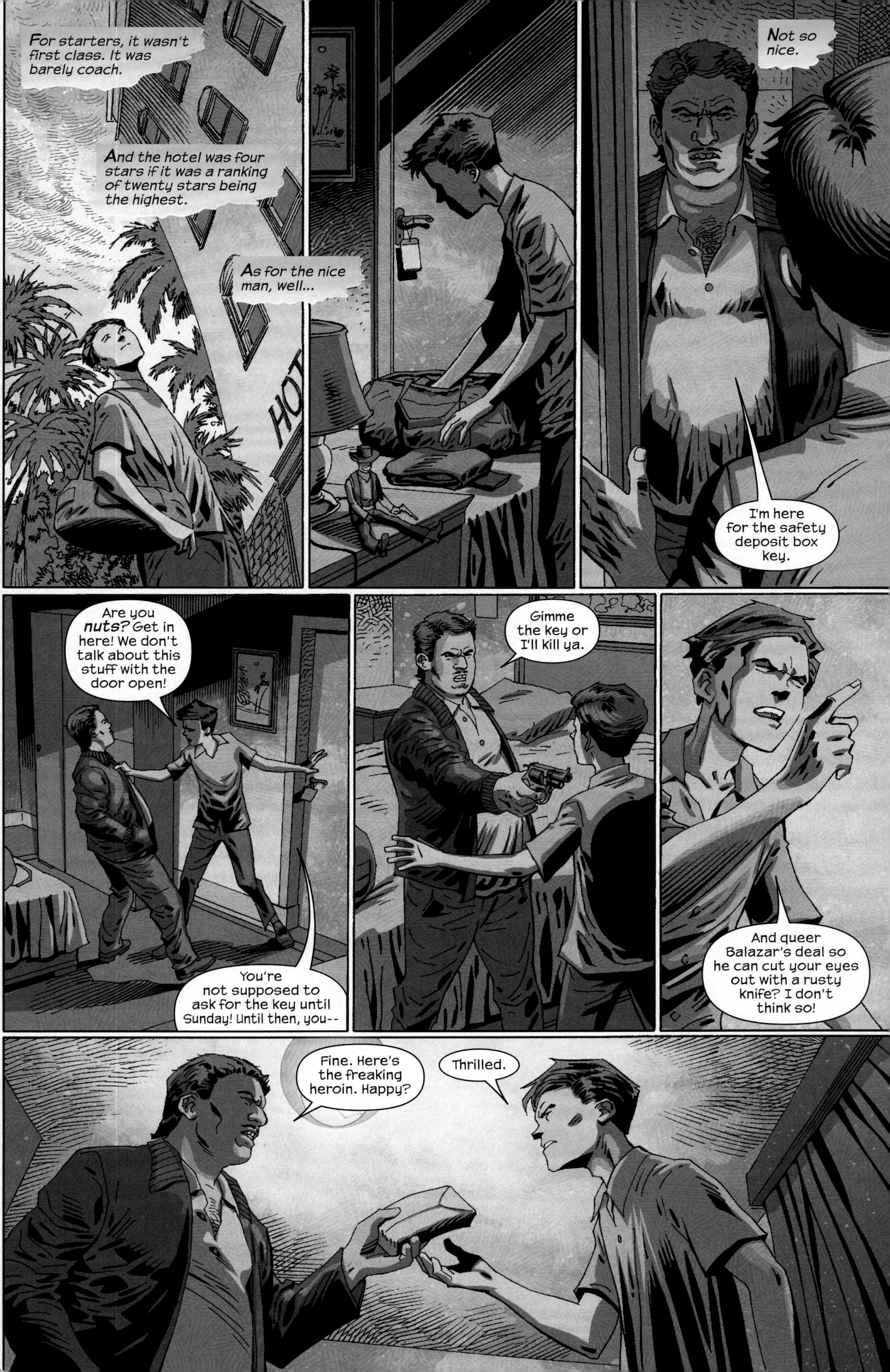

For starters, it wasn't first class. It was barely coach.
And the hotel was four stars if it was a ranking of twenty stars being the highest.
As for the nice man, well...
HOT
Not so nice.
I'm here for the safety deposit box key.
Are you nuts? Get in here! We don't talk about this stuff with the door open!
You're not supposed to ask for the key until Sunday! Until then, you--
Gimme the key or I'll kill ya.
And queer Balazar's deal so he can cut your eyes out with a rusty knife? I don't think so!
Fine. Here's the freaking heroin. Happy?
Thrilled.

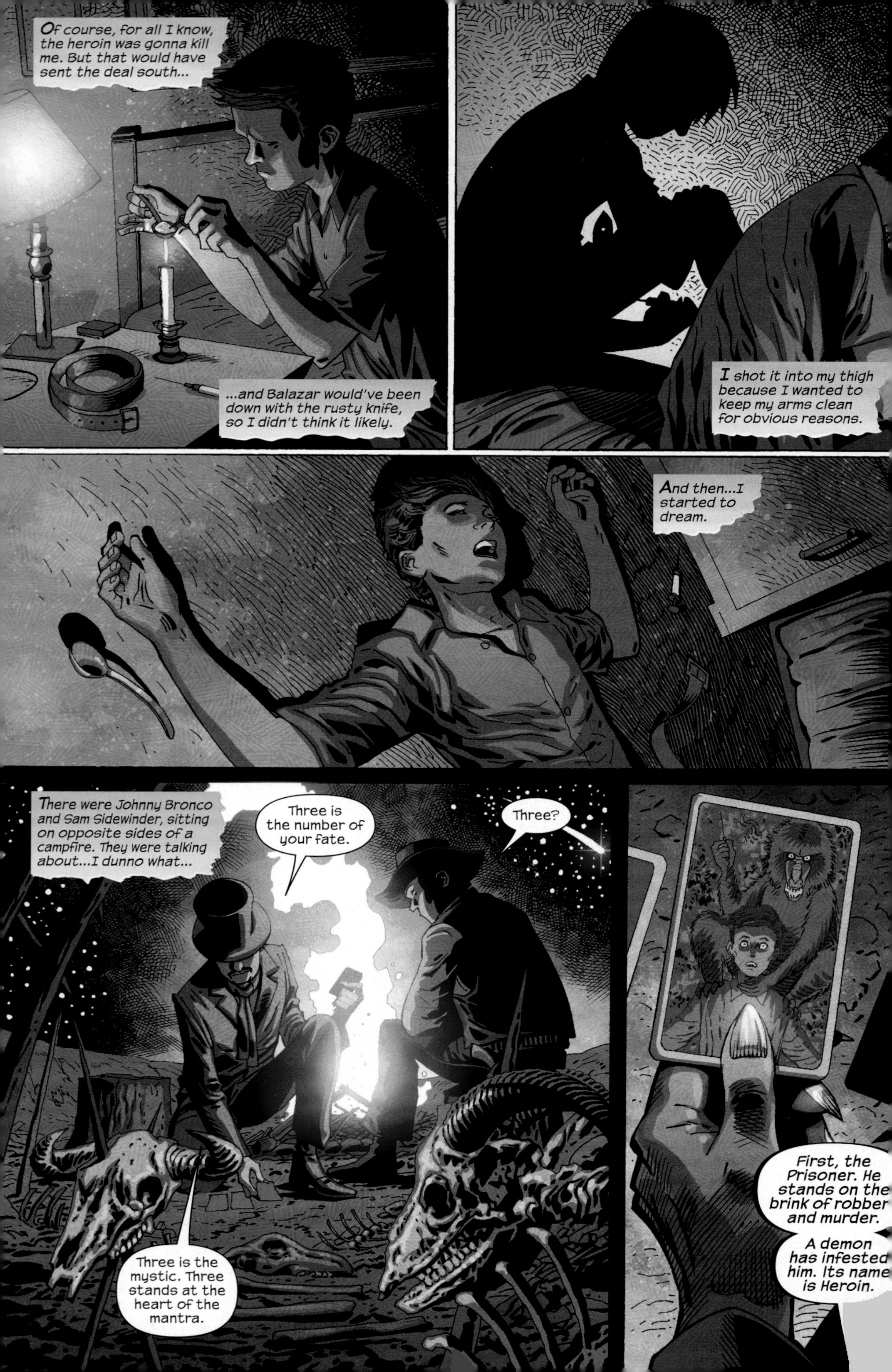
Of course, for all I know, the heroin was gonna kill me. But that would have sent the deal south...
...and Balazar would've been down with the rusty knife, so I didn't think it likely.
I shot it into my thigh because I wanted to keep my arms clean for obvious reasons.
And then...I started to dream.
There were Johnny Bronco and Sam Sidewinder, sitting on opposite sides of a campfire. They were talking about...I dunno what...
Three is the number of your fate.
Three?
Three is the mystic. Three stands at the heart of the mantra.
First, the Prisoner. He stands on the brink of robber and murder.
A demon has infested him. Its name is Heroin.

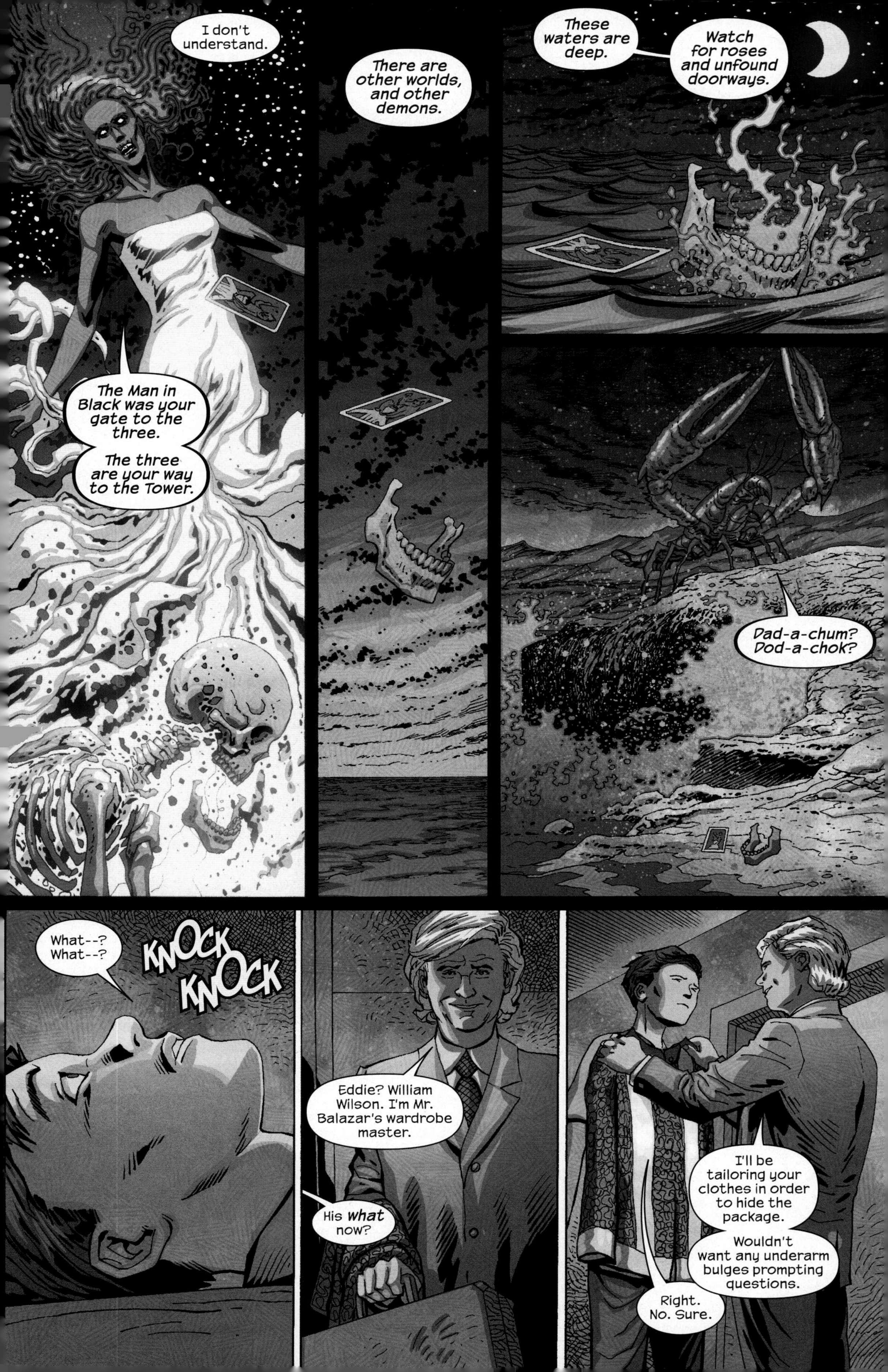
I don't understand.
The Man in Black was your gate to the three.
The three are your way to the Tower.
There are other worlds, and other demons.
These waters are deep.
Watch for roses and unfound doorways.
Dad-a-chum? Dod-a-chok?
What--? What--?
KNOCK KNOCK
Eddie? William Wilson. I'm Mr. Balazar's wardrobe master.
His *what* now?
I'll be tailoring your clothes in order to hide the package.
Wouldn't want any underarm bulges prompting questions.
Right. No. Sure.

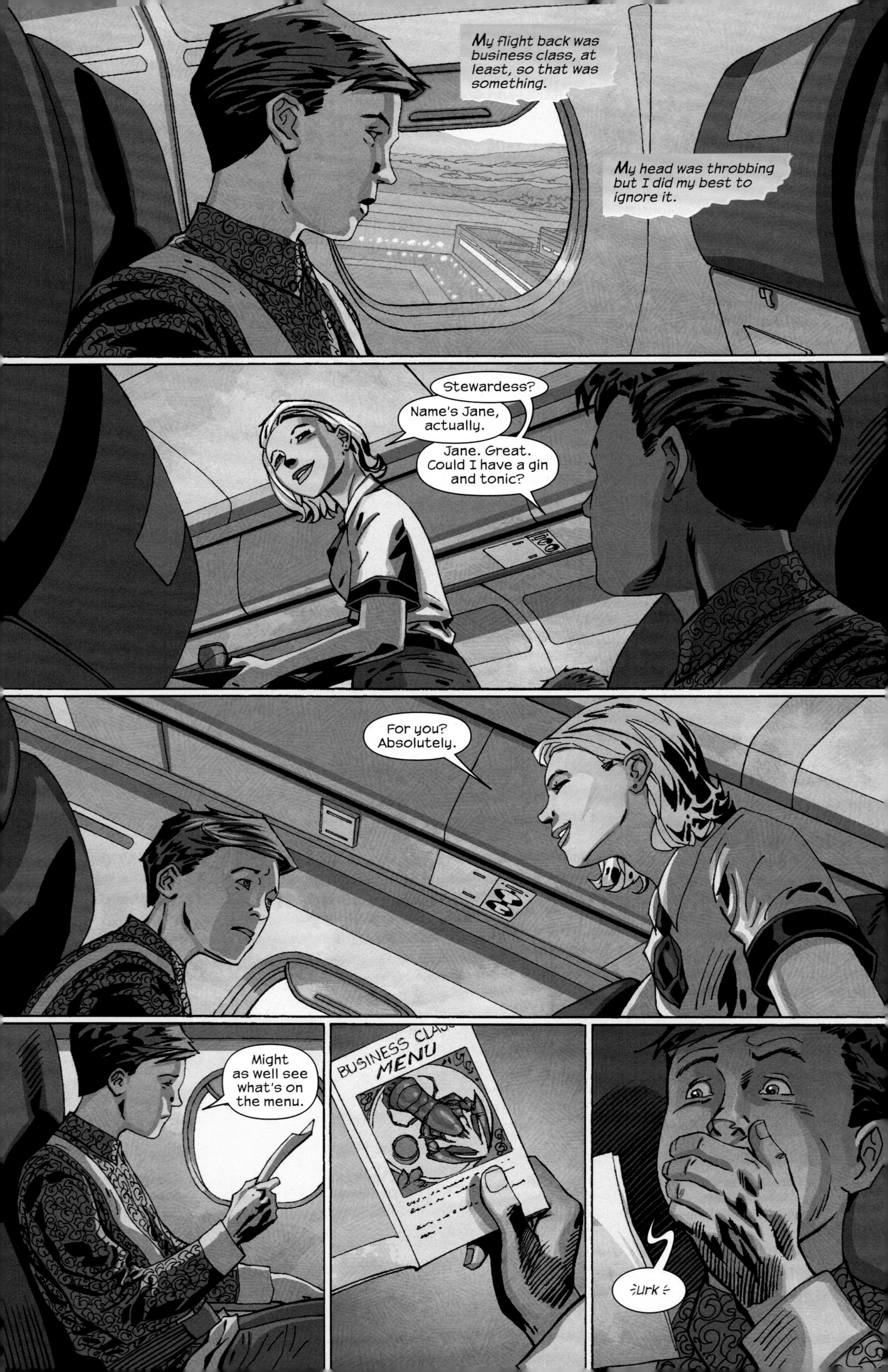

My flight back was business class, at least, so that was something.
My head was throbbing but I did my best to ignore it.
Stewardess?
Name's Jane, actually.
Jane. Great. Could I have a gin and tonic?
For you? Absolutely.
Might as well see what's on the menu.
BUSINESS CLAS
MENU
urk

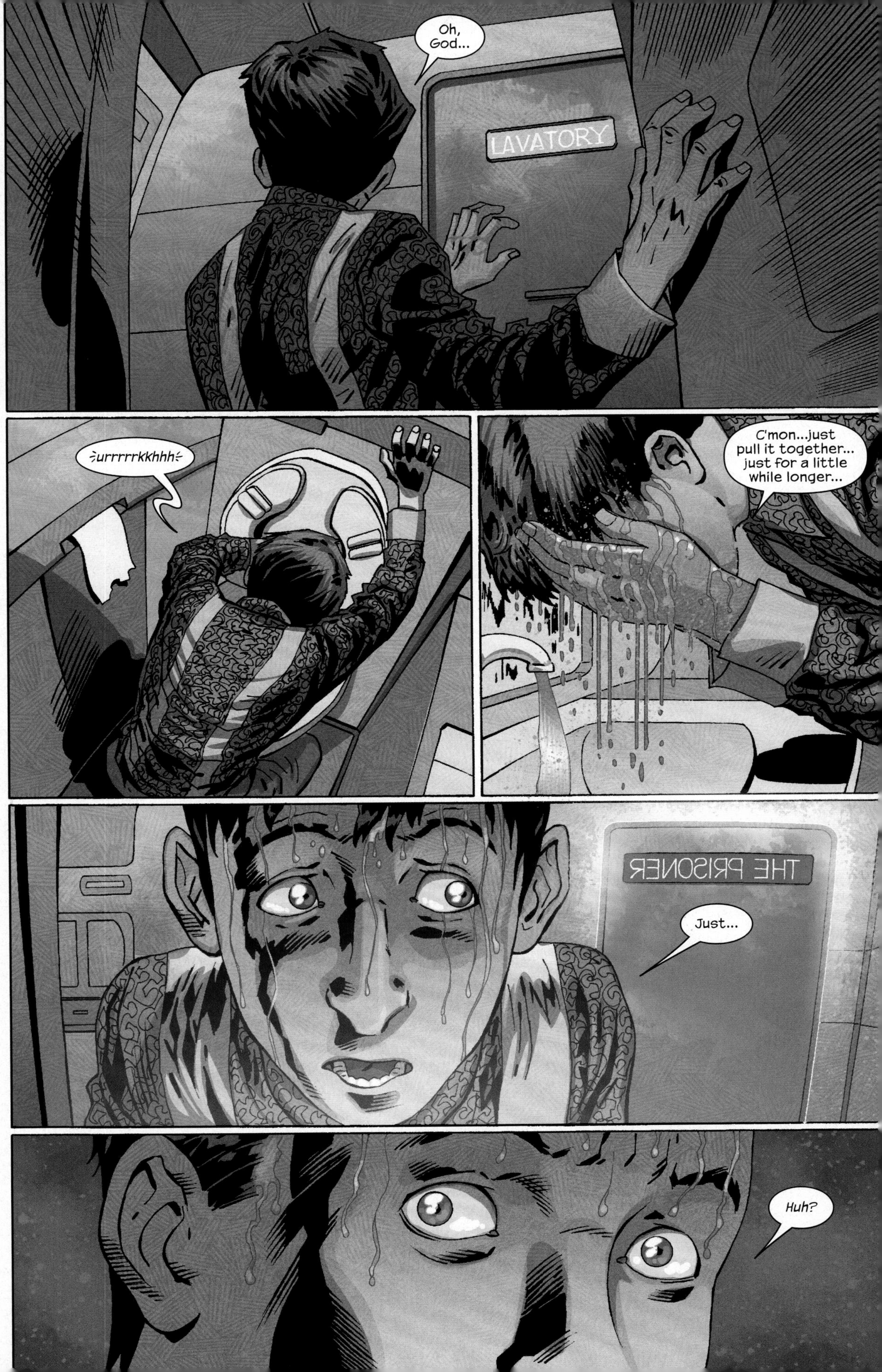
Oh, God...
LAVATORY
=urrrrrkkhhh=
C'mon...just pull it together... just for a little while longer...
THE PRISONER
Just...
Huh?

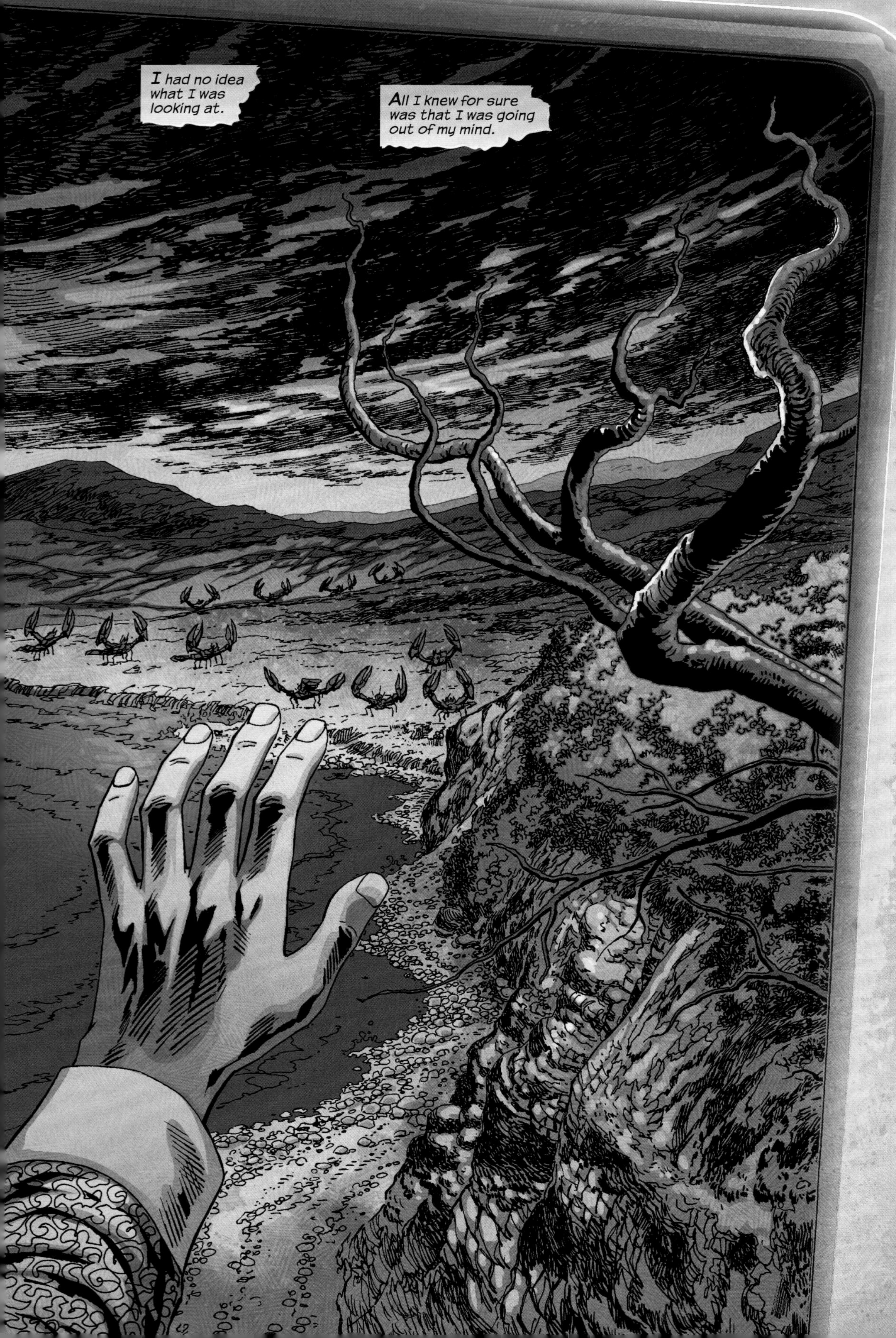
I had no idea what I was looking at.
All I knew for sure was that I was going out of my mind.

THE DARK TOWER
THE DRAWING OF THE THREE
STEPHEN KING

The Prisoner

THE PRISONER
CHAPTER FIVE

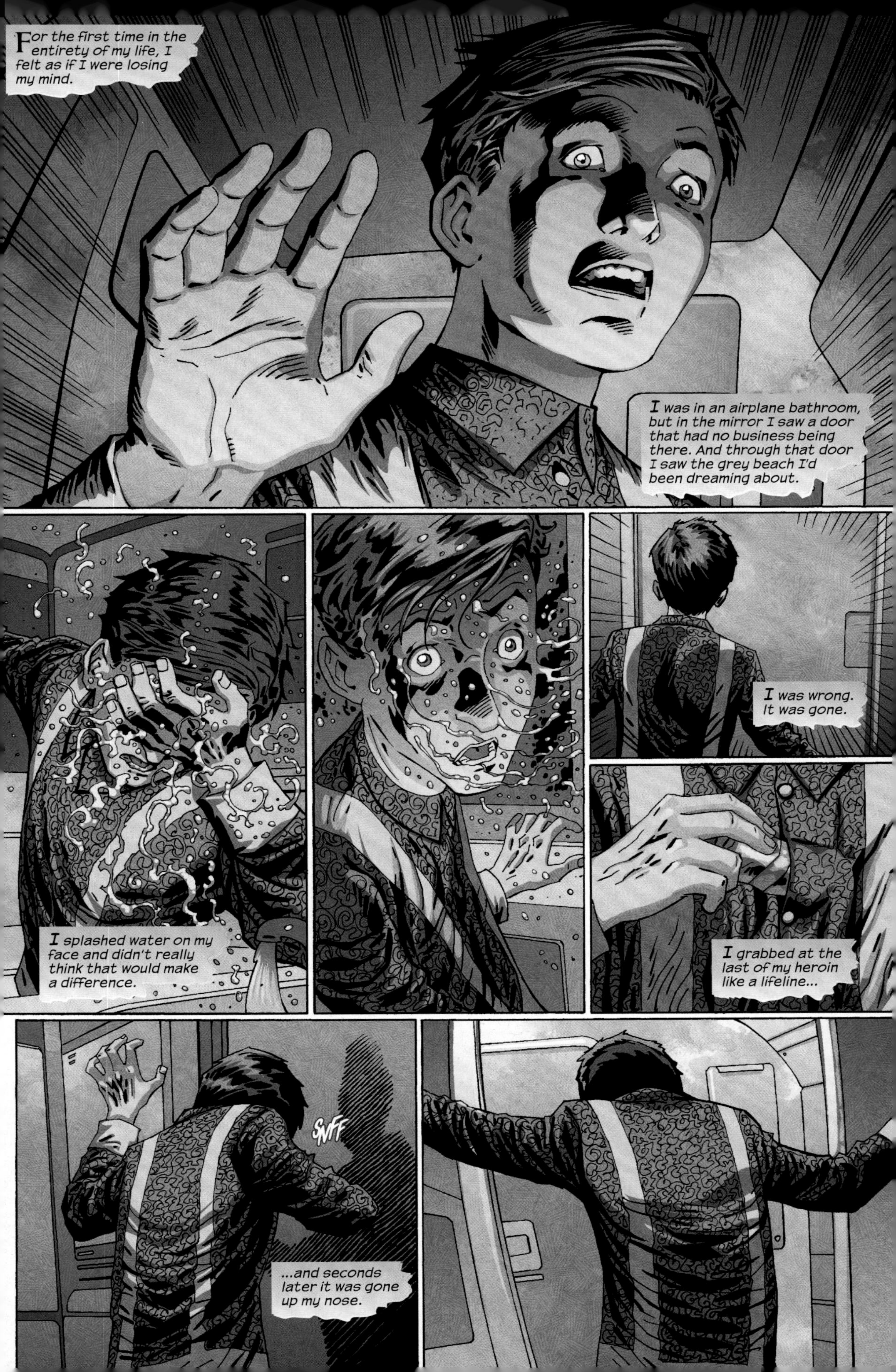
For the first time in the entirety of my life, I felt as if I were losing my mind.
I was in an airplane bathroom, but in the mirror I saw a door that had no business being there. And through that door I saw the grey beach I'd been dreaming about.
I splashed water on my face and didn't really think that would make a difference.
I was wrong. It was gone.
I grabbed at the last of my heroin like a lifeline...
SNFF
...and seconds later it was gone up my nose.

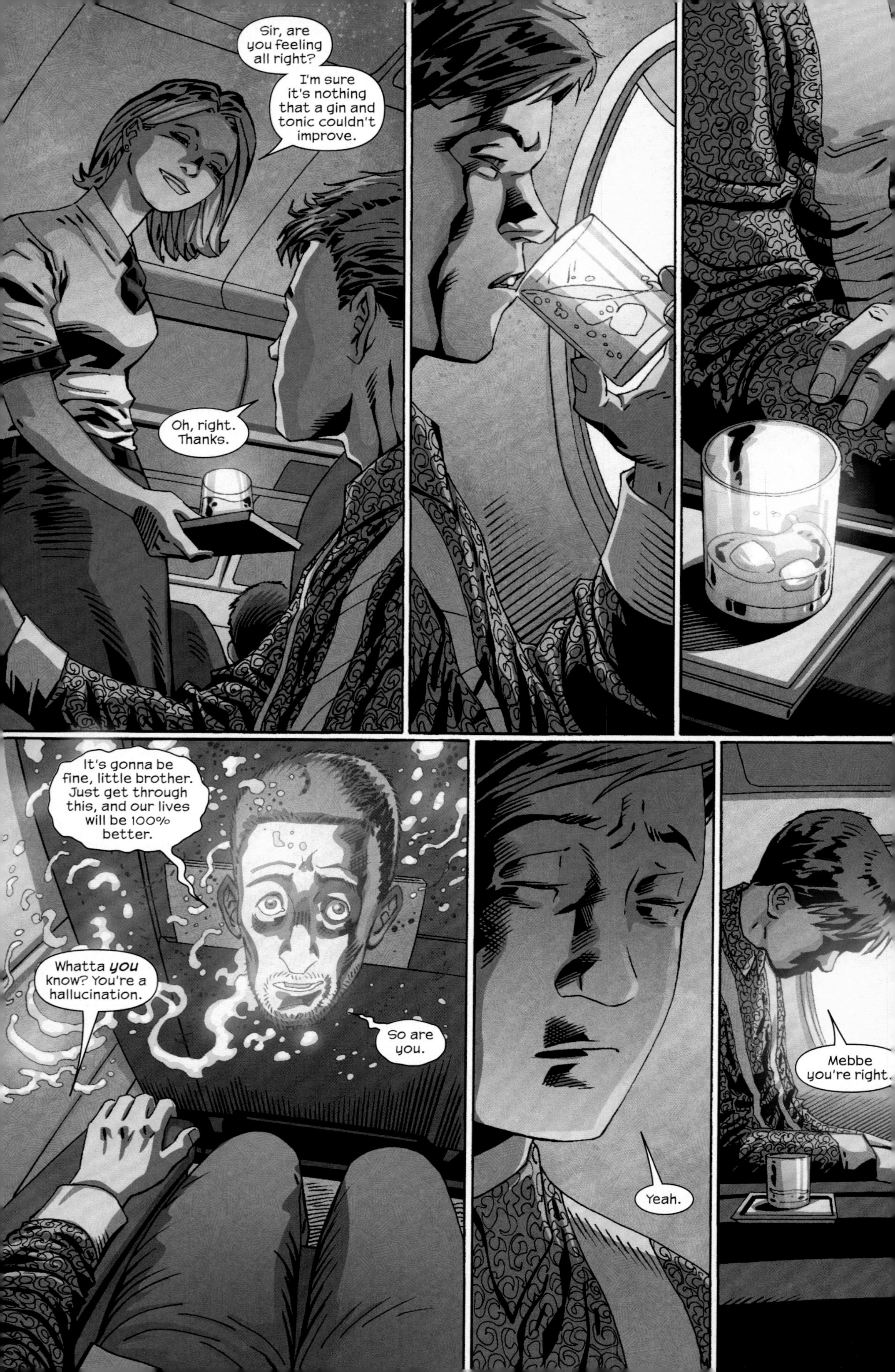
Sir, are you feeling all right?
I'm sure it's nothing that a gin and tonic couldn't improve.
Oh, right. Thanks.
It's gonna be fine, little brother. Just get through this, and our lives will be 100% better.
Whatta *you* know? You're a hallucination.
So are you.
Yeah.
Mebbe you're right.

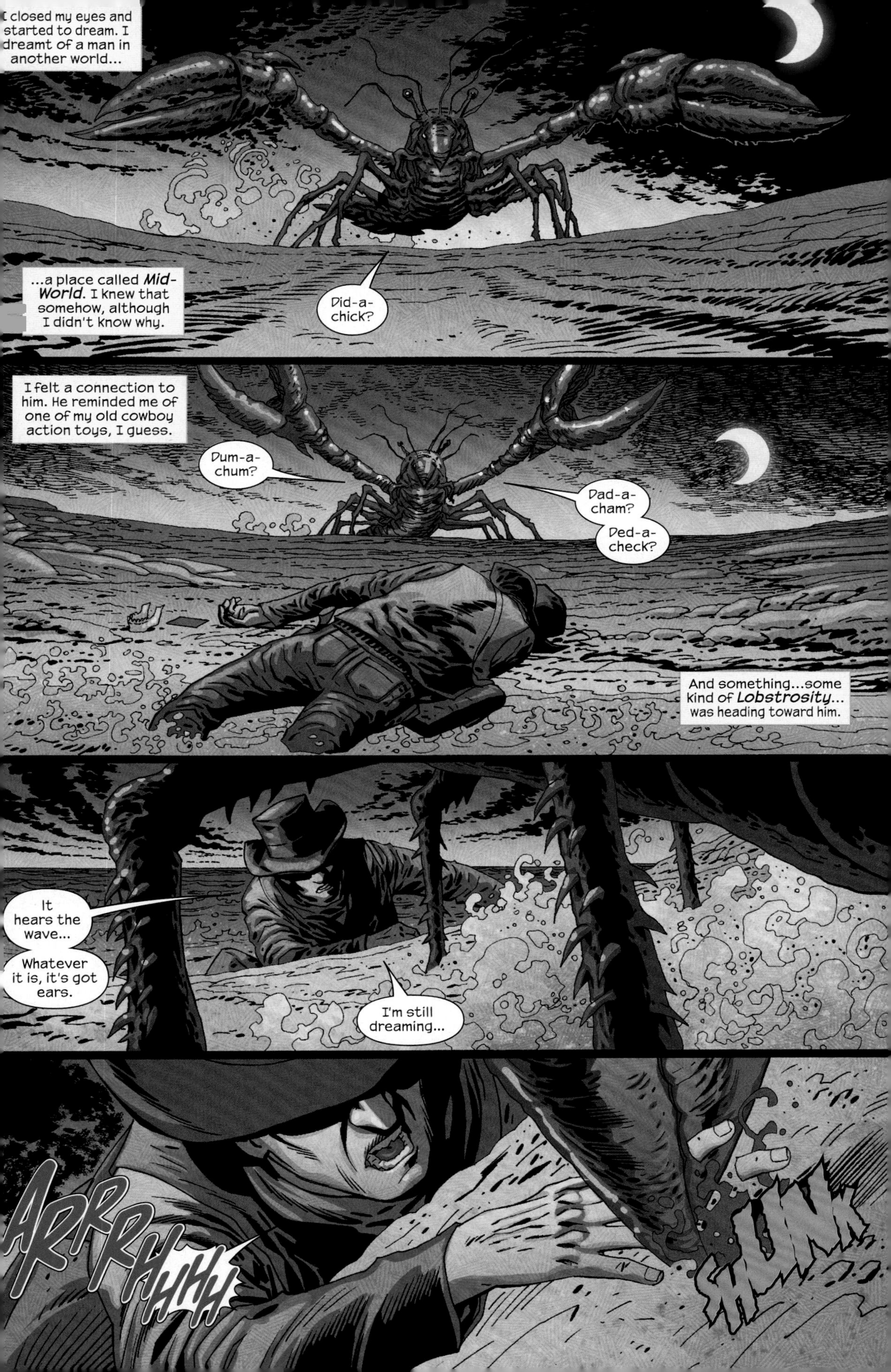
I closed my eyes and started to dream. I dreamt of a man in another world...
...a place called *Mid-World*. I knew that somehow, although I didn't know why.
Did-a-chick?
I felt a connection to him. He reminded me of one of my old cowboy action toys, I guess.
Dum-a-chum?
Dad-a-cham?
Ded-a-check?
And something...some kind of *Lobstrosity*... was heading toward him.
It hears the wave...
Whatever it is, it's got ears.
I'm still dreaming...
ARRRHHHH
SHUNK

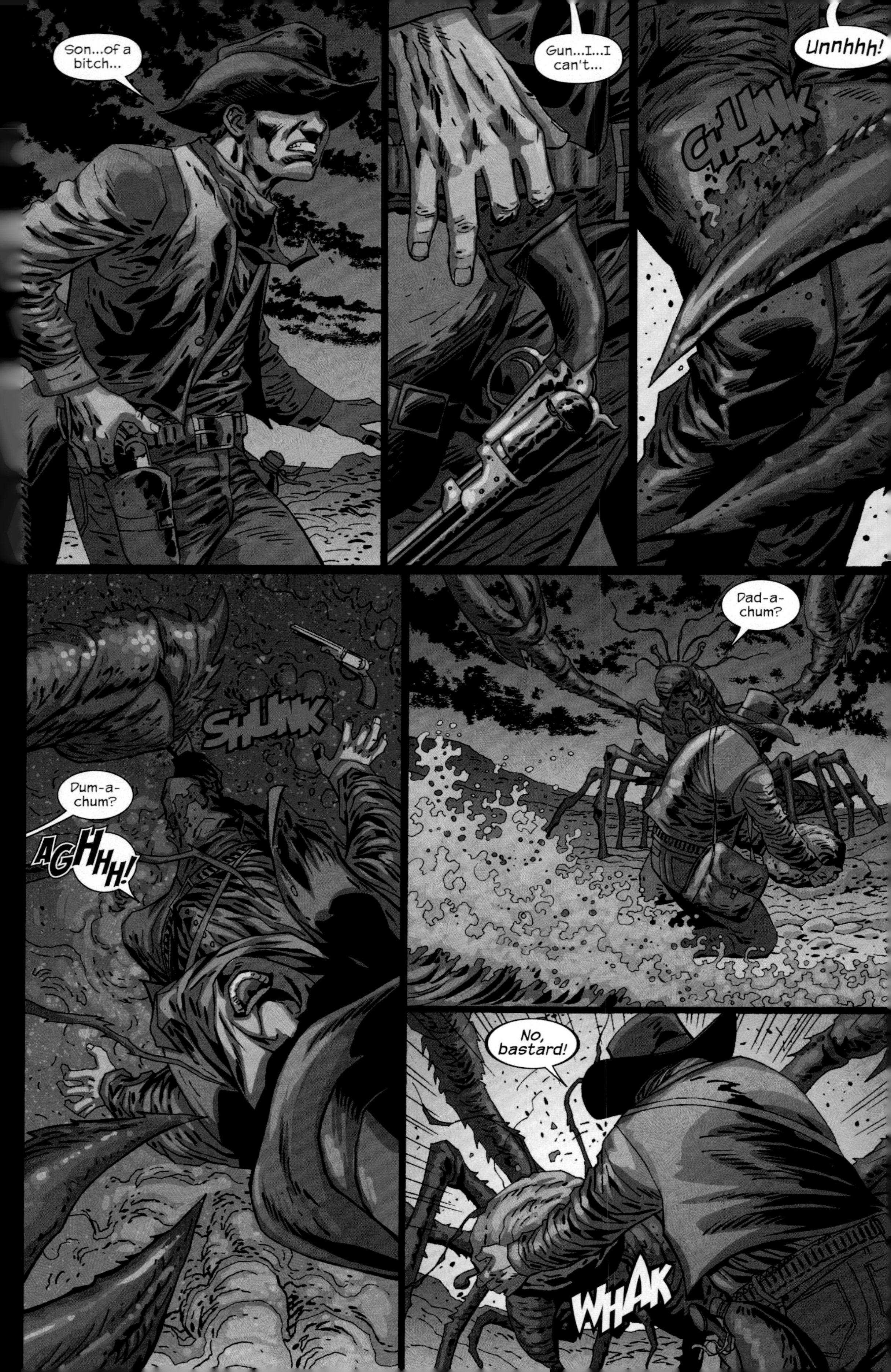

Son...of a bitch...
Gun...I...I can't...
Unnhhh!
CHUNK
SHUNK
Dum-a-chum?
AGHHH!
Dad-a-chum?
No, bastard!
WHAK

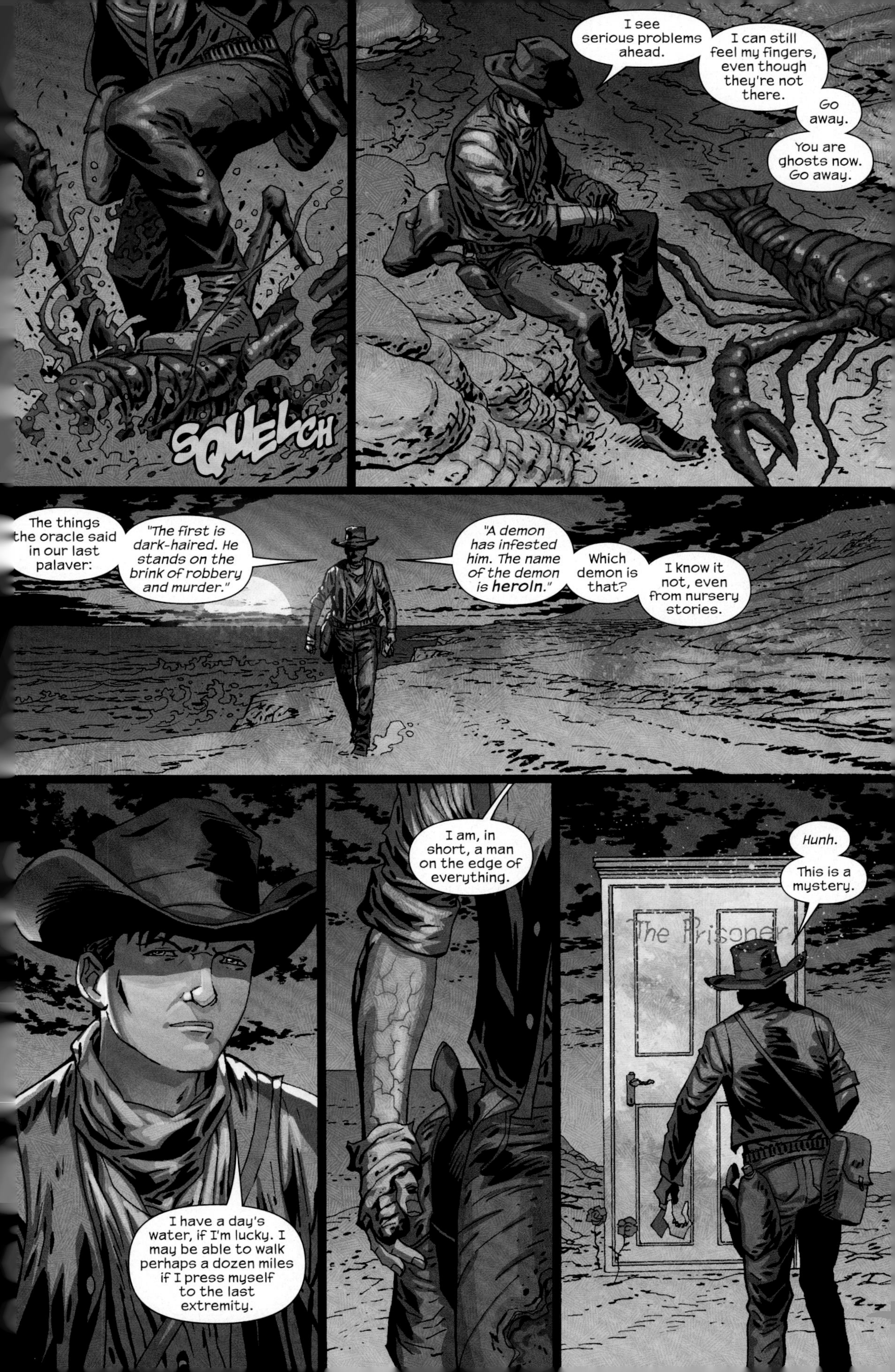
SQUELCH
I see serious problems ahead.
I can still feel my fingers, even though they're not there.
Go away.
You are ghosts now. Go away.
The things the oracle said in our last palaver:
"The first is dark-haired. He stands on the brink of robbery and murder."
"A demon has infested him. The name of the demon is **heroin**."
Which demon is that?
I know it not, even from nursery stories.
I have a day's water, if I'm lucky. I may be able to walk perhaps a dozen miles if I press myself to the last extremity.
I am, in short, a man on the edge of everything.
Hunh.
This is a mystery.
The Prisoner

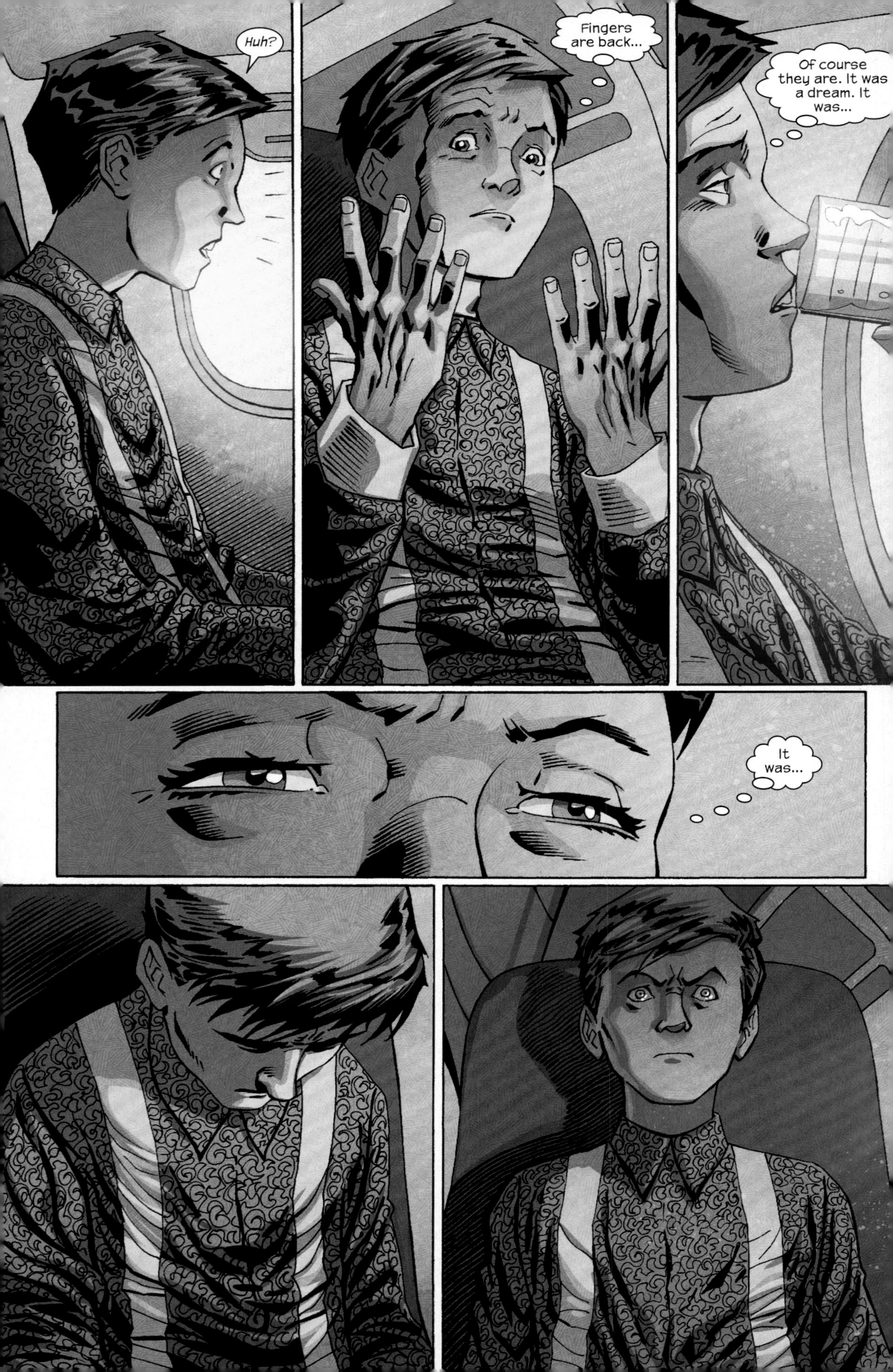

Huh?
Fingers are back...
Of course they are. It was a dream. It was...
It was...

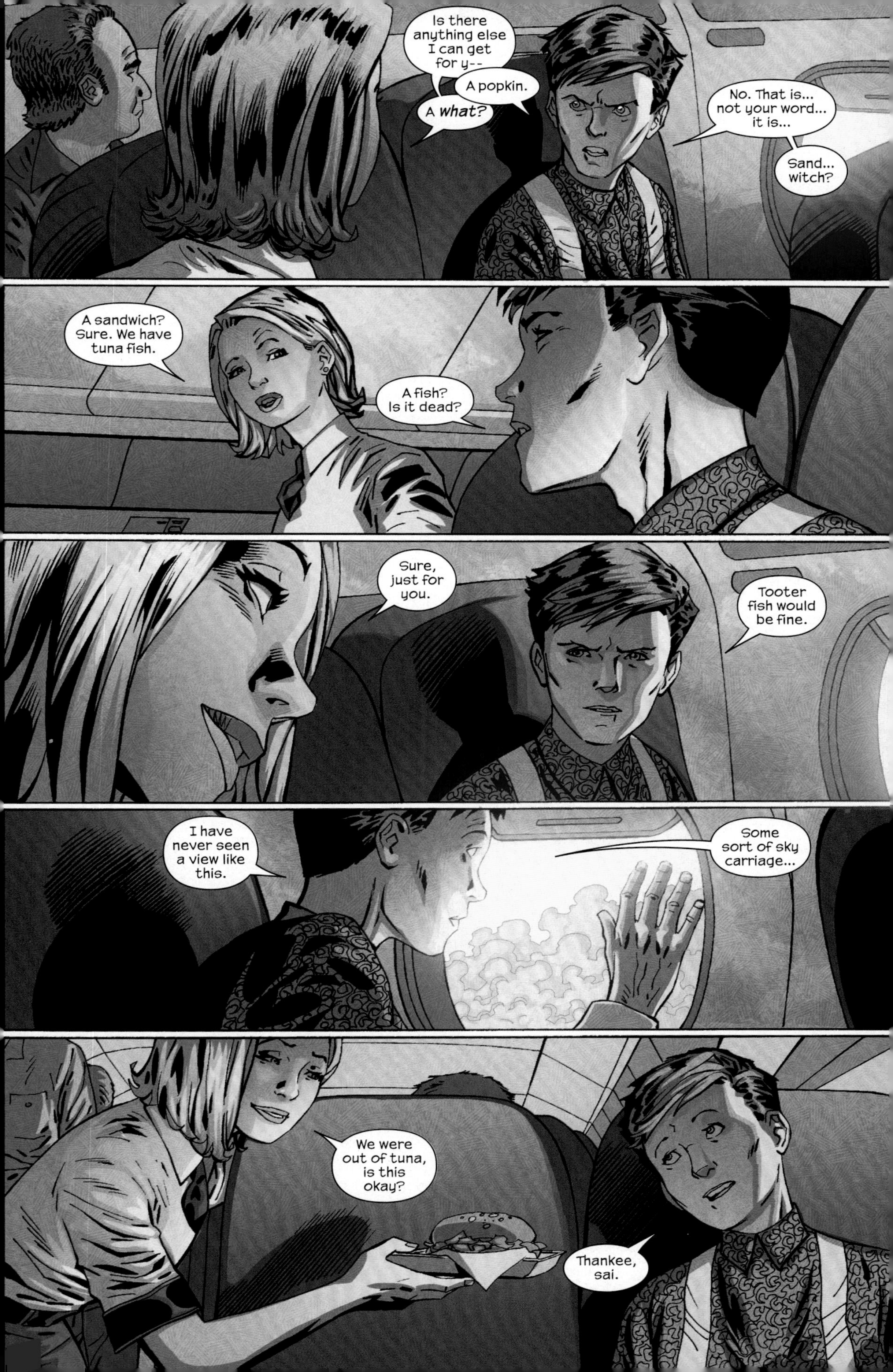
Is there anything else I can get for y--
A popkin.
A what?
No. That is... not your word... it is...
Sand... witch?
A sandwich? Sure. We have tuna fish.
A fish? Is it dead?
Sure, just for you.
Tooter fish would be fine.
I have never seen a view like this.
Some sort of sky carriage...
We were out of tuna, is this okay?
Thankee, sai.

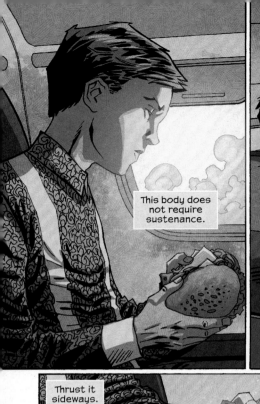

This body does not require sustenance.

Mine does.

Focus on it.

Thrust it sideways.

It worked.

Dammit!

Don't care.

I'll eat it with sand on it.

Appropriate for a sand witch, I suppose.

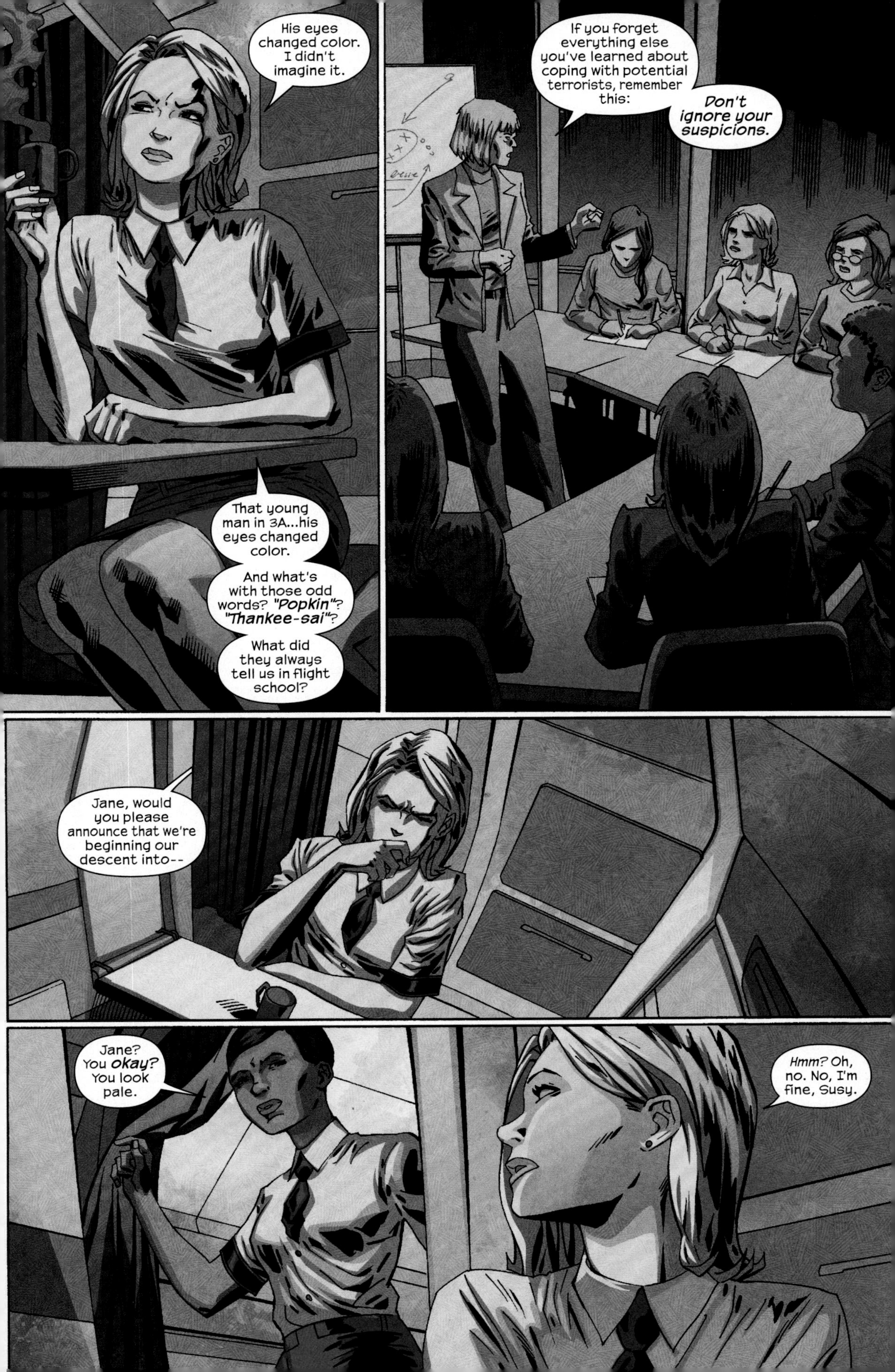
His eyes changed color. I didn't imagine it.
If you forget everything else you've learned about coping with potential terrorists, remember this:
Don't ignore your suspicions.
That young man in 3A...his eyes changed color.
And what's with those odd words? *"Popkin"*? *"Thankee-sai"*?
What did they always tell us in flight school?
Jane, would you please announce that we're beginning our descent into--
Jane? You *okay?* You look pale.
Hmm? Oh, no. No, I'm fine, Susy.

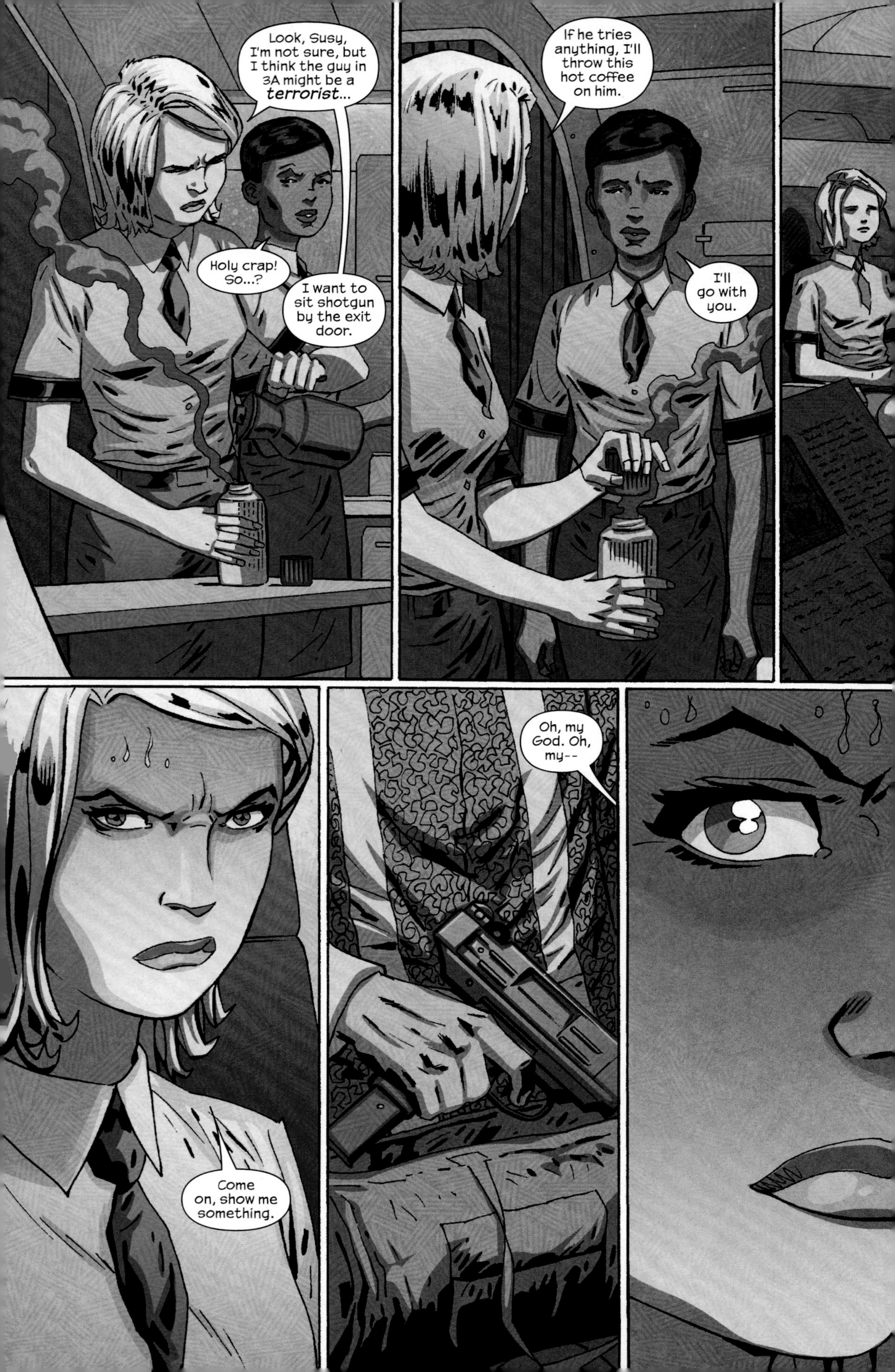
Look, Susy, I'm not sure, but I think the guy in 3A might be a *terrorist*...
Holy crap! So...?
I want to sit shotgun by the exit door.
If he tries anything, I'll throw this hot coffee on him.
I'll go with you.
Come on, show me something.
Oh, my God. Oh, my--

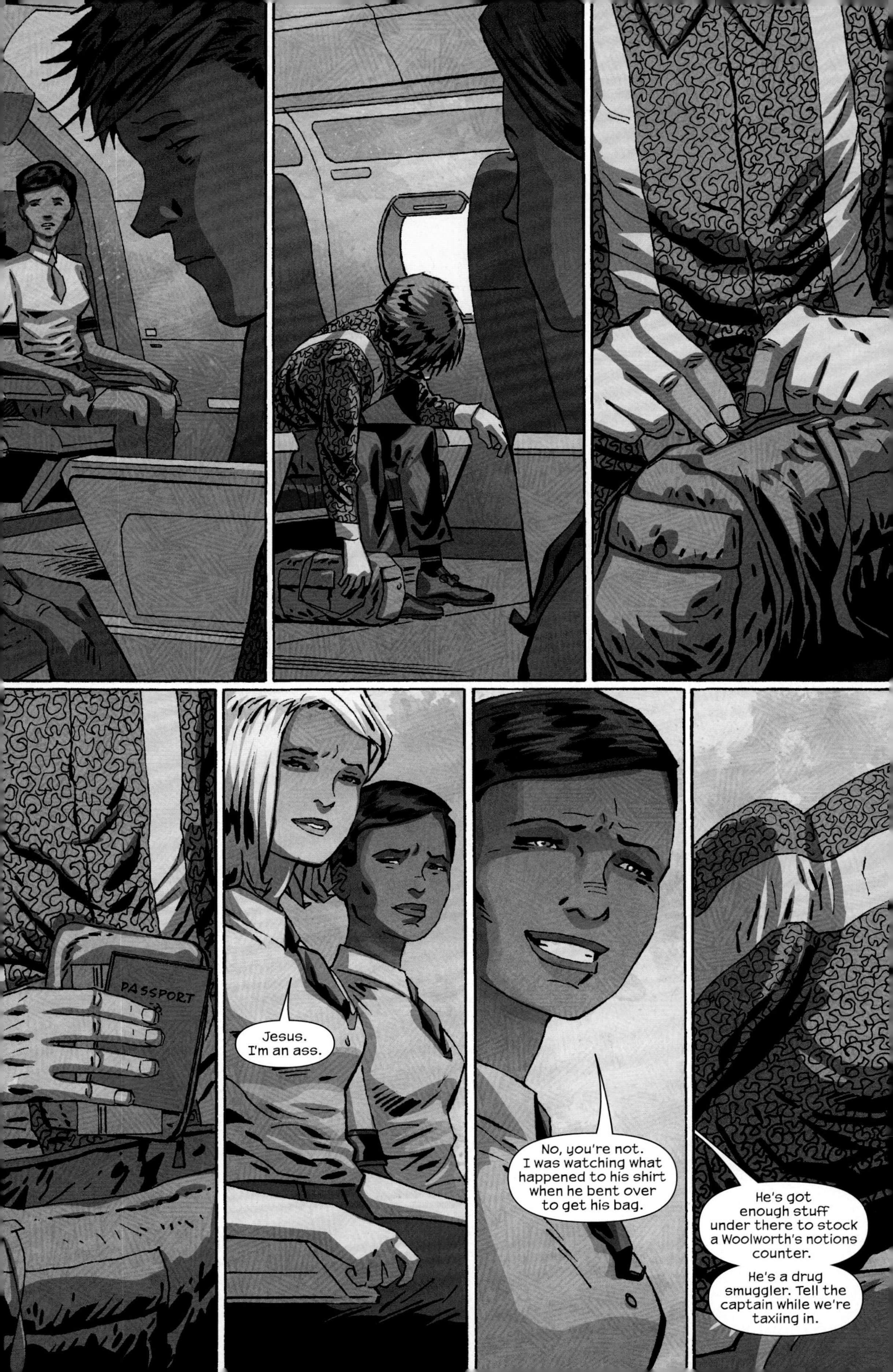
PASSPORT
Jesus. I'm an ass.
No, you're not. I was watching what happened to his shirt when he bent over to get his bag.
He's got enough stuff under there to stock a Woolworth's notions counter.
He's a drug smuggler. Tell the captain while we're taxiing in.

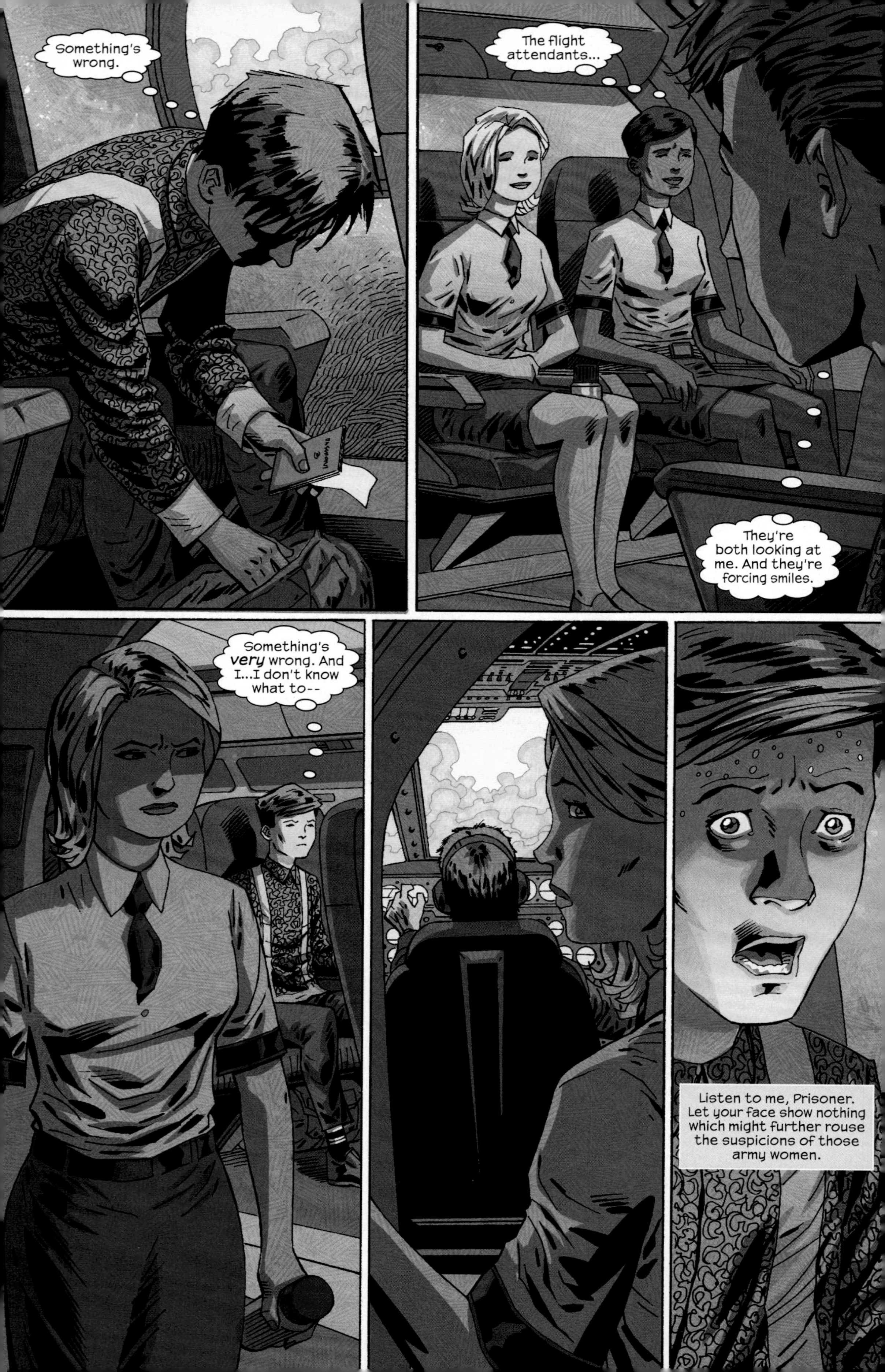
Something's wrong.
The flight attendants...
They're both looking at me. And they're forcing smiles.
Something's *very* wrong. And I...I don't know what to--
Listen to me, Prisoner. Let your face show nothing which might further rouse the suspicions of those army women.

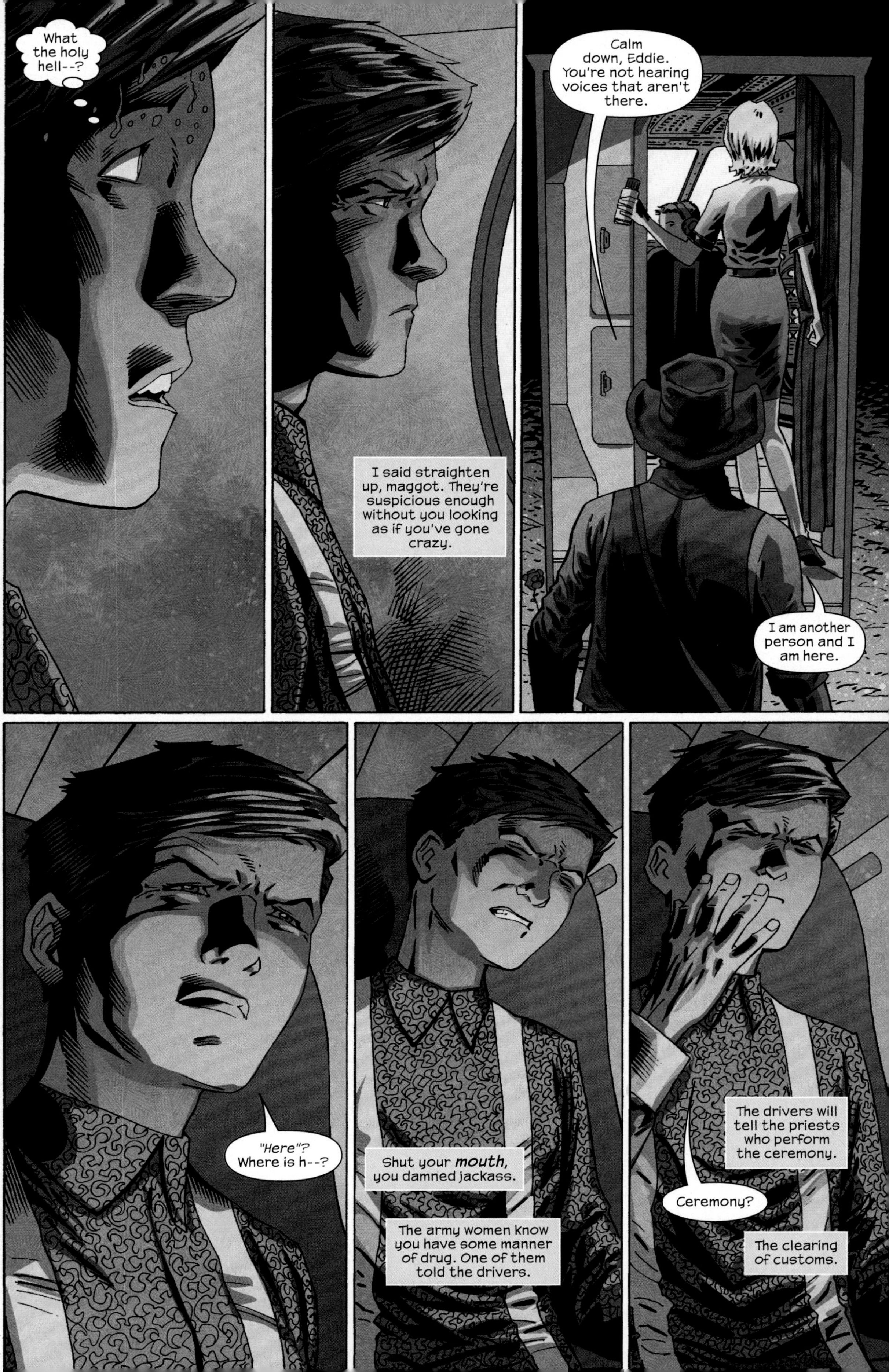
What the holy hell--?
I said straighten up, maggot. They're suspicious enough without you looking as if you've gone crazy.
Calm down, Eddie. You're not hearing voices that aren't there.
I am another person and I am here.
"Here"? Where is h--?
Shut your *mouth*, you damned jackass.
The army women know you have some manner of drug. One of them told the drivers.
The drivers will tell the priests who perform the ceremony.
Ceremony?
The clearing of customs.

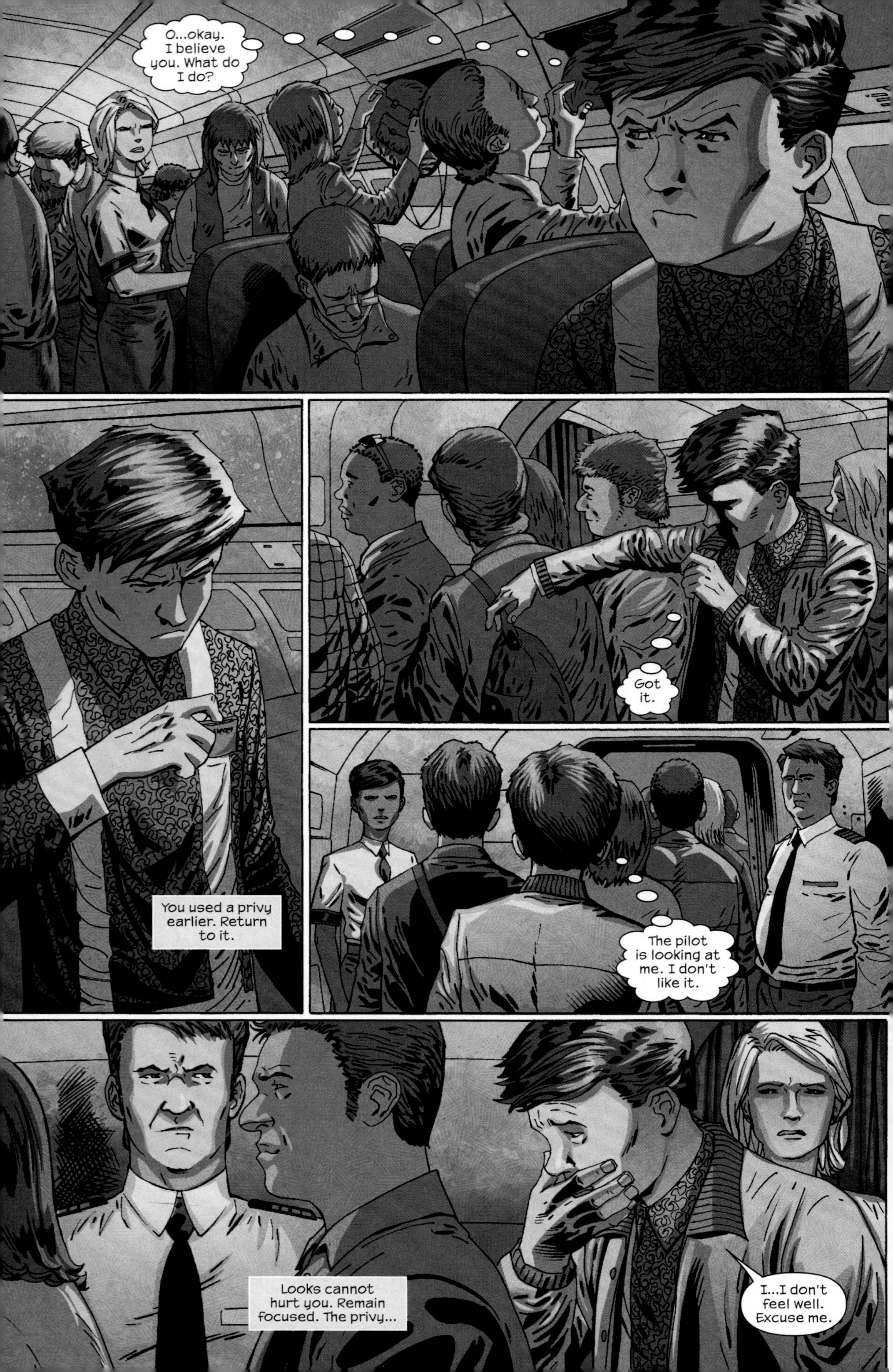
O...okay. I believe you. What do I do?
You used a privy earlier. Return to it.
Got it.
The pilot is looking at me. I don't like it.
Looks cannot hurt you. Remain focused. The privy...
I...I don't feel well. Excuse me.

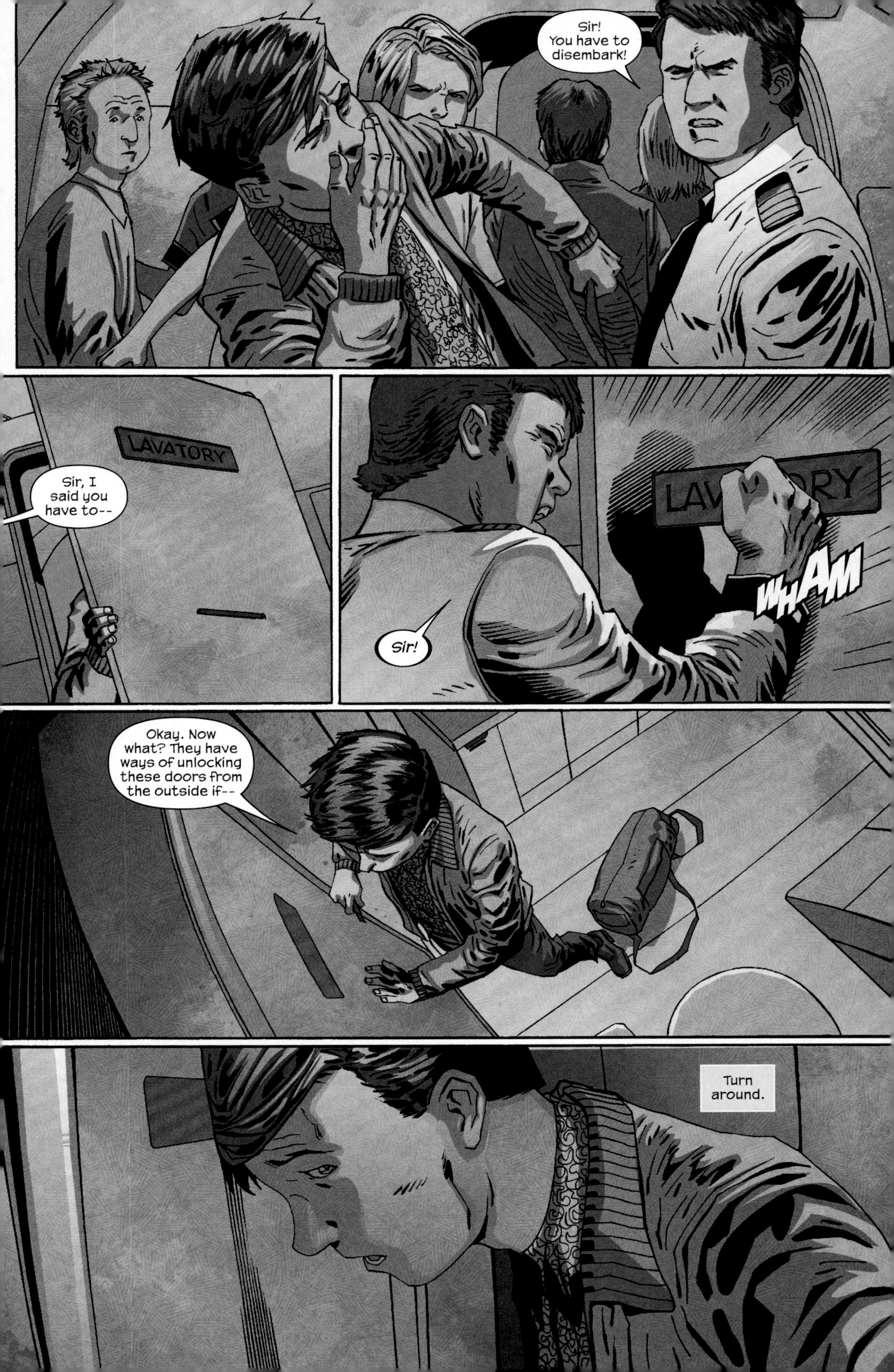
Sir! You have to disembark!
LAVATORY
Sir, I said you have to--
LAVATORY
Sir!
WHAM
Okay. Now what? They have ways of unlocking these doors from the outside if--
Turn around.

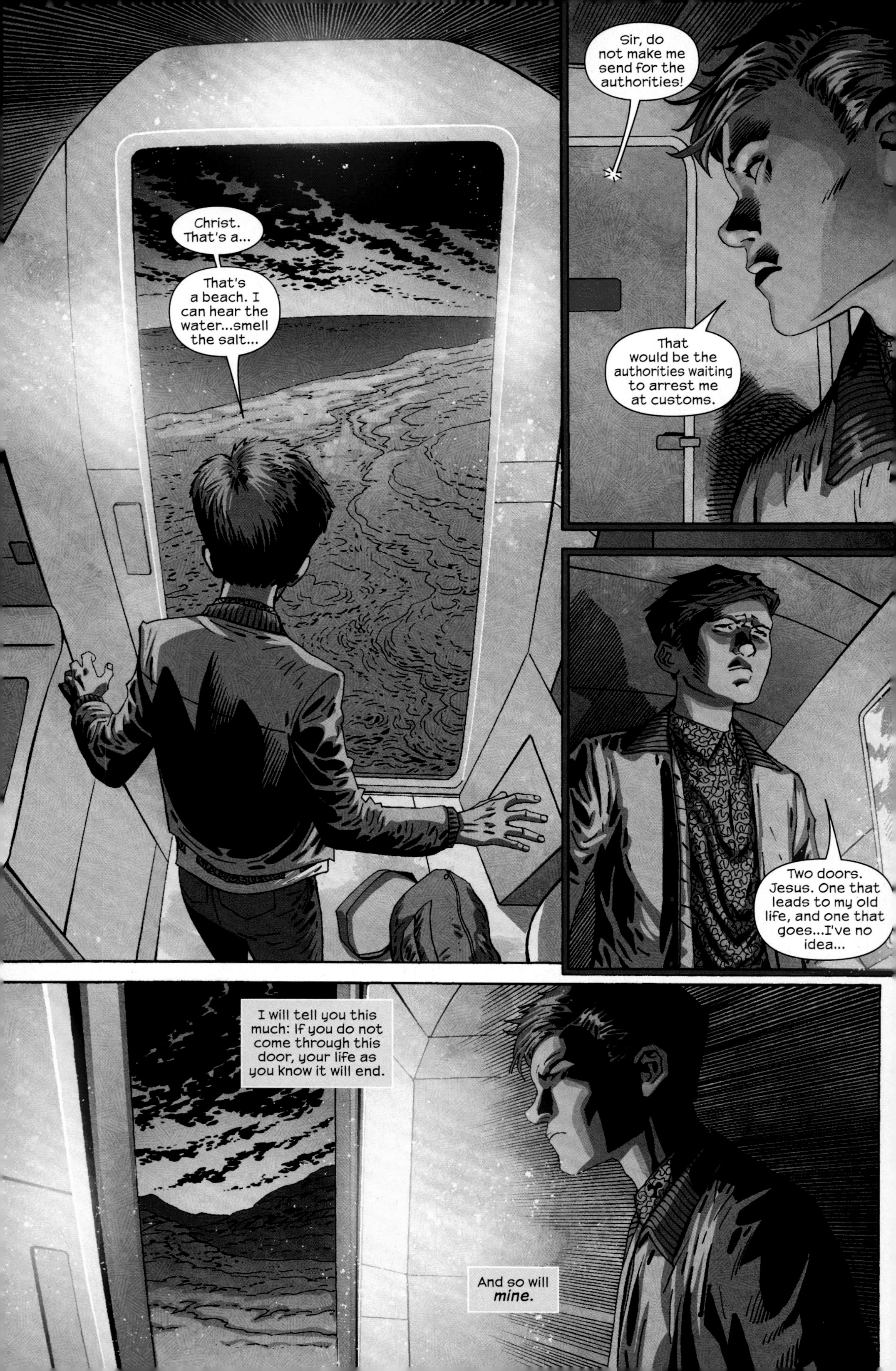
Christ. That's a...
That's a beach. I can hear the water...smell the salt...
Sir, do not make me send for the authorities!
That would be the authorities waiting to arrest me at customs.
Two doors. Jesus. One that leads to my old life, and one that goes...I've no idea...
I will tell you this much: If you do not come through this door, your life as you know it will end.
And so will *mine.*

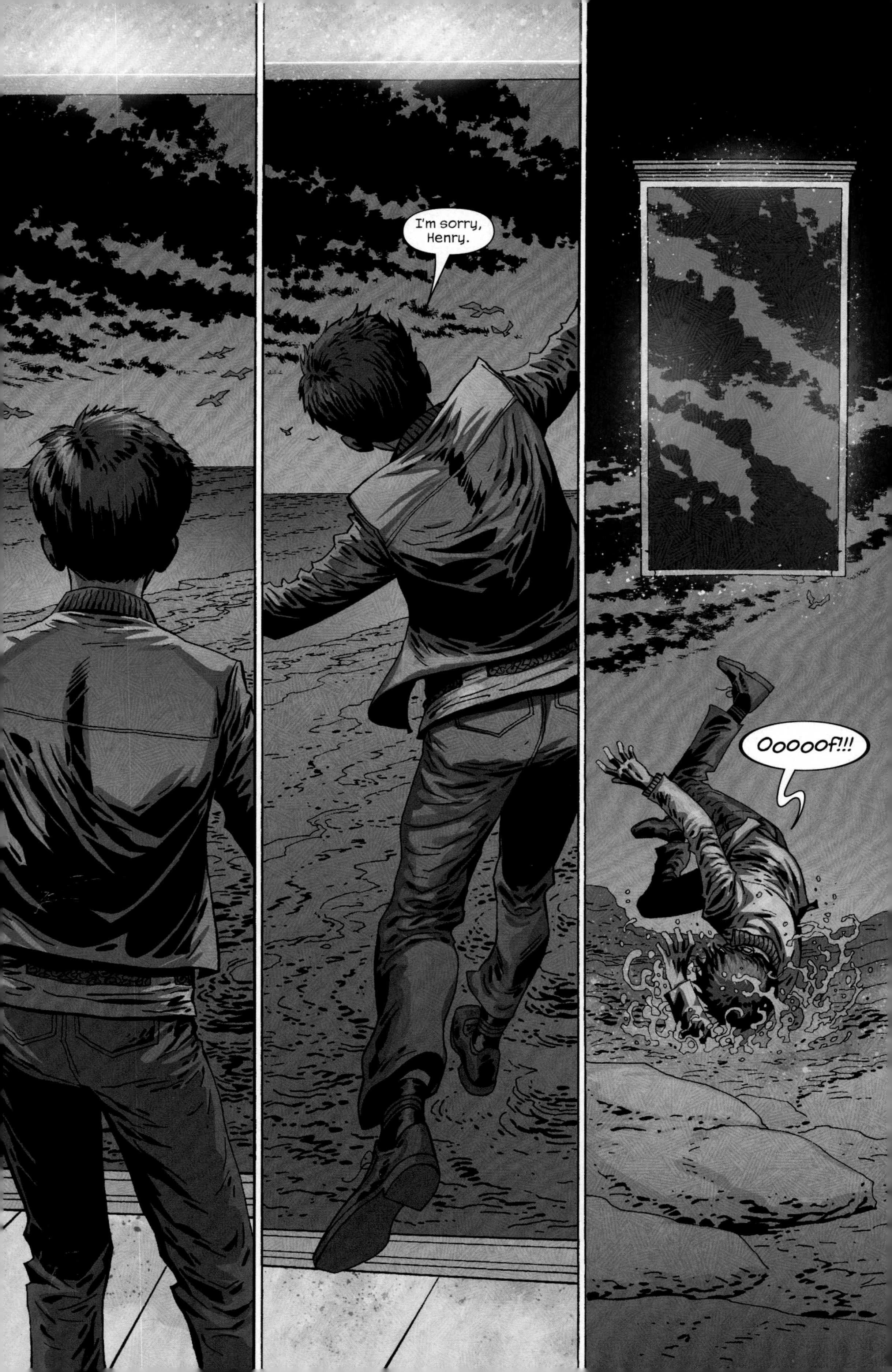
I'm sorry, Henry.
OooooF!!!

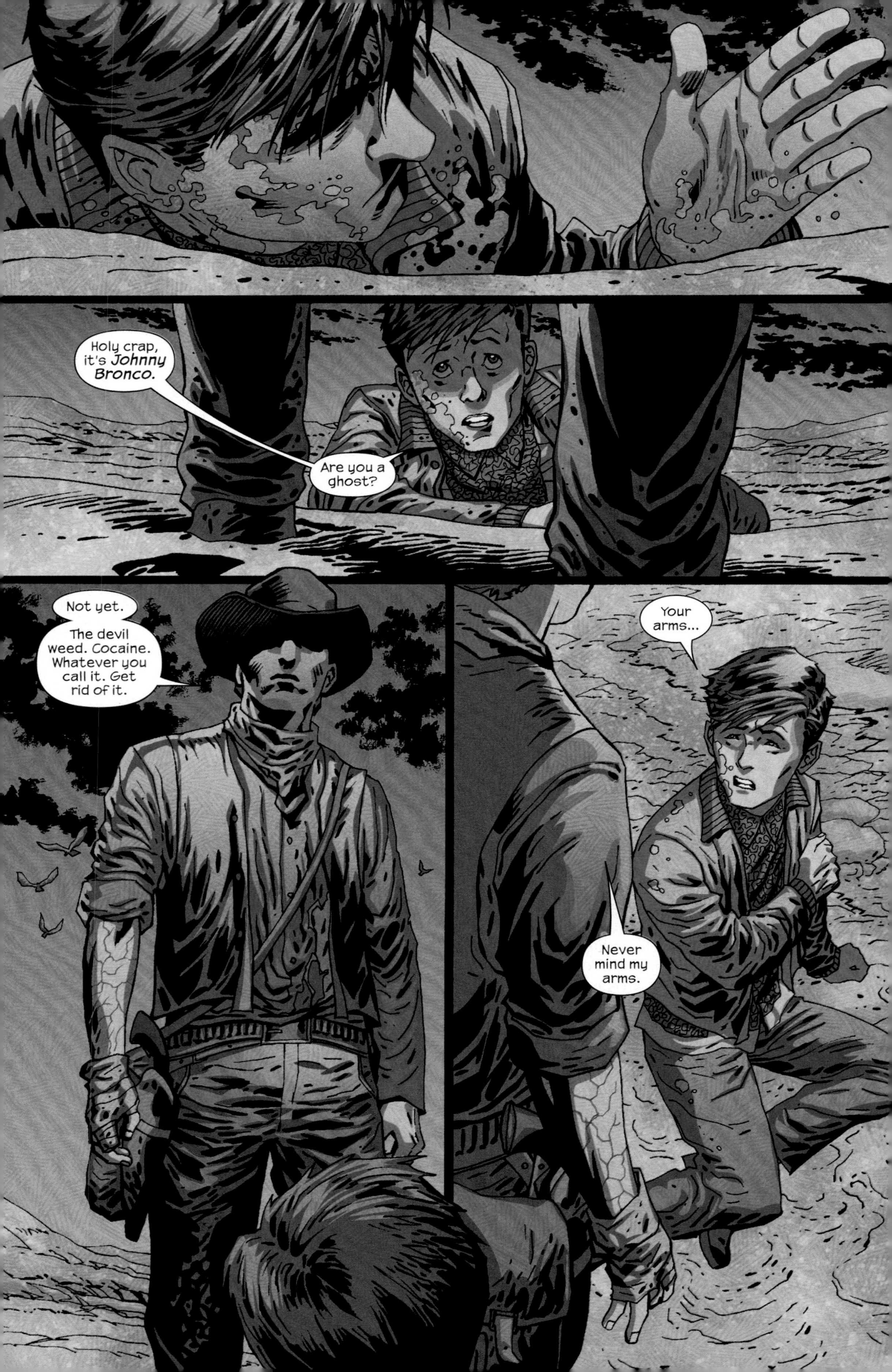

Holy crap, it's *Johnny Bronco.*
Are you a ghost?
Not yet.
The devil weed. Cocaine. Whatever you call it. Get rid of it.
Your arms...
Never mind my arms.

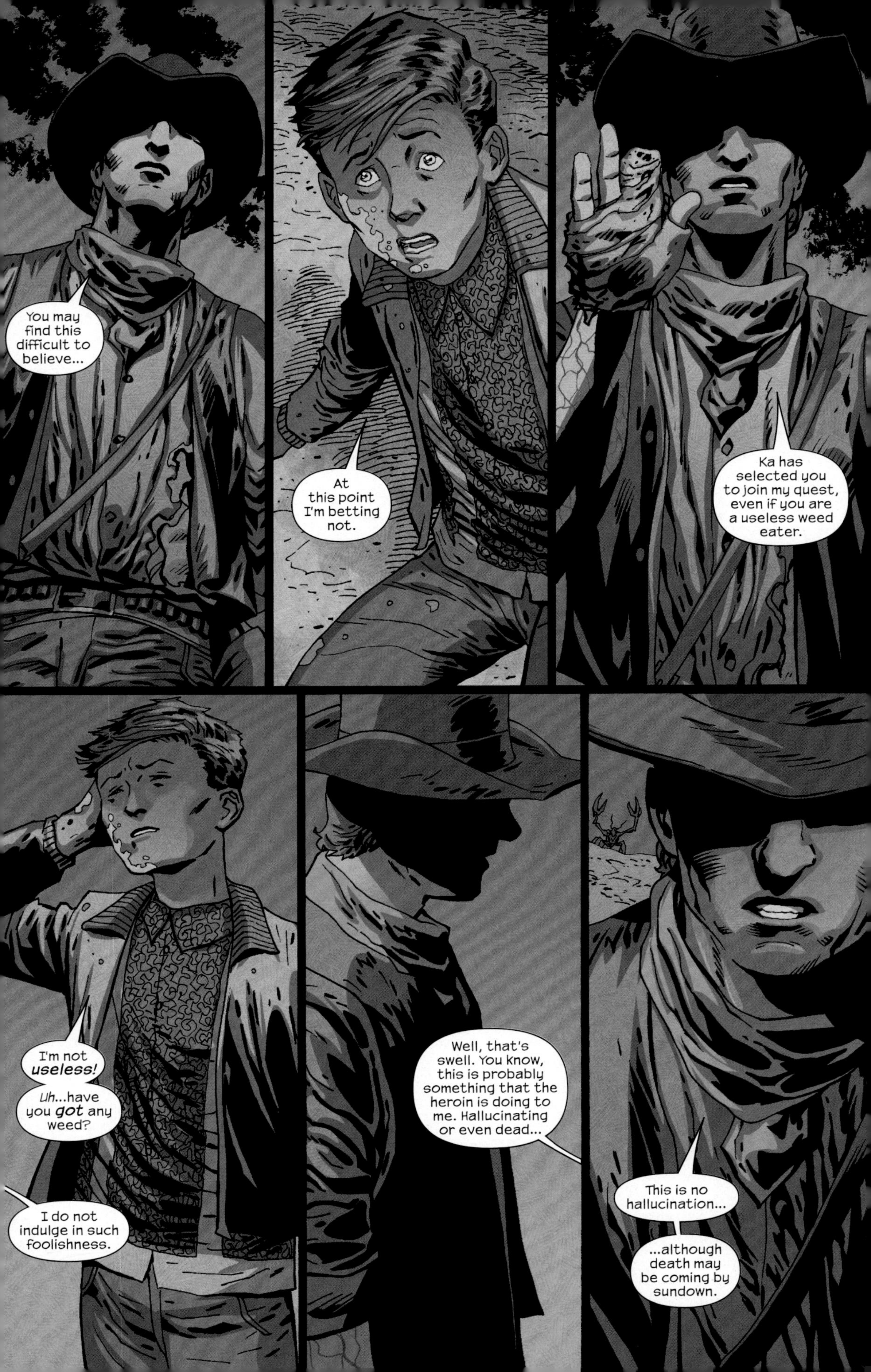
You may find this difficult to believe...
At this point I'm betting not.
Ka has selected you to join my quest, even if you are a useless weed eater.
I'm not *useless!*
Uh...have you *got* any weed?
I do not indulge in such foolishness.
Well, that's swell. You know, this is probably something that the heroin is doing to me. Hallucinating or even dead...
This is no hallucination...
...although death may be coming by sundown.

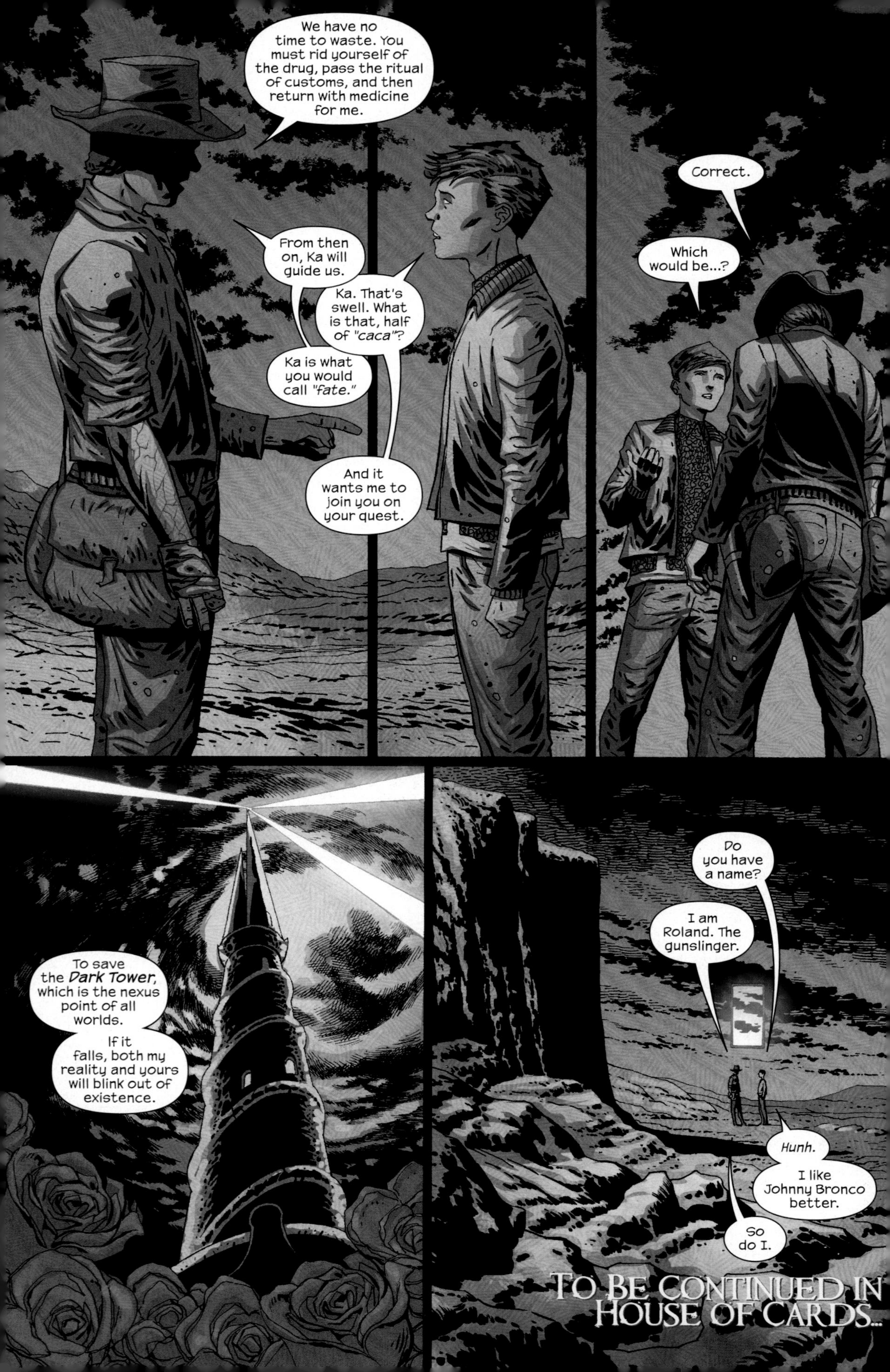

We have no time to waste. You must rid yourself of the drug, pass the ritual of customs, and then return with medicine for me.
From then on, Ka will guide us.
Ka. That's swell. What is that, half of "caca"?
Ka is what you would call "fate."
And it wants me to join you on your quest.
Correct.
Which would be...?
To save the Dark Tower, which is the nexus point of all worlds.
If it falls, both my reality and yours will blink out of existence.
Do you have a name?
I am Roland. The gunslinger.
Hunh.
I like Johnny Bronco better.
So do I.
TO BE CONTINUED IN HOUSE OF CARDS...

The story continues in *The Dark Tower: The Drawing of the Three — House of Cards*

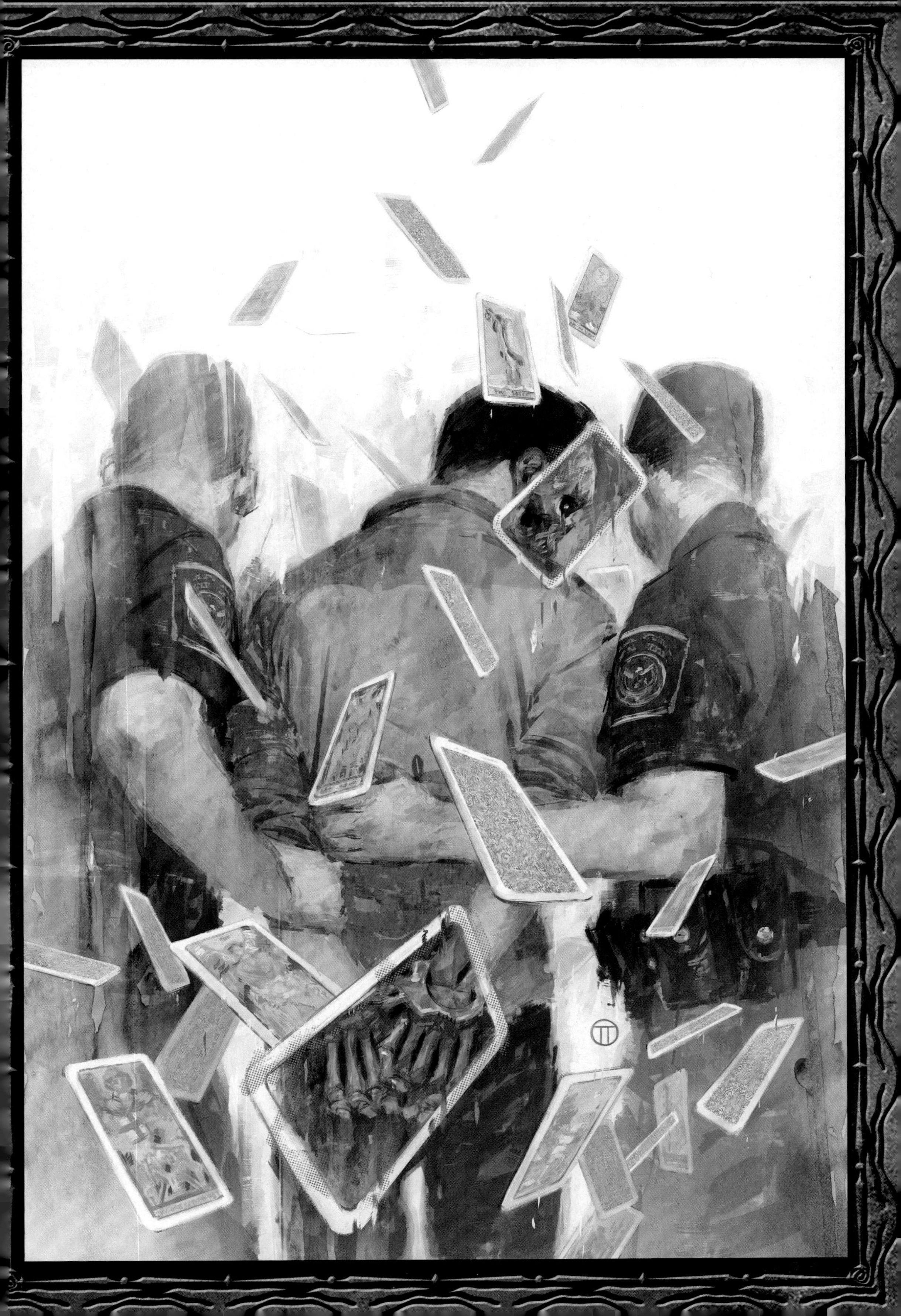

The Dark Tower: The Drawing of the Three — The Prisoner #1 **Cover by Julian Totino Tedesco**

The Dark Tower: The Drawing of the Three — The Prisoner #1 2nd **Printing Cover by Julian Totino Tedesco**

The Dark Tower: The Drawing of the Three — The Prisoner #1 **Variant Cover by Christian Ward**

The Dark Tower: The Drawing of the Three — The Prisoner #1 **Variant Cover by Skottie Young**

The Dark Tower: The Drawing of the Three — The Prisoner #2 **Cover by Julian Totino Tedesco**

The Dark Tower: The Drawing of the Three — The Prisoner #3 **Cover by Julian Totino Tedesco**

The Dark Tower: The Drawing of the Three — The Prisoner #4 **Cover by Julian Totino Tedesco**

The Dark Tower: The Drawing of the Three — The Prisoner #5 **Cover by Julian Totino Tedesco**

The Dark Tower: The Drawing of the Three — The Prisoner #1 **Cover Sketches by Julian Totino Tedesco**

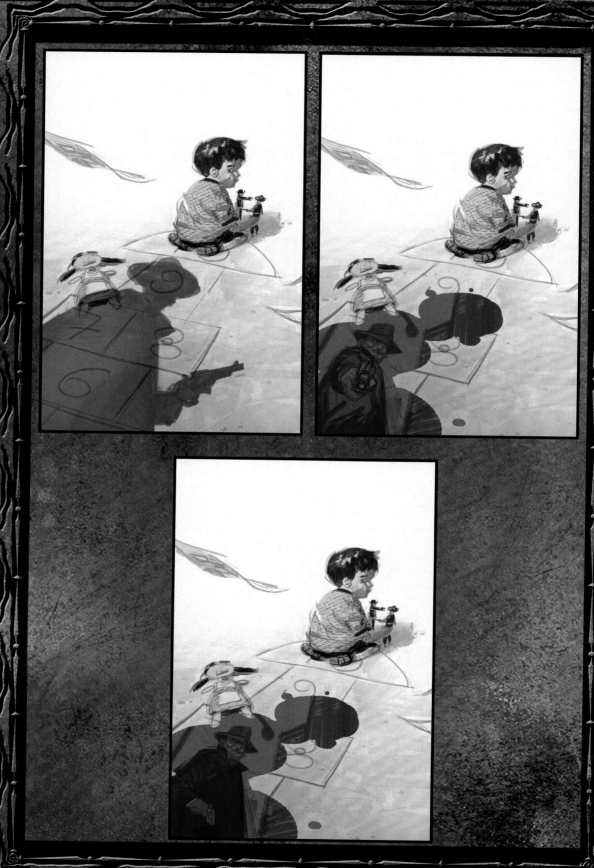

The Dark Tower: The Drawing of the Three — The Prisoner #1 **Variant Cover Sketches by Christian Ward**

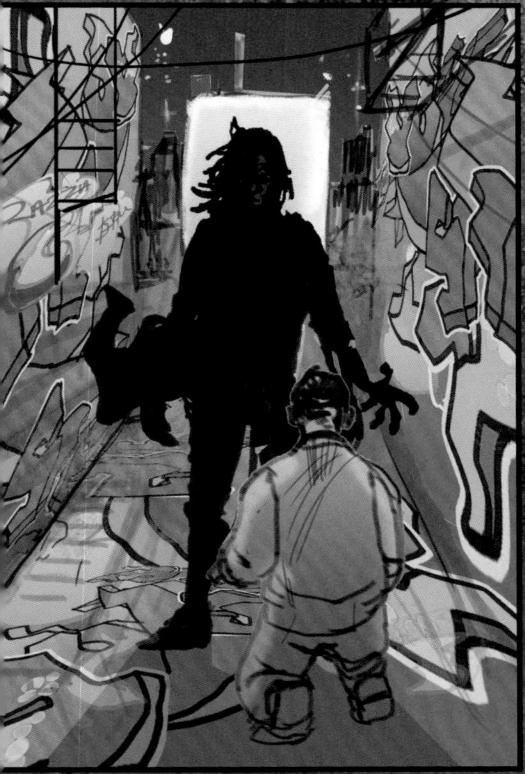

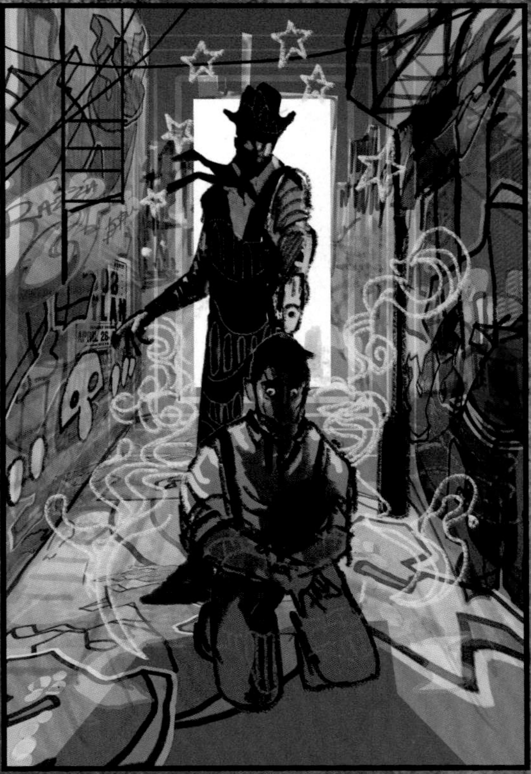

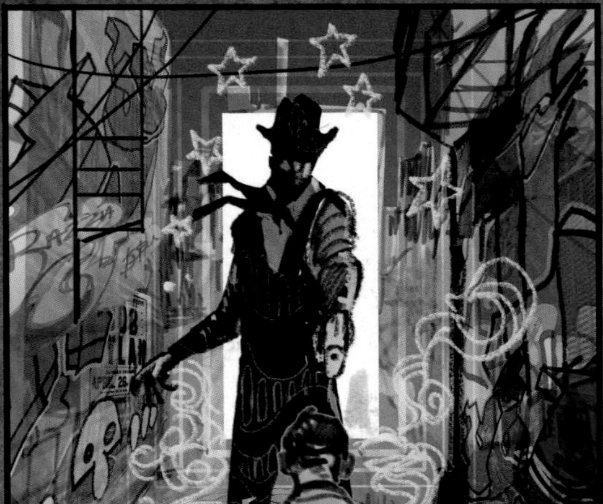

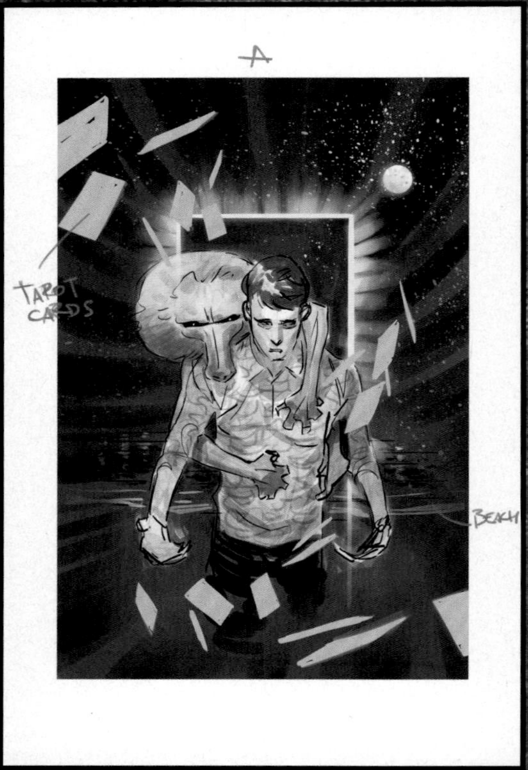
A
TAROT CARDS
BEACH

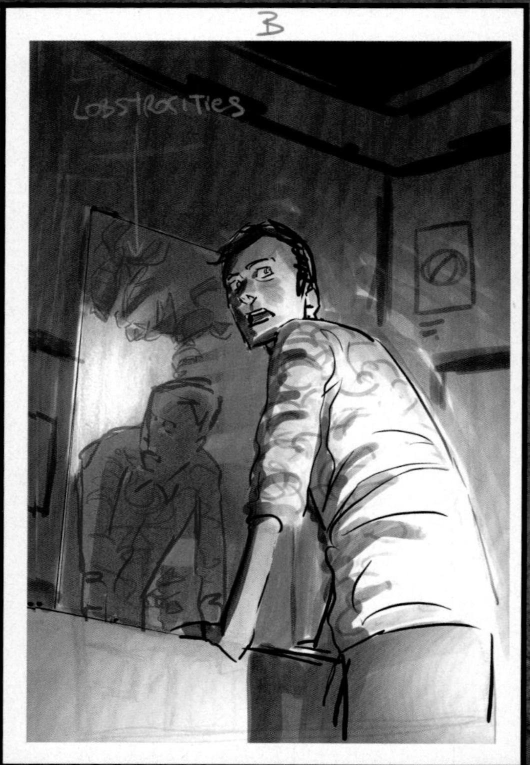
B
LOBSTROCITIES

Page 7

1. Henry and Tommy are walking away, but Mrs. Dean is now scowling at the bulge in Henry's turned up t-shirt sleeve. She calls to him, her hands on her hips. Guiltily, Henry looks at her over his shoulder.

2. Mrs. Dean is holding out her hand.

3. Hanging his head peevishly, Henry is placing a pack of candy cigarettes into his mother's open hand. (For image of '60s candy cigarettes, see appendix.)

4. Mrs. Dean is walking down the street, but she addresses Gloria from over her shoulder. Eddie, still clutching his cowboy doll, is beaming.

5. Gloria's friend has just finished her turn and is handing the stone back to Gloria. Eddie is about to throw a two-year-old tantrum.

6. Still dragging his Johnny Bronco doll (but with Sam Sidewinder on the ground next to him), Eddie KICKS Gloria's doll. It is skidding across the hopscotch. Horrified, Gloria's hands have flown to her cheeks.

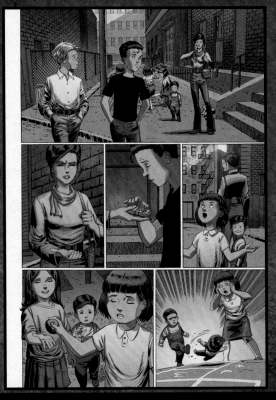

Pages 8-9

1. Eddie has picked up the stone. His expression is gleeful. A few feet away, Gloria is cradling her doll. From off-camera, we hear the roar of an engine.

2. Eddie has dropped the stone onto square 3. He is smiling. Gloria is walking toward him. She is FURIOUS. Meanwhile, Frank's car is careening towards the pavement. It is heading directly for Eddie, but the two arguing children are unaware of it.

3. Running at Eddie, Gloria is SHOVING him off of the hopscotch. She also is shoving him OUT of the way of the oncoming car.

4. Quick shot of Frank's wide-eyed, horrified face as he realizes he is about to kill the wrong child but can't do anything about it.

5. The camera focuses on Gloria, who clutches her doll. She is wide-eyed and frozen, like a fawn in headlights. She KNOWS she is about to be killed by this car.